THE BOOK of NUMBER

INTERPRETATIONS

Being the complete Book of Interpretations for all aspects of Pythagorean Numerology

Companion volume to the Book of Number: Practical Workbook

*By understanding perfectly a single drop
so too shall you understand the ocean*

The Book of Number: INTERPRETATIONS

Copyright © 2014 Michael Wallace

All Rights Reserved

This book is published under the Berne Convention. All copyright protected to the author. No prior use without permission except for excerpts for review or educational purposes. All enquiries via Email to: info.numberharmonics@gmail.com

Published by Ladder to the Moon Publications.
ISBN: 978-0-9756994-6-1
Mailing: PO Box 1355 Kingscliff, NSW 2487
WEB: www.bookofnumber.com.au
All rights reserved to the copyright holder.

Index

Introduction **4**

The Numbers of Fate **7**
    Being the Numbers One to Twelve

Dominant Numbers **54**
    Being the interpretation for prevalent numbers in the Numerical Chart

Composite Number **57**
    Being the Numbers Ten to Fifty-Three

Lines in the Matrix **74**
    Being the complete Interpretations for the Eight Lines in the Pythagorean Matrix

Trines in the Matrix **99**
    Being the complete interpretations for the Seventy-Six Trines in the Pythagorean Matrix

Patterns in the Matrix **180**
    Being the complete interpretations for the Fifty-Eight Patterns in the Pythagorean Matrix

Doublets **252**
    Being interpretations for the Nine Doublets

INTRODUCTION:

Welcome to the Book of Interpretations. This is the companion volume to the Practical Workbook. Here you will find every possible Aspect within Pythagorean Numerology. When you want to work out what an Aspect means, this is the place you start.

Obviously, these are all generic interpretations that will change in accordance with the other Aspects included in the chart. It is up to you to determine how the various ingredients will combine. Think of a chart before you as a recipe with many spices. The differing combinations alter the presentation taste and texture of the dish that is served.

The person you are dealing, their mood, their attitude, all will determine what part of the mix is stronger, weaker, or not of particular importance. This will affect the answers you offer to the questions you are asked.

Understanding the questions you are asked is core to this process. As an example, if a person asks if it is likely they will become an artist, the first response you are likely to have is a question: "What are you painting at the moment?" You would be amazed how many "would be if could be's" there are. The "real" question they are asking is probably, "Will I be recognised as something more than a worker bee at the factory".

A Number Chart will accurately provide you with the various potentials. You are the one who must determine how these are to be applied. As I have said many times in this course, seeing the obvious in the chart and understanding what a person are really asking will give you an insight into how the various aspects of their chart will combine, and thus indicate what their probable destiny might be. It's a Jig Saw.

EVERY SINGLE INDIVIDUAL only has a few main themes, a small number of things they have to master or resolve in this lifetime. There are no exceptions to this. There is only a question as to the number of core issues we have to resolve, but rarely more than three important "core karmas".

If you can remember this, despite the myriad of Aspects in a Chart, you will learn to keep looking for, and finding, core "themes".

RHIND TEXT: Ancient Egyptian text book for Mathematics

Numbers Of Fate: Introduction

Let's take a quick rewind to the beginning. The first step in any reading we will do is to determine the "Key" number, or Birth Number of an individual. It is a very simple thing to do. Simply add up all the digits in their date of birth.

Someone born on the 13 April 1956 gives 1+3+4+1+9+5+6 = 29

29 is the COMPOSITE Number for the birth date 13 April 1956.

Now add the 29 Composite Number down. In this case 2+9 =11

Eleven is the Primary Birth Number. But we need to go a step further for 11 is what we call a "Higher Order Number" (10, 11 and 12), We add these down again to get a second Birth number. Obviously 1+1 = 2

The date 13 April 1956 therefore equals: 29 into 11 into 2 birth number.

NOTE that I add all numbers separately, it isn't 13 + 4 + 1956 which would give 1973 which then adds to 1+9+7+3 = 20 into 2. While in all cases it adds down to the same last digit (This is how Vedic Math works) there can be many changes in the Composite Number Values. As an example, "losing" the 11 like this can affect a chart significantly.

Similarly, the date 24 June 1943: 2+4+6+1+9+4+3 = 29 into 11 into 2

The 23 Oct 1965: 2+3+1+0+1+9+6+5 = 27 into 2+7 = 9

We have specific meanings for each and every number and aspect in this Book of Interpretation. Words are not enough. If we are to truly grasp these meanings, we need to understand how the Ancient Greeks looked at a Number as a doorway to an archetypal consciousness. The number One did not mean "one" as we understand it, but possessed a whole series of meanings, ranging from Logos to pigheadedness, for instance.

Further: The meaning of any number in a chart is *qualified and defined by the numbers in relationship around it*. As a reader you obviously need to have an understanding of the range of meaning each number represents. But this is not enough. You must also develop a sense of "interaction", of how the other numbers present work in with each other. Only then will the various combinations begin to 'talk' to you in ways that make sense.

Understanding the Language:

It is all about understanding the LANGUAGE of Number. When we see each number as a letter in an alphabet, we learn that different groups of numbers "spell" different words, and thus have very different meaning.

It is quite remarkable when you click into this Number Consciousness. Things like a simple birth date suddenly become open doorways into understanding the reason and purpose for a person's existence on Earth.

It will take time and application to understand this, but follow through one step at a time, and it will unfold in a natural and relatively easy manner.

The Ancient Greeks were not alone in the belief that Number represented god-like power. The Hindu Pantheon of Gods IS a "Number System". The Sacred Music, the Raga's, are all number systems, based on specific mathematical principles. All the Hindu Chants are *mathematical formula*. An Example: Om Mane Padre' Hum *Om Mane Padre' Hum* is Vedic Math for "Pi", written as a "tone equation".

When you see the patterns and clear truths that evolve from number sequences, you realize that there is a divinity in Number. You will discover, like the ancients, that this divinity is associated with each and every aspect of our lives. We ARE divinity hidden in flesh, and this divinity is encoded with Number. We are sparks of light, pure energy that is ordered by the various sequences of Number in our lives.

As you get more proficient at reading charts, you will surprise yourself. You will literally start to pick up the frequency of a Soul, and tune into it like a radio station. As you go through someone's chart things will "occur" to you. Ideas just pop into your thoughts and you say, "It seems to indicate that this is the case in your life" and so often they will answer "How could you have POSSIBLY known that?" It soon becomes obvious to even the most rank novice that there is SOMETHING at work here.

However, this is to come. The journey of a thousand lifetimes starts with the first step. Your First Step in Numerology is understanding the meaning associated with the Twelve Fadic (or Fate) Numbers.

Let the descriptions of these numbers soak in. Book learning, memorizing and trying to recite things by rote really does not work here. We need to let the meaning of every number osmose into us, so allow it to become a natural part of your vocabulary. Let it become your new language.

The Numbers of Fate

Being the Birth Numbers One to Twelve

This series of Number are known as the Fadic (Fate) Series. These indicate the primary focus for energy in the individual's life, and are comparable to your "Sun Sign" in Astrology.

They are also like the Tonic Note in music. There are many notes at work in any given piece of music, but the Tonic represents the harmonic point that all the notes in this music refer to.

The Pythagoreans held that Life is a Song. Your nature "sings" what it is, and as you express this, you become what you sing. Likewise, if you fail to be true to yourself, your "song" is unsung, and you become inhibited, locked up and frozen.

The Numbers of Fate represent the archetypal doorway you were given, or you chose, prior to incarnating here on Earth. They shape all else that is to come in the individuals chart, yet these of themselves do not determine what we manifest. The Fadic Numbers are more the rudder of the ship, not the cargo it carries.

The purpose of this section is to give an overview on the basic nature of the numbers One to Twelve. It is essential if we are to practise the Art of Numerology that we gain an insight into the meaning of each Number. Primarily, One to Twelve, but also the Numbers Ten to Fifty-Two as well. (The Composite Series, not related to the Mathematical Composite Numbers)

Book of Number: Interpretations

ONE

Mikhail Gorbachev 2/3/1931 2+3+1+9+3+1 = 19 = 1

Chuck Berry 18/10/1926 1+8+1+1+9+2+6 = 28 = 10 = 1

Positive Characteristics: Forceful, realistic, ingenious, determined and broadminded. One always desires improvement, and accents ambition, individualism, determination, intelligence, intuition, and the love of family.

Negative Characteristics: One's can become extremely selfish, pessimistic, stingy, and manic. They can suffer deep melancholy, with a fear of failure that makes them blind to the obvious. Backed into a corner they be stubborn, unscrupulous and materialistic.

ONE represents the primitive and basic elements within man. It is a dynamic, active force, yet as the number implies, somewhat solitary. One's are sober, single minded, blunt and pointed in opinion. The characteristic of the One Energy is singularity and so we find those affected by this vibration to be single minded. Like a tree growing in nature, the energy here only knows that to survive it must grow, and so the One Energy tends to push all others aside and demand it's rights.

Or it is the exact opposite. The roots do not go down, the growth never happens, and the One energy feels utterly bereft and alone. This is why the One energy often yearns for others to rule, it gives a sense of being "rooted" and removes their deepest fear: stagnation and decay.

Generally those srongly affected by the One are slow to anger, but they are fiery by nature, and like a volcano that has been dormant for years they can suddenly explode. The One personality very much wants things done their particular way, and can be capable of a very great anger and resentment when opposed by those they consider underlings.

One's can thus be unstable and unpredictable, acting (like a volcano or any force of nature) as an undirected, singular minded force for change.

Book of Number: Interpretations

Naturally the reverse for all of this is also true. In particular emotionally undeveloped One's can be irreconcilably stubborn, dogmatic and unchanging, often to the point of disbelief.

The One is very single minded about most things, and will barge on regardless of opinion or criticism. Indeed, opposition only encourages them! The parent of a One child with an opinion must either: learn to divert attention to more favourable subjects, be very interested in what their little One has to say, or suffer the very loud consequences.

The psychology of the One vibration is subject to an odd paranoia, a sense that everyone is "out there" while the individual is inside a system that needs change. This creates a sort of tightrope effect, and a specific sense of single mindedness, to the point of excluding all that does not conform to their own set of values. If you do not agree, you are wrong.

Women strong with the vibration of the One can be very career-minded, and sometimes brutal in their desire for the top post. It is not the job but the need for recognition that drives them. Yet these same women will be devoted mothers wanting to spoil their children with every luxury. The One woman cannot stand "fluffery" and resent insecure men who beat about the bush, yet so often they will marry someone just like this. Why? Often it is simply because they feel secure when they are in charge.

They will will be practical, frugal and considerate, or the complete opposite. Rarely will the One women be the quiet stay-at-home type. Yet if she is, she will be VERY quiet, and will probably have agoraphobia.

The same goes for the men, though as a rule in business the One man seems a touch more diplomatic and less ruthless. The One male will love outdoors, sports, fishing and all sorts of active "life" games that also allow a certain solitariness. If they play in a team they like to be the leader, or at least a star player, and the same goes for their business life.

You will often find a One man at the top of the organization, and also find them surrounded by men and women who are Two's and Fives. This is because Two's and Fives have an appreciation of diplomacy that the more blunt One cannot stand, but recognises a need for.

This is a powerful number, and works either as a cohesive driving force to accomplish, or a very devisive force to negate progress. Any effort that invokes a combination of creative effort, practical success, and physical ability needs the One energy, for this will be the glue that holds it all together. One's are the movers and the shakers, yet without the courage of their convictions, the One-based persona degenerates to the most unemployable type imaginable. Drug addiction, welfare dependance, and an almost total lack of drive indicate the inverted One energy at work.

Its opposite is the Nine, the representative number of silence and power. Here a curious fact emerges, which is an odd circumstance of the Noumenal Order, and this is that is we are to master the vibration of one number, we must also master the vibration of its opposite. As an example: If someone falls into the negative energy of the One, the solution is to silence the mind and rediscover their own inner power.

If the One individual chooses to work with inner silence as their guiding light they will find life will smooth out considerably for them. What is most opposite to us is also what we are most connected to. This why so many married couples seem to be in complete opposition to each other. It is a natural balance of nature at work.

The main lessons for the One revolve around Courage and Patience.

Book of Number: Interpretations

TWO

Henry Kissinger 27 5 1923   2+7+5+1+9+2+3 = 29 = 11 = 2

Michael Bulble' 9 7 1975   9+7+1+9+7+5 = 38 = 11 = 2

Cliff Richard 14 10 1940   1+4+1+1+9+4 = 20= 2

Positive Characteristics: Sensitive, tactful, diplomatic and cooperative. Diplomatic, loving, studious and patient. A Two will often express many musical or feminine qualities and also tends to be sensual and intuitive.

Negative Characteristics: Two's are often discontent and can be seen as spoiled or lazy. They can be careless, particularly with the truth, and when criticized for their faults, they can be oversensitive.

The TWO vibration is the first point of duality in the Noumenal Order. It is also the number of balance, intuition and beauty. We find the Two energy can encompass both utter double-faced bitchery (such as we see in political animals) and a delicate appreciation of all that is subtle and fine, and do so all in the same breath.

The psychology of the Two is one of schizophrenia, in-as-much as the individual has a tendency to feel displaced within themselves, and constantly on uncertain ground. This "ocsillating" is like a generator that creates the driving force inside the Two, but also a sense of stress and neurosis. The perception and pursuit of beauty stabilises this energy.

Its opposite is the Eight, and so we will often find Two's draw to money, business and also persons of great and noble natures. Its position in the Noumenal Matrix connects the numbers of Creativity to the Emotional Plane, and thus has an important role in the way of Balance.

Children vibrating to the Two are lovely Souls. They often are wide eyed and will gaze at things with wonder, listening to tales and stories with such intensity that they often begin to live in another world. Then without notice they can snap back and become hugely practical, with feet planted firmly on the ground.

Two is the first number of duality, and people under this energy often seem to be able to flip to opposite viewpoints, without any apparent contradiction inside themselves. Women work well with the Two vibration, and, as with all the even numbers, the Two has a feminine energy.

Ladies with this energy usually exhibit tremendous intuition, and are often involved with helping with the Arts in some manner. Also, as having strong intuition tends to lead a soul to separation from the hustle and bustle of life, we often see quite a few Two's in the Holy Orders. Even though Two's have a great need for affection, they will often choose to be celibate because of the difficulty they experience in dealing with, and balancing, the energies of a partner. Some are fortunate and find that special Soul, but most languish in poor marriages, not wanting to leave because it might hurt their companion.

There is a darker side to the feminine aspect of the Two, of course, and this is the plotting, manipulating creature who lives in a world of gossip and petty pay-back politics. This unpleasant type is characterised by the uplifted outer edges to their eyes, and their sharp tongues.

Interestingly enough, all the varied numbers have specific facial and structural identities, as well as an affinity to the twelve basic mineral types that form the human body. For example: Calcium vibrates to a similar frequency as the Two. This is not mere chance, but merely another reflection of how the Noumenal Order is vibrating throughout all the universes, creating a specific pattern by which matter takes shape.

The Male Two is often found in the corridors of power, not because they want power personally, but because the constant juggling and balancing of politics fascinates them. Many become leading bureaucrats, but rarely those upfront who deal with the public. The negative Two often tends to seek out secrecy and intrigue, which appeals to the sense of duality as well as the sense of beauty, yet many times it is the nature of these same Two's to change sides, giving away all the secrets because their courage failed them. In other words, a double agent!

Double-mindedness destroys the Two person, and could be considered their worst enemy. "The double minded man is unstable in all his ways" is a quote from the Bible. Many philosophers vibrate to this energy, and the ensuing struggle to resolve paradoxes is a common theme with this type of mystic.

Book of Number: Interpretations

Curiously the Two has an oddly male homosexual energy to it, though rarely do we find homosexuals vibrating to this energy. Normally this field is connected with the Four, but the emotional intensity of the Two, as well as the fragility of its nature, does attract the Gay male.

We find many poets tuning into the Two vibration, and mystics seek it as well. The ideal of beauty drives them, sometimes to the point of converting their natural energy to that of the Two, in order to more fully experience this. We can, in fact, alter the energy vibrations about us, but be warned that this can often cause more problems than it solves. It is wise to see a good Numerologist first.

The Two is a very odd vibration, for while it is inherently unstable and is constantly seeking balance, this uncertainty of and by itself can become a curious pleasure for it.

Dedication to an ideal is the easiest way to create balance with any frequency, but with the remarkable adaptability of the Two energy we find Two's inventing all sorts of wild and wonderful ways to keep themselves together. A truly interesting number to observe, for it so often involves both the highest ideals with the lowest immorality in a single person!

The prevalent lessons for the Two are always around developing emotional and mental balance, and in the process learning the art of right discrimination. In this regard, it is important for Two's to observe and connect with the seasons of life. By understanding the natural cycles around them, the Two will find the inner peace and clarity to finally see things as they are, not as they are imagined.

From the solitary One, which is drawn into the Two in a somewhat disharmonious relationship we find the resolution of both in the number Three. This is because of the Ancient LAW of THREE's that states "From One unto a Second, from whence a Third must appear."

In other words the nature of life is that when there is Two, they will get together and make a third.

THREE

Cloris Leachman 30 4 1926 3+1+9+2+6 = 21 = 3

Ann Landers 14 6 1918 1+4+6+1+9+1+8 = 30 = 3

John Malkovich 9 12 1953 9+1+2+1+9+5+3 = 30 = 3

Positive Characteristics: Imaginative, expressive, and good with communication. Creative in business and art. Three's are tolerant, joyful, optimistic, inspiring, talented, jovial, youthful, dynamic.

Negative Characteristics: Disingenuous, vain, extravagant, prone to complaining. Intolerant, hypocritical, impatient and superficial

The THREE is unique in that it can combine creativity and organisation. If they are not artists, they will be running an art gallery, if they are not a writer, they will be involved with publishing. Many successful business people are strong in the energy of the Three.

The Three is a risk taker, a gambler, and often an alcoholic to boot. They can swing between opposite emotions and thoughts like a monkey swings through the trees. This is a number that "breathes": the inward breath being the sad, whimsical effect, the outbreathing, the positive uplifting effect. The Three energy may put you through bouts of huge depression, but as soon as things get active in your life, suddenly everything becomes fine and life is wonderful once more.

The Three child is a joy to have around when they are happy for they literally glow with smiles, but when the dark clouds descend they become unreachable and very moody. The problem with the Three is identity, or more to the point, a lack of it. They are so ready to explore and express every imaginable possibility that they often get lost in their dreams, and tend to become sullen and withdrawn, rather than ask for assistance.

However, put a Three up on a pedestal, just stroke their vanity a little, and they will soon purr like pussy cats. Grudgingly at first, of course, but be assured that even if they know you don't mean it, they will love you hugely for loving them enough to bother.

This is both the strength and weakness of the Three vibration. They adore recognition, yet so often fear this very thing, thus creating a virtual storm of discontent that, in an odd way, forces them to create something. Creating "stuff" is part of their inbuilt survival factor. This natural tension within the Three is what activates the creative force inside them.

You will see this pattern again and again in the lives of most creative artists. Beethoven always had some tremendous upset in his life that somehow triggered the production of another symphony. Artists and writers classically become sullen and withdraw shortly before they begin work on major projects. By understanding the energy of the Three we can avoid all of this, and just get on with the job at hand.

The core issue with the Three wraps around issues of self worth, or more to the point, the lack of it. This is why Three children need quiet praise with every thing they do, and a very soft criticism when they err.

The Three needs to understand the Law of Completion (opposite Number is the Ten) for, with their boundless creativity, they tend to jump from one project to another, getting lost and confused. This can cause them to distrust their own creative process, and nothing seems to get finished.

This is why so many Three's end up in the lower end of society. They are the misfits and dreamers who have so much promise, yet produce so few results. But it is not that they are impractical of irresponsible, it is mostly a simple lack of confidence in being able to DO as well as the other person, yet with the inner tension of knowing they can do better!

Three is a combination of the one pointedness of the One, with the paradoxical nature of the Two. How is it resolved? By getting off our rears and doing something useful. It is this simple, but of course finding motivation is not always easy.

The Three always looks for freedom, and often take to task what they see as the oppression of the masses by covert and overt forces in society. They are the true idealists, totally disregarding practicality and common-sense, and indeed if you suggest this, they will see such a thing as some sort of compromise to be despised.

Three women generally love to dress their children as brightly as possible, and lavish them with affection. They make wonderful, reliable employees, but generally poor managers. What they lack in methodical application, however, they make up for with enthusiasm. Money tends to run through their fingers, but often the money will be spent to buy the basic material to create something else, like the fabric for a dress for instance. Even the extravagant shopping sprees will contain useful items.

The men vibrating to the Three are much the same. Give them a house and they will want to renovate it, give them a car and they will love polishing it, and improving it. Give them a girlfriend, and they will wonder what her sister is like in bed. Curiosity runs high with the Three, and it truly is what kills the cat in this case, because the Three Male just takes things too far, gets lost, and leaves things unresolved and unfinished.

Again and again the Three vibration has to learn the Law of Cycles, or Completion, which states "All that has begun must end." Not finishing things weakens the inner nature, and leaves it psychically unbound. Like a rope that has unwound itself, the non-completion of projects weakens our hold on life, and throws us into a state of dreamlike emptiness.

Three's survive best by setting up some big project, often doing so just as everything is about to collapse on top of them. This impending doom gives them the focus to survive. To avoid this extreme swing, Three's need to learn to categorise and plan their lives in order to feel content, even though they think they hate organisation.

Three is a curious and wonderful Number which gives much flair and character to the Noumenal Chart of so many people. The psychology tends to be based on escaping the present restriction in a search for freedom. One of the really great dangers inherent here becomes abuse of drugs, which promise just this, but generally fail to deliver anything but further confusion in our lives.

The stronger personalities survive even this, however. Their will to create overrides everything else. This then becomes the great saving grace for all under the influence of the Three, that if they create something positive it will uplift their life and make all things seem worthwhile.

Book of Number: Interpretations

FOUR

Meryl Streep 22 6 1949 2+2+6+1+9+4+9 = 31 = 4

Mark Twain 30 11 1835 3+1+1+1+8+3+5 = 22 = 4

Positive Characteristics: Four's are disciplined, strong, stable, pragmatic, down-to-earth, reliable, dependable, hard-working, extracting, precise, methodical, conscientious, frugal, devoted, patriotic and trustworthy. Distinct urges for adventure.

Negative Characteristics: Four's pay for their stability and pragmatism by tending toward the boring side. This will express itself with a lack of imagination and compassion. Fours can be careless in appearance, and their social awkwardness can make them seem vulgar, crude or jealous. Gambling is a serious illness.

The vibration of the Four is often greatly misunderstood. This is the first stable point in the Noumenal Flow, and indicates solidarity, organisation and physical world capability. Yet underneath the apparent steadfastness many Four's are extremely emotional individuals needing constant reassurance.

Four children have a wonderful humour as a rule, and are content to play for hours unattended, but they need to know someone is about. They will work hard at school, usually going on to some form of higher learning, but if not they will move into substantial trades that require the use of hands.

Many Four's are accountants, instrument makers, computer repairers and operators. They generally work as efficient support people. We also find many Four people in the armed forces, as this suits their need for regimentation. They make excellent soldiers.

The Four woman is a solid organiser at home, often running her own little business or doing odd jobs to help pay the bills. She needs constant reassurance that everything is alright, and is often a devout believer in faith-based religion and/or charitable causes.

Book of Number: Interpretations

The lady running the local party plan outlet is most often a Four, or working with the Four vibration, as is the woman who runs the local child care centre. They are pragmatic and capable, yet also somewhat distrusting, which colours their view of life.

The major failing of the Four is that the natives tend to be quite judgemental. This appears to contradict their naturally warm and humourous personality, but understand that making fixed judgements gives the Four a sense they are on solid ground. As stated, the Four has an essential insecurity, and this can drive them in odd directions.

The curious psychology of the Four is that they cannot trust themselves. So often they hide behind well tailored suits and well organised lives, living in the better suburbs, yet all the time they can possess this fear of some terrible creature inside themselves. Often this simply is a sexual need unfulfilled, but all these negatives come about is because the Four simply cannot bring themselves to open up the shutters, and ask another for the experience which they crave.

This gives a tight knot in the stomach, and you can actually feel this in so many who are negatively affected by the vibration. In physiological terms the Four vibration, in its need for solidarity, will often put a clamp on the expressive part of the personality, which places stress of the Vargus Nerve, thus creating tension within the sympathetic nervous system.

Naturally, when the individual learns to fully express themselves this knot goes away. Thus we find many actors and performers, particularly those in the circus (as this provides a family atmosphere) have affinity with the Four. It is the secret wish of every accountant to live some exotic lifestyle, and this is the key to understanding the Four, they exist on two levels, but the condition is not schizophrenic, it is more agoraphobic.

The Four man suffers his whole working life because no-one seems to be as bothered as he is with getting the details right, He will constantly check and recheck everything in his environment. They are the pedantic engineers that make sure the plane stays up, but are rarely the person flying it.

We often find inspectors, tax officers, accountants and money people in general vibrating to the Four. And yet we will also see firemen, crop-dusters, and lumberjacks with the same energy. Why? They have learned to express themselves in different ways, but generally one will be introverted and the other extroverted. Introverted Four's tend towards office and money, Extrovert Four's tend towards adventure and outdoors. The Four vibration tends to accentuate polarisation of the personality.

As a further note on the somewhat obsessive nature of the Four, you will often find them in gyms as budding body builders, even the girls! However, once the focus is lifted out of the physical world, the Four personality becomes a dedicated and genuine follower of any path they choose, never giving up or giving in to disappointment as a rule.

This cannot be stressed too much, for the Four personality has more than an inner and outer person, it has a higher and lower as well. (Get it, four sides?) If the focus is on the higher aspects of life; Ideals, Truth, Compassion, etc. then they will progress with remarkable ease in a spiritual sense. This is because, at heart, the Four is methodical. Method and dedication always have greater success than plain talent in this and all the lower worlds. Those with what are considered higher order numbers can learn a lot from the apparently lowly Four.

Spiritually speaking, Four is the number of the common man and is represented by the element of Fire, with Three being Water, Two being Air, One being Earth, and Five being Spirit or Essence.

We also see the Four Seasons, the Four Winds, the Four points of the compass, etc. The Four is a major number in the forming of patterns, and is the base of the physical universe. The mineral it vibrates to is Carbon, the linking atom of life, which gives us a clue to the inner nature of the Four.

The lessons involved with the Four vibration are to do with getting on with others. The destiny involves sharing and holding a non-judgmental attitude. Its symbol is the square.

At present there are very few highly evolved Fours on this planet, simply because they have so much natural affinity for the common things of man that they simply do not overmuch seek out the higher aspects. However, those who do lift up their eyes to the heavens achieve spiritual greatness, for they can apply the principles of focus, building and achievement to all they touch, thus creating a solid platform for spirit to build upon.

FIVE

Clark Gable 1 2 1901 1+2+1+9+1 = 14 = 5

Willie Nelson 30 4 1933 3+4+1+9+3+3 = 23 = 5

Thomas Jefferson 13 4 1743 1+3+4+1+7+4+3 = 23 = 5

Positive Characteristics: Five's are energetic, adventurous, daring and freedom-loving. They also tend to be versatile, flexible, adaptable, curious, social, sensual, quick-thinking, witty, courageous and worldly.

Negative Characteristics: Five's can be unstable, chaotic, self-indulgent, irresponsible or careless. They often fall into patterns of drug abuse and unhealthy or confused sexual relations.

The Five is considered the Lord of the Noumenal Order, because it is at the connecting point for all the numbers. It is indeed a pivotal number, affecting all around it with a subtle, yet profound effect. Five is the number of communication and connectivity. Its symbol is the Cheops Pyramid, and its power is that of ancient Egypt in that within the vibration of the Five lies mastery of the psychic forces.

This is the number of communication, and is governed by Zinc, the pervasive element that is intrinsic to every living cell. The Five personality is broad and persuasive, often seen prominently with entrepreneurs, architects, movie directors, and all other fields where many people have to be coordinated to achieve a goal.

They are not the builders, but the organisers. They are not the thinkers, but they get what others have said, and can translate lofty ideals into a pragmatic approach. Fives are often motivators and trainers.

As a child the Five is a little sparkling jewel, but always ready to turn their angelic faces to mischief if, and when, the opportunity arises. Opportunity is always seen as a gift from the heavens, and not to be missed, thus little Five's often get their whiskers burnt on various nefarious adventures.

They are also dreamers, like the Two child, but they like to fit their dreams into some framework that is meaningful to them, We find the young Five will dream of flying above the ground, and thus in that moment choose to be a pilot. Of course, the next dream might change the goal to being one of a fireman, but this is not the point! The Five child's dreams give purpose to their lives, for however long.

The Five child is gregarious and full of laughter. They love to be centre stage, and will often organise theatrical performances for friends and family. They are very easy to work with, and have little stubbornness that will not respond to reason. They are often fair haired, and need lots of fresh foods, in particular those containing the Potassium, Phosphorus and Zinc their bodies, as a rule, crave.

The psychology for the majority of Five individuals involves a great need for recognition. This is not to be confused with approval, the Five basically thinks they are OK, but recognition for the Five affirms in them an essential sense of emotional balance.

The Five tends not to be a thinker, rather they rely on instinct, which rarely lets them down. However, if the Five energy does start thinking too much about things, they will become quite clumsy and constantly put their foot in their mouth in social situations. This is prevalent during puberty.

Five's do not like to see things unconnected or broken. They are the ones who will pull the broken clock apart to see what the problem might be, yet not be able to put it back together again. But they will still put everything back into the case and shake it, in the hope that the miracle will occur. They are forever hopeful, and even when they grow up, have the lurking suspicion that there is a Santa Clause out there, somewhere.

They can be chatterboxes, and will happily talk to plants, birds, anything that they think is alive. Often they will get a secret reply, that they will tell you about if you ask nicely. Young Five's tend not to be afraid of much. Storms excite them, spiders intrigue them, but if they are worried about something, they will likely be phobic about it.

They get sullen with authority, mostly because authority is a one-way street, and allows no room for communication. Because of this they can be quite rebellious at school and university, but this natural rebellion serves them well as a rule, for it gives them a new perspective on things.

Fives like to work WITH power, but tend to be uninterested in actually wielding it. For example, they will often co-ordinate many strong personalities on a football team, acting as a manager, but they would not like to actually be the person who OWNS the team. They are more communal in their outlook, and generally prefer the concept of sharing to that of ownership.

Five women are generally very sensitive to others feelings, and many work as clairvoyants and tea ladies. Five is a volatile number. THis means tempers can flare, yet they will remain malleable, and be able to integrate with other viewpoints. Thyey resonate easily with all other numbers, and like a mimick, they will pick up the traits of anyone they are in a close working, or personal relationship with. Women are particularly sensitive, by virtue of their more yielding nature, and thus have to be very careful with whom they associate. This empathy can be disartrous if they associate with evil minded souls, and can lead to a sense of isolation.

It's the cucumber princple: If we put a cucumber in a jar of pickles, one day we will look about, and there will only be pickles in the jar. So it is with the Five in particular that they should be careful in choosing friends, and parents of Five children should take care with whom they associate.

Their malleability makes them desirable companions, and Fives generally do well in marriage situations, but are generally completely flummoxed when the partner wants to leave.It rarely occurs to the Five to leave a stable relationship. If there are difficulties, they will happily take on an external affair, but divorce is not a process they enjoy. But when they do divorce they really know how to enjoy themselves. Characteristically this immediately causes the old partner to become jealous and want them back. But Five's rarely turn back the clock.

Fives, for all their apparent whimsy, are very forwardly orientated. They like to progress, to forge new ground, to make new friends. They will not so much as forget the past, rather they will remake it into an image they prefer to see. If it was a bad experience, it will almost always be seen in the light of what has been learned because of it. A good experience by the same token can become overburdened with nostalgia.

The Five wife is a wonderful soul, but don't expect the house to be too clean. They are usually organising the local church raffle or chatting to the teachers about how the kids are coming on at school, and are too busy to worry overmuch about a little dust. They are clean, but not fussy, and go by the proverb "An immaculate house is a sign of a wasted life".

Usually people with like numbers do not get on so well in a marriage, but the Five is the exception. (along with the more developed Eight's and Nine's) The Five nature is so easy going, as a rule, that they can get on with almost anyone!

Book of Number: Interpretations

Five men can be real career types, always on the look out for the better title, even if no more pay goes with it. In this way they can be quite impractical, dragging a family from city to city on the climb to the top, and then not feeling quite pleased when the big job is landed. This is actually a symptom of instability in the emotions. This is a fatal Five failing, one that cause huge problems on the home front and in their personal life.

The energy of the Five man can be severely affected by poor health, so they must take care of it, and ensure that there is a holiday each year. Generally, though, the real cause of ailments with the Five is introversion, and especially sexual guilt. Fives tend, or wish, to be somewhat promiscuous, but social upbringing usually convinvces them that it is "wrong" even when their nature says it is "right".

Instead of accepting their nature, they often have several marriages. However, because of divorce proceedings and property settlements this generally means they stay poor. Again, it is really based in the misunderstanding of the emotions, and this is, in reality, the only major fault with the Five nature. But there is also a truly negative Five.

The Five energy is so affable in their outward personality that the really negative, power mongering aspect of the negative Five stays so well hidden that few suspect it even exists. This, if anything, is the great failing for most Five's: That they simply cannot deal with real power until they are quite highly developed. Many Fives are drawn to politics because they truly see that can help others, but with success that old contradiction between success and service arises and this usually puts a twist into their ambitions, making them quite avaricious, and sometimes malicious.

There is a truly dark side to the Five. Perhaps more so than the other numbers because even the native is often unaware of what lurks in the depths of his own subconscious. One of the major lessons of the Five involves delving into, and seek to understand, their unconscious needs and drives.

As a result of this, we find many psychiatrists and psychologists vibrate to the number Five. Also we will find many hypnotists and stage magicians carry this vibration as well. Indeed all of those with a fascination for the inner workings of the mind often have a Five somewhere in their chart.

However, the truly negative Five is rare indeed. Usually it is a vibration that loves to bath in undue attention, and is often given this because the number lies at the crossroads of one of the Twentieth Centuries greatest difficulties, that of matching our need for compassion with our drive for success. The Five is also at the crossroads of another traditional conflict area, the need for emotional love as opposed the desire for the perpetuation of our personal will.

Neither of these apparent conflicts could hope for a resolution without the Five's communicating ability, and we will often see in an individuals matrix the pattern of the cross that signifies the working out of these conflicting desires. If we consider deeply the above two paradoxical situations, we will see reflected in them much of man's present set of woes. Which will lead us to an appreciation of how important the Five is.

In the 21st century the energy moves from this "cross" to one of every increasing malleability. In spiritual terms, the Astral Plane is starting to mix with the physical, and those who can bridge this gap will be important in business, politics and social situation. The new energy is one of cooperation and coordination, both of which are natural to the Five energy. This condition will survive for 300 years.

In all the Five nature could be considered the "glue" of the Noumenal Chart. Because of this, many choose to represent it as the Spiritual Force, but this is really best represented by the Six.

SIX

Dwight D. Eisenhower 4 10 1890 1+4+1+1+8+9 = 24 = 6

B.B. King 16 9 1925 1+6+9+1+9+2+5 = 33 = 6

Positive Characteristics: Sixes are responsible, loving, self-sacrificing, protective, sympathetic and compassionate. These loyal, maternal figures are domestic, fair and idealistic. They often work as healers or teachers.

Negative Characteristics: A Six can overdo its inherent protectiveness and become anxious, worrisome, suspicious, paranoid, emotionally unstable, cynical or jealous. A blind acceptance of convention makes them immune to new insight.

The Six is the first representative number of Clarity, or Truth. It marks the beginning of the higher numbers, and represents SOUL, the conscious spark in all living things.

The Oxygen atom has SIX electrons, and by Its nature it is short the seventh that it needs for stability, thus it will form with anything that will offer that needed electron. The chemistry lesson repeats itself in a spiritual vein with the number Six, whose element is Oxygen.

The Six energy is a binding and building force that, like the Five, has a harmony with all the other numbers. However, the Five acts like a relay that allows other numbers to express themselves through its energy, whereas the Six is a catalyst that activates the latent force in all that it meets, and then binds it into some course of events.

This is why the Six is often both representative of the Home and of Business. An apparent conflict until we understand that running a business and a home are similar in many respects. Someone needs to be in charge, there are many people and duties to supervise, there are budgets to meet, goals to achieve and many tasks that occupy our time.

The psychology of the Six mind is to do with balance and activity, and so is symbolised by the tightrope walker. This implies a balancing act, and also a sort of neurosis with anyone not fully balanced with this energy.

Book of Number: Interpretations

Unbalanced individuals who fall in with this numbers vibrational spectrum tend to find the energy unleasant, and can become extremely non-social in outlook. Hermits, recluses and monks in orders of silence are often in this category. Another exceedingly negative trait of the Six is selfishness, as opposed to its positive end, which is self-sufficiency.

Sixes seldom work well with large groups, essentially because they are very intuitive and they find too many people in their world corrosive to their sense of harmony. Working with like-minded or understanding people, however, brings their many talents to the fore. Many artists have an affinity with people strong in the Six energy, and so you will see them moving in artistic circles. Often, they are the people running the gallery.

Six is also the number of study and higher learning, which gives a sense of aloofness to the Six nature. This type will have little to do with the common man, yet when they generate an understanding of the base aspects of human nature, the Six energy turns them into a formidable business person. This is because they have the breadth of vision that allows the individual to set and achieve realistic goals.

The Six child tends to be finely built, sometimes anaemic looking, yet if their diet is good they are surprisingly robust. They are prone to such things as Asthma, Colds and Flu and generally react badly to refined sugars. They are rarely heavy meat eaters, preferring chicken and fish as a rule. They will be practical and forthright, sometimes tyrannical to younger members of the family, and generally expect to be listened to. They like firm authority, and respect their parents for being strict, but they will look for flaws in your character if they suspect weakness in any shape of form. And if they find them, you will be told about it.

A Six child will spend many hours in contemplation, doing things like gazing at the full moon, etc. They are loving towards animals and often tidier than most children because they dislike clutter as a rule. They are not leaders, but neither are they followers, and often simply go their own way with a small group of friends in the playground.

The Six woman is very hard working, both at home and in business. They are perceptive of others feelings and do well as secretaries because they know who to let in to see the boss, and who to keep out. They will very often be seen working in large corporations, and will be part of the backbone staff who are central to the efficient running of the organisation.

Six women deal well with money, and have a good sense for both horses and the stockmarket, as well as when to buy and sell real estate. This alone can account for why they often have successful marriages, but only if the male partner understands and accepts their intuition. No man has ever won an argument with a woman, but most especially if she vibrates to the Six. They have such active and penetrating minds that no matter what you say, there will be another angle to prove you wrong.

If they have the courage, Six women make tremendous administrators and politicians, for as a rule, they really do work for the good of the whole. However, on the negative side they can also become terribly power conscious. What is more the Six knows how to wield power as well! This makes them dangerous opponents, though usually they are more caring as a rule.

Sixes make extremely efficient wives and mothers, coping with all life throws and rarely if ever complaining. They know how to make money work for them and how to find ways if it won't. They are resourceful, independent and astute and heaven help anyone who dares insult their husband or children in any way.

You will also see the Six woman in the armed forces, learning karate, or out their on the running track, pushing herself to the limit. She will often exude an aura of warmth, but have an underlying current of fire that men find virtually irresistible, especially as the innate chemistry of the Six will be firing away in the background. She asks pointed question of those she meets. It tends to give men the idea she is interested, when she is merely curious.

The feminine aspect of the Six is also often involved in natural healing, but persecution of this energy throughout the dark ages has given this vibration an acute sense of caution. Hopefully as this wears away in the Twenty First century this wonderful race of healers will once more step forward to fulfil their major role as doctors and administrators. It is in fact crucial that they do. Resonance medicine will only come forward when the Six energy rises to control the field of healing.

The Six man is the true philosopher. Contemplative and considered you will often find the elder statesman has a strong Six vibration in his chart. The men have the healing gift as well, but are generally not as intuitive as the female. The male has a greater sense of method, and a stamina that belies his often pale appearance, but this is because phosphorus is an integral mineral in the Six vibration. Not the ruling mineral, which is Oxygen, but each number works best with a different set of minerals and enzymes in the human body, and it is these which help to give specific physical and emotional characteristics with each chart.

Book of Number: Interpretations

Quietly, the Six will work in the background, until one day the fire breaks out, and everyone says "Hey, I didn't know Harry had it in him!"

This is only because the Six really thinks things through before acting. At their highest levels they epitomise patience, and yet carry a dynamic few can resist. This is another part of the reason the Six does so well in business, but they are also often on the frontiers of important research projects, offering innovative and unsuspecting ideas to help solve what appear as insurmountable problems.

Dreams will often be one way the Six finds his inspiration, but it is essential that these be written down, or else much will be lost. Only by writing down our dreams do we learn to interpret out unique and personal language of symbols found therein, and this is not only for Sixes! It applies to all people, because the act of recording dreams, writing journals, etc. brings in the balancing energy of the Seven.

When someone is "at Sixes and Sevens" with themselves, it really means the energy inside tham has not been grounded. The simple act or writing down plans, dreams and aspirations will lessen the sometimes querelous nature, and give the individual more direction in life.

Remember, the characteristics of any particular number are shared according to their weight in any given chart. You might be a Four by your birth chart, but carry a strong element of the Six within it and thus be affected by this vibration.

The strong, negative characteristics of the Six are mostly to do with the urge for a hermit-like existence. This is because of their inability to deal with the world, and the paradoxical desire to be recognised, which can seriously affect the way they deal with others. Its opposite number is the Four, which indicates that the Six needs to learn solidarity, to become more worldly and Earthy in outlook. Otherwise they tend to become somewhat ephemeral and/or intellectual in their day to day dealings.

SEVEN

J. Edgar Hoover   1 1 1895   1+1+1+8+9+5 = 25 = 7

John F. Kennedy   29 5 1917   2+9+5+1+9+1+7 = 34 = 7

George Gershwin   26 9 1898   2+6+9+1+8+9+8 = 43 = 7

Positive Characteristics: Spiritual, intelligent, analytical, focused, introspective, studious, intuitive, knowledgeable, contemplative, serious, persevering, refined, gracious and can display much inner wisdom. Lucky Seven is an archetypal notion, but it holds true. Seven is both the "Dark Horse" and the lucky one

Negative Characteristics: Sevens can be aloof, distant, sarcastic, socially awkward, melancholic, cowardly and downright nasty on occasions. Carping, biting cynicism is a characteristic of someone lost in the negative Seven energy.

The Seven is the Dark Horse of the Noumenal Order. Often greatly misunderstood, this vibration holds the key that unlocks all the universal secrets and as such indicates great learning and often apparent misfortune. This is merely apparent, and if the native survives the testing periods that come with the Seven energy, all the hard times will have been necessary steps to the higher platform of consciousness.

Its contradictory nature comes from the fact that it represents both the higher nature and the lower form, or that of the divine incarnate. Not that every Seven is destined to become the next Messiah, but there is often something very sacrificial about them.

In truth, it is simply that the lower self (Ego) must learn to step aside for the higher self (Soul) when we are passing through the energy of the Seven Ray. It is closely allied with the Eleven Vibration, as well as the Three, which if these occur in an individuals chart is certain to produce a spiritual dedication, and also a sense of disconnection with others.

Many Seven who fail themselves in this chosen incarnation become paranoid and depressive, exhibiting excessive behaviour in manner and dress as a rule. They are drawn to experiment with drugs, in particular the hallucinatory, calling this part of their spiritual quest. This is invariably destined to create heath problems and obsessive behaviour. However they also have the ability to snap completely out of this self-deluding sphere and, oddly enough, end up the richer for it.

Seven is the meeting point for the paths of inspiration, compassion and the physical world, and so we can easily see why so many develop a Messiah complex. This is because they have not yet discovered themselves as Soul and thus gained a sense of spiritual perspective.

Only when we can look into our own inner world and see the pure light of ourselves shining back can we truly feel balanced inside. This is an essential part to the journey of the Seven.

The child working with this vibration is often quiet and thoughtful, many times not needing the company of other children. If they do, it can often cause stress, for the solitary Seven energy will often-times sit wrong with other children. It appears to generate a state of slight unnaturalness, but this is only the Seven child considering deeply his thoughts and actions before he actually goes ahead. They are the most considered, but not necessarily considerate, child in the Noumenal Order.

This hesitation can only be overcome when the child is very secure within themself, and so it important that they KNOW they are loved. They may not appear to need hugs and cuddles, but they do, more than any other child. Curiously we find a lot of orphans are Seven children. It seems that detachment is a very important lesson for them to learn, which of course involves coming to terms with the Ego. A very difficult path indeed.

Many black magicians are of the Seven vibration, as well as many of the white ones! They are drawn to the occult like moth to the flame, and very often get their fingers burnt as a result. The women often become practising witches, yet also often lead otherwise normal lives as housewives and career girls. This is part of the two-leveled nature of the Seven, and is not indicative of a deceptive personality.

Seven women tend to be somewhat accusing in their manner, not because they wish to, but because their personality is like a razor blade, dissecting all it encounters. They are the girls at school who looked forward to chopping up the frog in the biology lesson. As a result of this natural curiosity they make good doctors and psychiatrists, as well as good writers. This is true of the men as well.

In fact most writers vibrate well to the Seven frequency, even if they are not naturally blessed (cursed?) with the energy. Many famous writers have been born on Seven days, many more than would account for mere chance. Writing is a particularly strong point with this energy, because it symbolises the drawing of the higher energy down to the lower. It will encourage thoughts and emotions to reform into physical reality.

The female and the male aspect to the Seven is very close, except that the female has more compassion as a rule, and greater patience as a result. The ladies find their life progresses along very well, as long as they keep their patience, and consider the needs of others.

As a wife, the Seven woman is intriguing, for you never know what she will come up with. Her mind is articulate, though often they find difficulty with words, (another paradox considering they are usually good writers!) and the way she will express her thoughts will be quite odd. They can be adorable, warm Souls who are a pleasure to share a life with, and things will never become boring unless you, yourself, are an ill-considered bore.

Whereas the women will fit in, the men will invariably seek to stand out. They can often be nervous and edgy, needing solid dependable work to feel at ease, and will work on private projects into the late evening night after night. Surprisingly, after years of working for the firm the Seven male will suddenly decide he has had enough, and take the family for a trip around the world, on a camel, or some other equally absurd notion.

Somehow they will always find the obtuse way to do something, but as a result of this, we find that they make excellent computer programmers. One might say the Seven energy is almost inexplicable, but there is always a method in the madness. Naturally, the opposite end of the spectrum is the individual who has done nothing with his life. If this is a Seven, they will most likely be a suicide candidate.

The Seven will always look for a career or service post. We find many priests and religious figure fitting this energy. This is partly because of the solitary nature it is often associated with. This need to be alone is often really a need to resolve some inner question. Yet there is also a need to be of service in some way, which can conflict with the desire to be alone. This is shared by both women and men under the Seven vibration.

Oddly, one of the major karmic lessons here is to do with money and understanding the true nature of wealth. Often the Seven individual has come from a background of wealth, but appears to need to be poor for many of the lessons to come home properly. Because of this, the Seven will often hold up poverty as some sort of standard that is to be valued.

Book of Number: Interpretations

This is merely one section of the path they tread. Beyond poverty there is great spiritual and often material wealth for these people, but only if they can get over the failure/martyr consciousness they so often suffer.

The psychology is one of freedom. Freedom is paramount, yet the Seven native will enslave themselves to an ideal, a group or an individual thinking that their devotion will set them free. Perhaps, but in time we realise that most good shepherds are only here to shear their flock.

Rather than freedom, these natives should focus on individuality and expression of Love, wherein they will find their true freedom. The colour the spiritually seeking Seven will often choose to wear is blue, which indicates their desire to ascend to the next level, that of the Eight.

The mineral attached to the Seven is Manganese. Much of the activity of the vibration utilises phosphorous, but the principle agent is Manganese. A shortage of it will make these people depressive and moody, and so it is essential that they have live food, especially fresh sprouts and herbs like tumeric (which is mostly manganese and iron).

As we have said, Seven represents the Dark Horse of the Noumenal Order, one that is rarely understood, but which can spring forth with a font of wisdom. The Seven makes the true elder statesman, though because of the solitary nature, they are rarely drawn to politics. If there is an important ideal at stake, however, they will go through hell and back to see it is achieved. They are misunderstood, and usually they do not understand themselves, but when the Seven finds his or her wings he soars like the eagle and is an inspiration for all.

Book of Number: Interpretations

EIGHT

Nelson Mandela 18 7 1918 1+8+7+1+9+1+8 = 35 = 8

Ulysses S. Grant 27 4 1822 2+7+4+1+8+2+2 = 26 = 8

Aretha Franklin 25 5 1942 2+5+3+1+9+4+2 = 26 = 8

Positive Characteristics: Eights are authoritative, business-minded leaders. They value control and power but can be balanced, materially detached, successful and realistic. In management positions, they are efficient, capable, street-smart and good judges of character.

Negative Characteristics: The dark side of the Eight can be cruel, insensitive, violent, bullish and/or greedy. Negative Eights are intolerant of others and often tend towards being religious zealots.

The Eight must be approached on two levels, that of the double Four and the full Eight. In practical matters Eight represents overall stability, as thus is closely affiliated with money and finance. In spiritual matters, the Eight can hold a breadth of vision and compassion. If the two can be combined (Such as in the case of Nelson Mandela, born July 18, 1918 = 35 into Eight) great upliftment for all around them will occur. When non-judgemental and bi-partisan, the Eight can transform, inform and edcuate all around them.

Many Eight's feel a spiritual calling, and those that do find that money and other people opinions are not important to them. Self-sufficiency and having enough for the day is all that matters. They make fine philosophers and also great adventurers, like the type that go to the Amazonian jungles to find a new breed of butterfly.

The Eight is any form is not a light personality, and tends to be rather severe on first impressions, but this is only their considered and serious nature. They tend to have little interest in what other might think, and are happ as long as they are left in peace to contemplate.

Book of Number: Interpretations

This is especially true of the Eight children, who will sit for hours, and then come out with what seems a very obtuse question, like, "Why is Santa Clause being pulled along by reindeer in his sled:? Would it not be much easier to load it all into a big plane?" The pattern of the Eight is to ask a question with an answer already in it. This is because they have already decided inside, and are simply checking if you agree.

If you laugh at an Eight child they will be very hurt. They are unforgiving with any perceived weakness and/or stupidity, and if you are unfair, you will lose all respect. An older Eight child will simply discount you, possibly for life, if you do not measure up to their expectations. They need strong, yet gentle, guidance throughout their young life, and will be utterly faithful to those they care for, and those who care for them. Don't get on their wrong side, however, for they have elephantine memories and will bring up words you have said three years earlier if it will prove their point.

The Eight wife and mother is assiduous in their efforts to keep the children and house in complete order. And what is more they will do it while holding down a career! Capability reels off them as the orders fly, and the children will rarely argue. They don't want the clear and concise pulling apart and dressing down that their mother will give them if they are not well prepared with answers and reasons for their actions.

Let her have the bank account, for it will stretch forever in her hands. With the right husband, usually a Five, Four or Six and occasionally a Two or One, she will ensure that his prospects are looked after, and that promotions come. She will invite the bosses wife to bowls, and while ensuring that the lady wins, also make sure she recognises the advantages of having her husband on the company team. The Eight wife and mother is quite ruthless about looking after their own.

On the Negative side they will become preoccupied with finance and getting the better home, to the point that they will become nags and fishwives. They will ride the children, causing resentment, and create disharmony in the home.

The Eight male is usually very affable and makes an excellent employee. They are reliable and conscientious, taking pains to not waste company monies. They are also painfully honest as a rule, and tend to avoid gossip and the common type. They far prefer drinking wine with the boss than beer with the boys.

As a result, they are seen as good executive material, and are! An innate understanding of diplomacy combined with a forthright manner allows the Eight to open door after door for themselves, but if at any point they question their seemingly good fortune, or become introverted in their dealings with others, everything will be thrown into reverse.

The chaos that ensues when the Eight vibration turns sour is very painful, especially as the native of the vibration often refuses to see it, and insulates themselves in the Ego sphere. They would prefer the bank to repossess rather than to sell cheaply and escape with minimal losses.

The spiritual aspect of the Eight is important, for it carries the tone of resolution within the emotional sphere. Mispent and misunderstood emotion is the area that cause us the most pain, as a rule. The core issue here is essentially that we fear a loss, and insulate ourselves emotionally from this. The Eight energy breaks up the fear of loss, and innately understands the Law of Plenty. This key to the Eight vibration can provide a lever by which we can all solve many of lifes concerns.

The Law of Plenty states that that there is enough for each individual if they allow balance in their lives. The Eight vibration teaches balance, rather than compromise, and inner strength, rather than outer will, as the solutions to lifes concerns. These simple notions really work. When we abide these rules, we find that there is indeed enough for our families, and this holds as true in Ethiopia as it does in America.

The Eight is the double Four, which is the symbolic representative of the Merchants Principle of Added Value. Added Value is simply that if you have a tomato, and you want ten, you take the seeds from the one you have, and plant them. Pretty soon you will have lots of tomatoes. The essence is in allowing time for things to grow, and so we come to the Eight's greatest failing, a tendency to rush.

The psychology here is of the fear of failure, which lies buried in the combination of a lack of commitment and the lack of self esteem. If we look at anyone's life we will find that the source cause of most of their concerns come down to this fear of failure. It is accented with the Eight.

Lack of commitment and low self-esteem are the bogey men of the Eight vibration, and the interesting thing here is that the nature of the Eight is that of the Octave note, or keynote. Eight is the repeating energy of the first note in the scale, only higher. But if you fall into depression, you cycle down to a lower note, and have to start climbing all over again.

In music you can play a song in any key, and someone can play the tonic note to the song over and over, and it will fit in. This is the secret of the Eight. As the native more fully steps into this vibration they will begin to fully relax and be themselves, thus preparing the inner person for the vibration of the Nine that follows.

Eight is a most curious number. In China it is seen as a Lucky Number, yet in Cherio's Book of Numbers it is viewed as unfortunate. The key to understanding the bridge between the two is to see the different mind sets between East and West. The Chinese are incredibly hard working and prepared to sacrifice in order to obtain a long term goal. This suits the energy of the Eight. The seeking of short term gratification, quick results, easy money, all opposes the Eight vibration.

Eight is associated with Saturn Rising in Astrology. Traditionally a difficult period, but if a person is well prepared for emergencies, and hard working, it is a very healthy and beneficial aspect.

The greatest lesson the Eight will learn is the truth that there are no shortcuts. Only by fully grasping the inner workings of things can we learn to make the external things move more quickly, and the natural energy of the Eight is to look to understand the minutae of 'stuff' in the knowledge that this will become the building blocks to a greater future.

Eights are builders. The stones we use to build bridges are the same stones we use to build walls. When this vibration is strong in a person's life, they feel the need to ascertain with every situation in their life whether to build a bridge or a wall. The real secret is letting it all go.

When we forget we are the centre of the universe, and just strive to be part of the great flow of events, the Eight comes into its own. In stepping back from the limelight, by removing ourselves as the focus, we allow life to construct things as they are meant to be,

Book of Number: Interpretations

NINE

Mohandas Gandhi 2 10 1869 2+1+1+8+6+9 = 27 = 9

Baron von Richthofen 2 5 1892 2+5+1+8+9+2 = 27 = 9

Positive Characteristics: Nines tend toward positions of service. They can be helpful, compassionate, aristocratic, sophisticated, charitable, generous, humanitarian, romantic, cooperative, creative, self-sufficient, proud and self-sacrificing.

Negative Characteristics: Nines can become egocentric, arrogant, self-pitying, sentimental, discontent, fickle, cold or mentally unstable. In the negative, they use silence as a weapon.

The Nine is the next most misunderstood vibration after the Seven, for it represents the combination of Power and Silence within the human psyche. A good part of the journey of the Nine is learning how to harmoniously marry these two distinct, often warring, aspects.

Because of the internal "noise" from the need for attention that most of us are addicted to, few will grasp that true and lasting power is to be found in silence. This equates to a deep, impenetrable resolve to cease all unnecessary inner and outer activity. Silence creates the state of "No-Power", and practicing this as a this way of being opens us up to properly allow the force of life to flow through us. The paradox is that by using NO power, other than silence, ultimate power will manifest in our lives.

And what is this power? It is simply that nothing shall be kept from us that is in accord with the divine plan. This pure state of silent power is, of necessity, a paradox to the mind, but if you witness the way a cat will stare down a dog you will get an inkling of the process at work here.

The dog has eminently more power, and is symbolic of the universe, but the pure focus and intention of the cat will tip the balance in its favour. Thus the individual becomes, in essence, greater than the universe as a result of its focus. If the cat sought to use its own power, it would have the reverse effect. The dog would easily see that it possessed the greater strength of the two. Are we getting the picture of how the Nine works?

Book of Number: Interpretations

In Ancient Egypt, the Pharaoh and the priestcraft used Silence as the ruling force, and it allowed them to rule for thousands of years. The power of silence unleashes the ancient Dragon Energy, or the Mind Focus Energy, that is also the characteristic trait of Western Society.

And who runs Western Society? The silent, background force of beauroracy and the money behind it. The ancient Zen Coan states: Why does the king of the Ocean rule? Because he rules from below.

The Nine Energy can open up the psychic and spiritual corridors within man. It is not abrasive like the artificial means, such as drugs and ritual, and hides in plain sight. The Law of Nine is highly visible in our society in our modern advertising culture. This uses indirect means to control the minds of viewers on TV, etc. The proliferation of Mind Training seminars around the world also speaks of the awakening of the Nine Energy.

We have just left the 1900's and the Nine has been the ruling force for that century. The growth of silent controllers, the increase is rules, the slow restriction of freedoms, all speak of a negative Nine energy.

Yet the true, unlimited Nine energy cannot be controlled, owned, possessed or dictated to by external forces. It can only be awakened in your heart, and only through the sincere practise of Silence. This is the Power of the Nine: The individual only has to wake up to their natural state of Being, and no external fetters will control them.

The evolved Nine has an advanced sense of fairness and a powerful drive for independence. But the journey to this place often means traversing the chasms and pitfalls inherent in the mind. Many Nine's suffer simply because they think too much, and thus give away their sense of independence for a sense that the universe is much bigger than they are. And so they feel it would be best to just fit in. The cat versus the dog: the cat can only win with pure focus and intent. In this way, the Nine imprisons itself by inversion. Iron bars do not a prison make.

Compromise is deadly for the Nine, for it ties them into lesser energies, and yet the truth is we all have to get along with each other. Because of this paradox the Nine often feels the need to run things. If they are in charge, the Nine feels less like agreements are a compromise. Thus we will often find Nines working as directors of companies. They are the people who do not actually do anything themselves, but who organise others to do the job that most suits them. The cat staring down the dog.

Book of Number: Interpretations

Nines will also work behind the scenes as researchers and development officers. Here they do the groundwork, so that others can take over when there is a sound concept to create. We will find the energy of the Nine everywhere, especially as the last decade has been 1900's and so EVERYONE will have a nine in their chart, somewhere.

The 1900's have been the years of the technical revolution, with abuse of power via this technology growing on a grand scale. The 2000's will level this out, but an exceedingly difficult time will precede this. (Author Note: The financial crisis of early 2000's is the sign of the Nine energy breaking. The above words were first recorded in 1991) The end of the Nine cycle, the end of the decade, and the end of the century is an awesome combination Numerologically speaking. Our next few hundred years have already been charted, directly because of the 1900's.

The Nine Child can be difficult, as they often demand their own way. You might get cross with them, and they will in turn go cross at you for going cross at them. They have an unbreakable will, and if they feel they are correct nothing you can do or say will change this. They are hard to train socially, for they have little respect for the concept of right and wrong, yet they will learn well through games.

Like all children, they love to mimic. But even as they copy what they see, the Nine chaild is analysing the pattern. They want to know how things work, and will research, read and ask questions about anything that picques their interest.

They will keep something unspoken within themselves. If you are sensitive enough to notice, and simply ask what it is, they will often tell you. Otherwise the Nine child keeps its own counsel, or they will talk to their teddy bear about their discoveries that day. A sense of secrecy and privacy is all important. These are the children who have secret meetings in the cubby house, creating passwords and the like for admittance.

Iif you can understand them, these are amazingly easy children to raise. Quite simply, if they respect you, they raise themselves. You will be "on their team", so to speak, and this connection will last their entire life, and puberty will be far less troublesome. This period, by the way, need not be one of dissension and parental alienation. If you connect with your Nine child at an early age, they will keep no secrets from you later on.

Of course, the 1900's really oversaw an entire a new race coming to planet Earth, but the basic rules of understanding, teaching and directing still apply. Now more than ever we need to establish a respect bond as well as a love bond between ourselves and our children. We need this more than ever, because the Years 2000 will bring such a powerful energy that many children will feel pressed to cope, unless their home life is on solid ground.

Nine's need this stability more than most. Though they are independent they are also greatly aware that home is safety, warmth and love. If the Nine child is given these three things, they will grow up secure and positive in outlook. Without them, the Nine becomes tyrannical and demanding. Safety, warmth and love are essential to their harmony..

The Nine is a mixed mineral makeup, and so they come in all shapes and sizes, but they need to take care of the electrolytic action within their body. These minute electrical charges are extremely important, but particularly so with those strong in the energy of the Nine. This means the Nine has to be careful of the thoughts and attitudes, for negative thinking will suppress their electrolyte (plasmic) balance, which is what is all important in the exchange of minerals and nutrient in the body.

Self discipline is the keystone to the Nine's continuing happiness, and they are wise to have it instilled at an early age, for otherwise their own streak of independence will work against them, turning into defiance and the scattering of their attention into meaningless mental dialogues.

The Nine woman is a survivor. She knows instinctively when to shut up in the conversation, and also when it is time to walk away. You will often find them working with small companies, for the rush and bother of larger corporations tends to leave them cold. If there is no independence in the workplace, the Nine will be fighting for flexi-time arrangements, or to have a crèche installed, anything which broadens and deepens the view.

She will seek the top job, not because she wishes to climb the ladder, but because she sees that she is the right one for the job. Nine's are rarely ambitious, but they do not like working under those they feel are inferior to themselves. In such a circumstance the Nine woman can, and does, emotionally assassinate the personality of the one they dislike. The men are gentler, but this is because the masculine energy is more in tune with the Nine than the female. This is true of all the odd numbers, which are masculine, while the even are feminine.

The Nine wife often marries several times, for they simply wear out relationships. They demand a lot, but if they meet a man who can match them, they are docile kittens who love to make him breakfast in bed. Oddly this is rare, which I suspect has more to do with the weakened male nature in Western Society at this time.

Book of Number: Interpretations

If no success is found in love, the Nine wife will throw her energy into finding success elsewhere. She needs movement and positive growth as a rule, yet the very striving often puts her happiness that one inch away all the time. It is the paradox all Nine persons need to resolve.

The Nine male is forthright, critical of failure both in himself and others, and precise in speech. Futher, if they do not express themselves, they can become introverted very easily. Clear expression is essential to their sense of balance. Few choose to argue with the Nine male, mostly because when he does say something it has been well-considered and is fairly difficult to flaw.

They have an imposing presence in conversation, but many times this is a sham and a bluff, for many Nines are busy working on their self image, and they use social situations to brush up on appearances. Politics is high of the agenda of chosen professions, as are any positions of influence where their will might be extended. However, it is not until the Nine practises perfect inner silence that they discover their true identity, and thus their true sense of worth.

They seem tough, but in reality the Nine is a tender soul who needs a great deal of love. If it is missing in their lives, they will turn into hunters chasing down their quarry, but rarely do they truly find the secret their heart is looking for. The Nine will join the Masons, the Rosicrucians, and any mystery sect they can find. They will study old scripts, go on pilgrimages to ancient shrines, and finally realise that the hidden thing they have sought has been in their pocket all along.

It is only then that they learn the inner silence that gives the Nine its balance, and the freedom from the endless cycles of action and reaction.

This then is the key to the Nine: *It rests at that point between finalisation and beginning.* In any given moment, do you encourage and grow the situation, or end it? Therefore the Nine has always this element of choice in their lives, which is both a blessing and a curse, if you think about it.

Symbolically the Nine represents the Ninth note in music, or what is really the Second note, higher up the scale. This indicates it is the next step on the higher journey, but of course, this can be the lower journey is the attitude is negative.

It is interesting to note also that Beethoven was deaf when he wrote his Ninth Symphony. This is indicative of the silence of the Nine Vibration, and how it produces its power as the result.

TEN

Tom Hanks   9 7 1956   9+7+1+9+5+6 = 37 = 10 = 1

O.J. Simpson   9 7, 1947   9+7+1+9+4+7 = 37 = 10 = 1

Positive Characteristics: The Strong TEN personality can withstand life shocks, and stay focused on the task at hand. They are natural entrepreneurs and leaders. Clear, bright and determined, any task is viewed as a means to a specific goal. The positive Ten is like sunshine to the seeds of hope and aspiration.

Negative Characteristics: The Negative Ten cannot finish anything. They flounder in indecisive, contrary thoughts, and vacillate between all available options. Augmentative and weak, they brood over the past and generally fall into severe addiction or depression. They see conspiracy and subterfuge as the cause of their failures, and cannot accept personal responsibility.

The Ten, Eleven and Twelve are considered higher order Numbers, and as such they are called Volatile Elements. Yet they only work in a medium suitable for them. It is like trying to put electricity through a piece of wood, the higher frequencies simply do not flow unless the native has some connection to their higher self. Yet with this number present, there will be some area of the persona affected by it. The first thing that must be determined is where this number is active in a person.

This is really determining what aspects of consciousness are volatile, or awake. Socrates stressed the importance of knowing ourselves. This is the only way to bring the latencies of these high numbers into play.

This means that if you are doing a reading for a drunk, and he has a predominance of high numbers you can fairly well assume that he has either forgotten his inner nature, or is seeking to repel it for fear of the responsibilities they entailed. Some drunks I have dealt with, however, were very aware of the spiritual power connected to them. They simply did not know how to deal with it.

Book of Number: Interpretations

There is little point casting pearls before swine. If you are doing a reading, ask questions and work out where a person is at, then focus your interpretation in accordance with where they are at. How do you then pick an active Ten energy in a chart?

The Ten has the energy of the new, the budding flower of Spring, the turning of the season, the whisper of a new love in the heart. All this is the frequency of the Ten, which is the One and the Zero combined. The One signifies force and direction, while the Zero indicates the presence of Spirit. This adds up to a sense of purpose and a sense of fulfilment, but of course the reverse is also possible. Always the positive carries with it the shadow of the negative, because even angels can be tempted!

The Ten energy has an intense sense of purpose. A destructive Ten is a dangerous person who will create harm intentionally before burning out and destroying themselves. Polarised the other way, the Ten is the great builder, and thus is connected with the vibration of the Four and the Eight. A person carrying this trine aspected in their Noumenal Chart would almost certainly be an creator of great and noble things.

The perfection of architecture is natural to the psychology of the Ten, with the natural form and flow of life a source of fascination. The concept of architecture is an interesting one, for it is the highest of the arts. In this study the individual must combine beauty and form with practicality and longevity, and this is the destiny the Ten vibration seeks to fulfil.

If we add the basic building blocks of the Noumenal Order we find they add up to Ten. (1+2+3+4 = 10) This is the Pythagorean Decad.

The Ten is the mystic with the eyes forever searching the heavens. Their ideal is seeking the form of God in manifestation. The finest sculptors will vibrate to this number, as will surgeons and people of vision, but it is very difficult to categorise it any further.

Suffice to say the native affected by this vibration will have a certain spiritual quality to them. They will also have a certain surprising way of finding just what they need, even though the odds were against them. This is because they have the quality of Spirit in their lives, which is the ultimate resource, and things seem to find their way to them at the right time and place.

Naturally, if the native is out of balance, the force of this spiritual flow will internalise and be directed against the obstacle in their mind or emotions. The Ten person can have a very trying time until they learn detachment from their fears, inner wishes and hopes.

They have a curious trait, which is to question everything while giving the appearance that they believe all things. It is a sort of survival mechanism, for the Ten is inherently unstable in these lower worlds, and the native needs to learn to approach all things with a negative outlook. This gives them balance. All good builders view things from the point of what difficulties there will be, and because of this they work out what can go wrong. Therefore they minimise the problems before they start. It's a good attitude to adopt in this world, this sense of realistic optimism.

This could be said to be the attitude of the balanced Ten, a realistic optimism, and it is this which gives them the weight to wade through the darkest night of Soul, and to penetrate into the very heart of the matter when the need does arise.

The major lesson for the Ten is surrender.

The Ten is a composite of all the numbers, and so can be found in any field, with any sort of personality, but it carries an air of preciseness and spirituality about itself. A negative ten simply does not carry this vibration, but what does happen to natives who cannot hold its energy is that the Ten splits into the One and the Zero, with the Zero (spirit) remaining a passive background vibration.

We occasionally find what I term as "blind healers", or those who have no idea what is happening when they do healing work, but it works anyway. We find that these Souls usually have a latent Ten vibration in their chart.

Napoleon looked for Souls who carried this vibration, and his way of qualifying prospective Generals was to simply ask them at the end of an interview "Are you lucky?" If they said "No" they did not get the job. Napoleon was spiritually advanced, and understood the energy of luck, or what we might otherwise refer to as the Ten.

Book of Number: Interpretations

ELEVEN

Shirley Temple 23 4 1928   2+3+4+1+9+2+8 = 29 = 11 = 2

Bob Hope 29 5 1903   2+9+5+1+9+3 = 29 = 11 = 2

Positive Characteristics: The Elevel is the most intuitive of all numbers. It is instinctual, charismatic, dynamic and capable when its sights are set on a concrete goal. Eleven is associated with faith and psychics, yet also with teachers and higher learning.

Negative Characteristics: The Eleven can be anxious, shy, stressed, conflicted and scattered. When focus is not applied toward a goal, the Eleven can be self-sabotaging. It's positive characteristics turn into obstacles when not used properly.

This has been described by many Numerologists as the Number of Power, but we need to remove this idea of a "Master Number" because it is simply not part of the Pythagorean Teaching. This concept comes from Ancient Egypt where the spiritual mathematics invoked the Base 12 numerical System. (which was used in the higher circles of Egyptian calculation) In the Decimal System, NINE is the number that carries unique properties, in the Base Twelve, it is Eleven.

The essence of the Eleven is the combination of singularity with duality. The number itself gives a clue, two parallels, individual, yet combined as one. It is a number that represents a mixed blessing, because of the unique "variable" it seems to create in a person's life. If you are strong in the Eleven, you will constantly find change being evoked in different aspects of your life.

When you have an Eleven prevalent in your chart, it is an indicator you have chosen to study, or seek to grasp, the inner working of things.

The Noumenal Order is not a passive thing. It has it's own intelligence, and will reach us individually in the way IT chooses. What I can say is that the occurrence of the Eleven anywhere in the Number Chart indicates a stronger connection to this energy. But it is a potential energy, and if you want to use this energy you will have to learn ITS ways.

Eleven symbolises the balance between the use of Power and the use of Love. The dual paths are Love and Power, and when practiced properly there is only harmony between them. But when greed, lust, etc. take control of the heart, the power of the Eleven is ruinous to the individual,

By practicing the ancient Delphic proverb (Inscribed on the Temple of Apollo alongside "Gnoeth Sueton") "Nothing too much" we can learn to get in charge of the dual nature of the Eleven energy. If we can learn to combine Love and Power in our lives, this gives us the inner direction to achieve a great deal in this life. So in a sense we can say that the Eleven IS the Number of Power, but I go this circuitous route to more fully illustrate that true power must parallel a deep, abiding love, if it is to be effective and useful.

The greatest power in the universe is Perception. Perception is really the true secret of the Eleven. It gives us the ability to see the divine written in the heart of all things, to hear its sweet whisper as its agent (what we loosely term as Spirit) passes through and enlivens creation. By recognising the Divine in life, and in ourselves, we can emulate it, thus fulfilling the prophecy of Socrates that we "shall rise up through the ethers and of ourselves become as Gods."

Classically speaking, the Eleven represents the plane of Agam Purusha, or that sacred void that protects the Godhead from the vagaries of its own creation. This immense deity, by report, challenges all who wish to know the true heart of God. It takes a brave Soul to master this challenge.

And so it is with the Eleven. Persons with this aspect are capable of enormous leaps of faith that brings them into the understanding of truth. But beware, for if you fail the test of the Eleven you can easily become insouciant, and uncaring of others.

Most individuals are really not interested in coping with such an intense energy in their lives, and they retreat into "rational" thinking and conservatism. Hiding yourself in a "safe" job, burying yourself in dull circumstances, acting as if the world is too big to understand, all this is part of the negative backlash of the Eleven energy. An emptiness of failure can haunt you, because the Curse of the Eleven is that it demands perfection, balance and harmony. Few can really master its nature, and the nagging sense of failure to achieve this can warp the personality, and turn a decent soul into a depressive alcoholic.

Book of Number: Interpretations

What people with this energy need to learn is that there is a time and place for all things. If we experience failure we need to understand it is really just a rest period until the energy develops once more. As a child learning to walk, we fall over many times BECAUSE of the process of growth, not in spite of it. The only true failure is not getting back up after we fall down.

We are human. We are all in this together. Understanding this is core to unlocking the Eleven Energy.

As an aside, all the Numbers and number patterns have their particular tests which will be evidenced in both large and small things throughout our lives. By coming to recognise these for what they are we can more swiftly pass through them successfully. This is the really great benefit that the study of Numerology can offer the individual, a clearer life because of a developed perception. Note that I did not say EASIER!

Eleven has a phonetic key within it with the word "Leven". Though it has been lost to the history books, the two words were once related, for the Eleven has the power of levening the Human Spirit. In bread terms, levened bread rises in the oven, and in spiritual terms, the "Elevened" Soul rises through the heat of experience into the higher worlds of God, gaining more substance and personal truth as they do so.

Eleven is the power of growth and renewal, and this is what sustains the focus of the Noumenal Order. Coming after the Ten, which symbolises the finalization of one cycle and the beginning of the next, the Eleven is like the entire series of One to Ten energies all rolled into one. It symbolises ALL of the Decimal cycle, and so encompasses the vibrations of the decimal system in its entirety.

It is a terrible number for acquisition. If you are interested in increasing your earthly goods, beware. Everything the Eleven touches brings with it an entire set of learning curves to work through. It is a great vibration for those interesting in teaching and growth, but it has a never ending quality that often frustrates the person who just wants it done and dusted.

For these persons the Eleven in their lives will symbolise a series of conflicting decisions. This tends to activate the energy of the Two, and the Eleven frequency fades to the background. This is one of those curious realities on the Noumenal Order. When a person inwardly fails to grasp an energy, the energy itself switches down to lesser and lesser forms. In this case, the Eleven switches to the Two frequency.

Book of Number: Interpretations

The Eleven Soul simply cannot afford to be of two minds about anything, for where they place their attention they will activate this energy. If they are double minded, it will fracture their personality in very short order. (Leading in some cases to mental illness.) The inner survival mechanism of the individual will seek to avoid this, and shut down the energy.

Schizophrenia is common with those who tread the spiritual paths, even though most do not recognise this. It is a process of having ones head in heaven, yet dragging along their feet on earth. Until we adjust to this conflicting vibration, it will shake us, and rattle our sense of proportion, to the point where we will forget just who and what we are. And this is sometimes necessary for the true light of God to shine through the morass of social conditioning that inhibits and encloses our personality.

I mention this, because a very deep power hidden in the Eleven energy is one of resolving paradoxes. When the person in the Eleven Vibration reaches the state where there are no paradoxes, they become open to the higher forces at play in their lives. If not, the door doesn't open.

"Human all to Human" is the philosophical argument for the general frailty of the race. But we can see it another way: For those who know their ancient religious history, we can use an analogy. "HU" is the ancient word of God, and "man" symbolizes mankind in general. This concept of God in Man, or Hu-Man, has long perplexed the philosophers, but if we look at the word Humility, which phonetically is Hu-Man-Ability we can see the key that resolves the dilemma.

Humility is the lesson of the Eleven. We are humbled until we learn we are divine. A curious paradox!

Through humility and an understanding of internal divinity, we come to learn to embrace power and love in the same moment, and this releases the freedom and clarity inherent in the Eleven.

Note: The word Human is believed to derive from the dual Latin roots, Humus (earth) and Hominis (man).

TWELVE

F. Scott Fitzgerald 24 9 1896   2+4+9+1+8+9+6 = 39 = 12 = 3

Janeane Garofalo 28 9 1964   2+8+9+1+9+6+4 = 39 = 12 = 3

Positive Characteristics: Breadth of vision, expansive outlook, kindness and consideration. Twelve represents the capability for deep insight and a perception that removes all bias and doubt. Often we find an enhanced sensitivity, and the active Twelve will find it difficult living with others who do not respect nature or their surroundings. Service to a higher cause is their watchword.

Negative Characteristics: Negative Twelves abuse friendships, and play mind games. They reverse from a concept of service to a calculated and ruthless sense of self service. People are seen as minions to serve them, and only when you are subservient to them will they appear to give you any form of recognition.

Shakespeare's Twelfth Night, the Twelve months of the year, the Twelve hours for day and night, the base Twelve math system of the ancient Egyptians, the base 60 (5 x 12) math of the Sumerians, and Twelve notes of the musical scale. So much emphasis on Twelve.

Twelve is the completion of the cycle. It represents the ability to grasp the entire sequence of the Noumenal Order, and then BE it. This is Self Mastery at its highest level, and this is the key to the Number Twelve.

You rarely see the Twelve stressed as being important in any of the Numerology books, and yet it is the most important number of all! The enery of the Twelve, however, has so rarely been completed in the average Noumenal chart, that for the most part it may as well remain invisible, which is interesting for this is exactly its essential characteristic. The ability to be unseen and unheard.

If the Twelve is strong in a reading, you must judge for yourself whether it is worth mentioning or not. Unless a person has high aspirations, often it

Book of Number: Interpretations

is best to say nothing beyond asking what the persons goals are, and, if they are common ones, suggesting that they have the potential for more.

Twelve represents the dedication of an individual to God. If the vibration is strong, they will have seen in their contemplations, or perhaps in the time where they were dropping off to sleep, the great Single Eye. This is the ancient archetypal signature that represents this. Unless someone is ready, talking about the importance of the Twelve energy tends to only enhance the ego, thus making a difficult journey just that much harder.

On this point, it seems almost a prerequisite that those destined for higher growth seem to have enormous egos at the outset. This is likely because of the habit of comparison that comes with enhanced mental ability. It has been particularly strong in the 1900's, but even more so in the Years 2000 because the Two is the eternal shopper and comparer. This will accent ego difficulties, split personalities and poor self esteem.

As a result the indication is that the Mind Sciences will enjoy a boom period coming into the years 2000. It would be helpful if we understood that those with large egos need them for their own protection, to help cement the dichotomous struggle they feel is tearing them apart inside. Ego is not a dirty word, but Ego is not the natural personality of the child. The true attainment of the spiritual state requires that the individual may, on demand, set aside both Ego and Personality to become an Impersonal Channel for the higher truth. This is very much the power of the Twelve.

It is the power of neutrality. If a person does not hold it's energy, the Twelve adds down to a Three. A Twelve so affected will have a great desire to create, but that does not mean they have the talent to create anything worthwhile. However, the Twelve into Three is a powerful catalyst. It will trigger off change and growth in those around them.

In one sense the Twelve is the catalyst of the Noumenal Order, and any creative individual who is married or in partnership with someone who carries this Twelve vibration will greatly benefit by it. It is important to note that the Twelve never makes itself obvious, but that its presence will set things in motion if, and only if, those around it decide to get motivated and start manifesting. The Twelve energy is a Verb, it is active.

When surrounded by dull or insipid people, the presence of the Twelve will actually inhibit experience and growth, creating not a catalytic action, but one of an increasing negative inertia. It becomes a question of Physics: "What would happen if, in a state of no conflicting forces, an unstoppable object were to collide with an immovable object?" The answer is simple, and it is the answer to the riddle of the Twelve.

The force from one energy TRANSFERS to the next. Twelve is like a carrier wave that allows energy to shift, transmute, and transfer from one state to the next.

If we are simply what we are, then all that we do will take on the character of our beingness. This adds to beingness, and creates a new moment of experience. If we are of service to life, we move gracefully into the new state of Being that comes as a result of our actions. I am tempted to utilise the word "perfection" to describe the Twelve, but this implies an ending, something finished and complete. The Twelve is exactly the opposite, for it symbolises each moment as a new beginning.

This then is the character of the Twelve, that of the Spring of Everlasting Life, the River of Consciousness, and the Ocean of Love and Mercy, all as a single whole.

Naturally, this is beyond most peoples conceptions or desire, and thus much of the value of the Twelve is like the spilled water over the brim of the glass. But every now and then we meet that special Soul who might benefit from our words, and so it is very important that we, at all times, remember that this tone, this vibration of Twelve, is the ladder where we common Souls might reach up and touch the Divine.

Summary

These words are only a precursor, an outline of the Twelve basic vibrational energies. The interpretaions for One to Twelve are aligned with the colour spectrum, and the musical scale.

Go to www.numberharmonics.com.au for more information. For now practise adding up the numbers in our own, and our friends, birthdates. See how the description given that number fits them, or not!

If it does not seem to suit, first make sure you have added ALL the numbers in their birth date, because many forget to add the "19" and write their birth date as: 23/5/54. It should read as: 23/5/1954.

Also look at numbers that appear twice, such as the two Fives in the above example, and use the next section (Dominant Numbers) for the basis of interpretation for these.

ADDENDUM

Numerology does not promise an individual eternal life, nor does it preach a set of moral codes or hold out offers of heaven. At no time do the teachings of Numerology seek to assert themselves as a religion, unless required by law and/or taxation reasons. It does hold, however, that an individual who leads an ordered life with an attitude of goodwill will naturally accrue a greater inner wealth of wisdom and beatitude, and in this might be described the religious experience of BEing.

The essential premise of the Noumenal Order is one of addition, not multiplication. The reality of one manifest creation, be it thought, emotion or physicality, draws the other un-manifest likeness towards itself. The joining of the two begets the next expressed reality. Likewise the opposite is true whereby the un-manifest creates the manifest, in all proceeding according to the Law of Creation.

The individual journey along this ancient path is just this, an individual one, and as such indicates that these writings and interpretations will be absorbed and then expressed through the individual in their own manner. It is therefore your own personal responsibility to succeed of fail, and to accrue what benefit and/or detriment as your experience will grant you.

SUMMARY

This brings to a close the basic interpretation for the Fadic Number Series of One to Twelve.

You will have read many interpretations and will have noted that they seem to fit a wide variety of people you will have met and dealt with. Of interest: Someone may clearly seem to be aligned to the Three in the interpretations, but they possess a different birth number.

This is completely normal. As you go through the rest of their chart, the aspect of the Three will appear in different ways, and the meaning fo this will make itself clear.

These Fadic Numbers are like the Sun Signs in Astrology. It is a general description of what energies apply, a broad net cast to catch a general meaning. Yet we know that Astrology has many more aspects at work than just the month you were born into, and it is the cross-referencing of ALL aspects from an Ephemeris that gives you an accurate account of the individuals chart..

The same holds true for Numerology. It is not just the number of your birthdate, or the numbers of your name, but how they all combine in your Noumenal Matrix that creates the "map" we read.

The simple message is: Everyone has a range of Numbers that have significance in their lives.

What counts is how these numbers interact with each other. This is why it is so important for each of us to gain a sense of what each number is about. If we cover these basics and catch the spirit of each individual number, the rest becomes much easier.

DOMINANT NUMBERS

Dominant Numbers are created from any number having what is known as a a dominant position in a chart. They indicate that this frequency is being "called in" by the individual. These modify the Noumenal Chart in a similar way that a scale in music can be played in a different mode.

If someone has a One Birth Number that has a Five Dominant Number, then it is the same frequency adjustment as the Key of "A" being played in the harmonic mode based on the Fifth note of the Scale ("E")

The overall effect can be either significant or slight, depending on the number relationships around it.

Interpretation is simple. If a person's chart has a predominance of One in the Matrix, that is the dominant number. If the birth chart has a Three as the dominant number then in the area of Ancestral Past the Three is a strong factor.

When the combined (name and birth) Matrix has a specific number in the Dominant position then it is part of the Destiny of the individual. In a sense, it represents that which is to come.

You can also use these short interpretations for any number that needs highlighting in a chart. They are generic, to the point descriptions of the number energy, and can be applied wherever it is suitable.

Interpretations for Dominant Numbers:

ONE: Dominant, forthright, unforgiving, high in energy. Single minded and persistent, the person affected can become frustrated by resistance, with deep angers boiling beneath their hard exterior. This can burst out in unfortunate outbreaks of temper with loved ones, and must be seen as the person venting in what they feel is a safe environment. In the positive aspect the One can be focused and determined. In the Negative the One becomes dogmatic and opinionated. Courage and the ability to live in the moment are the greatest assets the One can develop.

TWO: Intuitive, manipulating, artistic, fragile. The greatest enemy of the Two is always themselves. Two can be very double minded, and thus lose all momentum in life. Dreamers and visionaries, or politically motivated and scathing, the Two always likes to imagine great things with themselves being a part of them. When the Two grasps that they are at the centre of both their problems and blessings, they will them learn and accept personal responsibility for their actions.

THREE: Creative, logical, inventive. Three likes harmony, but must learn that true harmony only occurs when we have inner freedom. They seek this freedom in many ways, often not realizing the overall goal and getting sidetracked into argument and ideals unsuited to their temperament. They are good in business, and creative, yet often Three's suffer from chronic low self-esteem. Success can accent this problem, oddly enough. Three's need love and tenderness, which resolves their inner tensions.

FOUR: Stoic, reliable, conventional yet adventurous. Four is a mixed bag, from the social rebel to the accountant. Four is a paradoxical vibration: they dreams of great things yet will count the pennies. They are generous, yet always remember the favours owed, and expect payment in due course. Four is generally patient, yet impatient with stupidity and thoughtlessness. Laughter and humour are needed to relieve the seriousness of their nature, and this makes them easier to live with. Otherwise there can be unpleasant, sullen silences from the Four. They also tend to like taking an opposite view against whatever is presented to them. In this sense they often play Devil's Advocate.

FIVE: Energetic, temperamental, faithful and yet sometimes fickle. This is a pivotal number, and is correctly placed at the centre of the Noumenal Matrix. It is the number of communication and its effects can be either good or bad, depending of the circumstance. Having a Five in a Dominant Position represents the ability to change. It's all about communication, and sorting out the jigsaw. Because of their natural curiosity, promiscuity, and other sexual matters often come to the fore under the influence of this numeral. The Five must learn to combine the stability of the Four with the constant love and intuition of the Six for success in life.

SIX: Clear, Intuitive, Loving. The Six can be extremely magnetic, easily attracting others to it. The only number that surpasses the Six in attraction is the Five, but the Six is generally more stable and can hold another's belief more readily. This number has an energy that tends to brook no opposition when roused to anger. The love here is more of a "mother" love rather than sexual. Sixes are highly affected by their upbringing and environment, and keenly feel social disruptions around them. This often leads to a career in publishing, journalism and the like.

SEVEN: Internal, Studious, Respectful. The Seven needs freedom, but often imprisons itself in circular thought and inaction. Sevens are driven to understand the details, and can lock themselves up with internal questions. It will appear to be a confusing wheel of self-created pain to those around them, yet this is their process. There is a tendency towards a hermit consciousness, where even if the individual does not actually live on a mountain top, they may as well for all the communicating they do. In time the Seven sees through the illusion of pleasure and pain, and life becomes more balanced inwardly and outwardly. Sevens need to learn to just DO IT, as the Nike Logo says.

EIGHT: The Eight is the number of Money, Karma and paradoxically, Indifference. It is represented as the harvest, which moves through the above three points in a never ending cycle. Finding a point of detachment from worldly concerns is the overall energy at work here, but this can put the individual through great difficulty because precious few can let go of their dreams and hatreds. Eight involves the preparation for completion, for the start of another cycle, and so the lesson is to focus. You cannot complete what you begin without a persistent focus.

NINE: Power, Strength, Silence. The Nine carries many powerful energies, but few ever fully realize its potential, because they are either too lazy or too talkative. Inner Silence is the keynote of the Nine. It is the number of completion, and depending on how you deal with matters you cycle into the higher subtle energies or revert backwards into physical world concerns. The Nine energy allows an individual to cut off from the world, and from their problems, allowing internal room to sort things out.

Note: Ten, Eleven And Twelve are not treated as Dominant Numbers, and should be looked at as One, Two or Three.

COMPOSITE NUMBERS

As we carry on from the Dominant Numbers, we come into the Composite Numbers. The term Composite Number is NOT RELATED to the Mathematical term of the same name.

These are using in adding down the birthday and name of the individual, and in the Noumenal Flow Chart. As you grasp their meaning, you will find that the Composites form an essential part of the language of the Noumenal Order.

They are fixed points of truth, and remain so even for people who have never heard of Numerology. As one example, they are of great use in Dream Interpretation. Someone may have seen 41 rabbits in a dream. First we ask what a rabbit means to the person, then look up the meaning for 41. (Finding a cause, learning communication)

Or you are travelling down the highway, and you have a question you are thinking about. A car pulls in front of you, and it has the number 61 stand out. You know as a Composite, you reverse numbers above 52, so you look up 16, and there is an answer to your question. (Which is: Make sure you plan well, because if you don't, vanity will cause thing to crumble)

Composites are the all purpose tool we use every day. These are the numbers that appear in your life as a continuing dialogue.

The best external reference on this subject is "The Life You were Born to Live" by Dan Millman.

COMPOSITE NUMBERS: Interpretations

10... Symbolized as the "Wheel of Fortune" and indicating negative Karma as much as the lucky turn of the dice.

This is a fortunate vibration in regard the sense that one's dreams are likely to be fulfilled. Yet manifestation where a bed of fear still controls the heart becomes nightmares. If the person is too involved in controlling situations, it is a good indication the fears run the show. If the need to control things is based on a fear that they will go wrong, the Ten energy has a habit of materializing your secret inner thoughts!

The lesson is simple: Learn to let things be, and be sure to keep your own porch swept. The Ten is subject to the inner nature of the person which in turn affects outer circumstances. These can easily be polarized to good or bad purposes. The ideals of honour, faith and self-confidence are an important consideration, and the person affected here would do well to look to their ethics. (if they are to have a balanced, worthwhile life)

The Law of Completion is highlighted when the Ten Energy appears.

11... A curious number. It is seen as the portent of power.

In truth the Eleven is really the number of direction, education and higher teaching. When the Eleven person finds a motivation, or a sense of purpose, they find that the Eleven energy seems to materialize what they need to complete it. However in the negative aspect it also indicates hidden dangers, treachery and difficulties relating to circumstance.

Symbolized as the Lion muzzled, generally Eleven is associated with the person struggling against convention, upbringing and authority. It is often in evidence with those who are breaking away from a heavy religious background. The lesson is one of decision and focus. The 11 likes to dominate the other numbers in a chart, and for this energy to be harmonious, the person needs to be very sure of their abilities. It is not a vibration for the faint hearted.

12... Signifies the completion of a task, often through great sacrifice.

The Cross on the Mount is the image here, as it indicates an individual giving all, often in ignorance of what may lay ahead. The overall lesson is one of self-sufficiency, and the person affected must be sure not to fall into the "martyr trap" of doing everything for others, and nothing for the self. There is a great ability to plan and organize with this vibration, and a tremendous capacity for love, but it must be a firm love or else the energy will not be contained. In this instance the negative effects are a weakening of resolve, infidelity and/or confusion as to the person's purpose and direction.

The positive aspects are organization, recognition of beauty, and happiness. In fact, those who work in harmony with the 12 vibration often seem to have a well of smiles inside them, whatever the outer circumstances.

13... Greatly misunderstood, and not at all an unlucky number.

This number represents a heightened awareness and an increase of energy. It is symbolized by Death, though in reality death is but a transition from one state to the next. The lesson of the Thirteen is that through ending the old, the new shall grow. It is growth, yet the power of growth wrongly applied becomes a cancer.

This number tells us to expect the unexpected, and to always go one step further than the average man. It follows the merchant's principle, which is that if you want to increase your wealth, plant the seeds of things that will grow. This is a good number for those in the fields of investment and advice, but if one cannot handle the "added" energy that seems to surround this vibration it can be a difficult path. The lesson is to simply always go one more step than what is absolutely necessary, and things will work out fine.

14... A number of movement, travel and new associations.

Fourteen is fortunate with money and business, but a strong element of risk seems to shadow it. Caution and prudence are advised, especially in the choice of associates. If a focus is kept on the obvious, things generally go well. Danger is minimal if the emotions of the querent are kept in balance. If not, there is often a swift climb up the ladder of success, but some unexpected turn sends you back to the bottom.

Investment in solid realities, both financial and emotional will counter much of the negative aspect of this vibration. Work as much as possible with trusted friends, but ALWAYS check the books yourself, just to be sure. Prudence is the main lesson.

15... A number of Magic and of the Fey (fairy) folk.

People with this number will often utilize magic (consciously or unconsciously) to carry out their plans, which involves the manipulation of natural forces. This is often done without the person realising this, and so you must take particular care of your thoughts and actions if you have this number aspected. There is a cost for using pyschic forces to attain personal ends. Fifteen is associated with eloquence and grace, and people with this vibration present in their chart generally have an ability to mix, and be accepted with people above their rank.

It is a dangerous aspect if the person who possesses this energy has few scruples. If so they cannot ever be trusted. We see such traits as charm and convivience present here, which can as easily be negative traits as they can be positive!

Many are uneasy with the unpredictability of this energy, but really, this is the fun of it. More to the point, the lesson is one where the person learns to accept and enjoy life as it finds them.

16... This number is associated with the Tower of Babel. It is a warning to be aware of one's Ego, and to make sure it does not rule your heart.

If your vanity gets away, with this number aspected your relations with others will sour and you will feel a sense of dislocation in life. Calamity will strike when you least expect it unless you build plans with the complete agreement of loved ones. The number can be especially difficult because just as life will seem to be paving a way before you, the uncontrolled Ego will go and ruin everything. We have to be aware of its influence BEFORE it becomes obvious to others.

This simply means that we have to set a goal of honesty with ourselves, and recognition of the good points in others. The lesson is to allow others to be good at what they are doing.

17... Highly spiritual. This vibration indicates that Soul will rise like the phoenix from all adversity, stronger and better for the trial.

Often housed in an attitude of detached love, this number can indicate tremendous growth for the individual, however, it is not considered fortunate in regard worldly matters.

A person with this number will often be remembered after their passing, if they have not succumbed to the difficulties of their life and become negative in outlook. Otherwise there is a quality of the far seeing eye to this energy, and if the person affected learns to look beyond the immediate concerns of the present they will see the greatness indwelling in all things. The lesson here is to do with purity.

18... This number is often symbolic of the material nature seeking to conquer the spiritual.

In the negative we might see here the image of a weapons dealer, or of someone trying to make a profit from another's fear and misfortune. As such these people are often financially successful, but at what cost a man's Soul?

If this number crops up in future plans one must take great care, for it indicates a need to choose between the higher and lower. On the flip side, if one chooses a spiritual view, which involves giving rather than taking, this energy gives tremendous strength and purpose. As such it has a slight missionary zeal to it. If kept in balance this means that this person can do a great deal of good for others. The overall lesson is one of setting priorities. What is really important in your life, and what can you do without?

19... Symbolized as the Sun. Extremely fortunate for finance, self esteem and honor, this number indicates successful outcomes in all associated with it.

You have to have a big heart and mind to allow all these good vibes in, and it can also be the case of the higher they go the harder they fall! So the person with this vibration must be sure to build a solid foundation in all they do, which will give the energy stability. In the negative these people can become extremely self-centered, to the point of expecting others to serve them. If this gets out of hand they lose friends, money and influence, and the positive energy dries up. Suicide is not uncommon.

In the positive, this energy literally shines, and those affected find popularity and good times rolling in. The main thing is to remember the Law of Gratitude, and not take it all for granted.

20... Recognized as "Judgment". This is often a call to a higher goal, and is a vibration not usually associated with worldly riches, unless these have been inherited or discovered in some way.

Otherwise the person affected generally does not have the intense desire to make money, and at any rate riches will generally be of little account for these people. Finding a worthwhile purpose, and the subsequent fulfilling of it, is their greatest wealth.

The number can also indicate delays and hindrances, creating an atmosphere where the native must develop themselves inwardly before the outer doors will open. It indicates that a turning point will be reached, and important decisions made in regard the ethical nature of the person affected. A good number when coming to deal with the self, and taking charge of one's life.

In the negative it indicates cynicism, bigotry and criticism, while in the positive it indicates service, clarity and wisdom.

21... Seen as the "Universe" in the Tarot. This is a number of achievement and honors. It is victory, but after a long fight.

The battle has really been fought in past lives to develop a belief in oneself, yet we still need to go over the ground again. Only when we realize this "battle" is won do we grasp the role of society and the reasons for the battles each of us have.

A very fortunate number if you stick to your principles, but very negative if you fall into apathy or sour emotions. In this case it can be a very black energy that can consume the heart, and the person can become very power conscious. Otherwise it is a good number for the counsellor, the intermediary and the socially concerned soul. The overall goal is the discovery of self, which is beyond the concerns of this world.

The message here is to always look beyond the immediate and transitory concerns, and find the deeper purpose.

22... Play the Fool. This is a raw energy, and the person with it often likes to clown around, but there is a satirical nature.

The Court Jester used to be an important position in medieval courts. By using satire, humour and wit in observation, the fool could speak of things that were never allowed to be mentioned. The energy is really about getting around the Ego to make a point of truth.

Generally the person finds they are directed into social issues and personal rights. We often see this type involved in trade, where they are their own boss and free to play all day with tools. In the negative there can be a deal of false judgment and poor perception associated with this number, which generally comes from associating and listening to others who have no clear vision and/or confused ideals.

New beginnings are indicated, but care should be taken to get off on the right footing with all ventures. Being involved with the right people, (Right Association) is one of the major lessons here.

23... The Star. There may be help from higher up. You could find yourself in the position of receiving "jobs from the boys".

There can be a spiritual aspect to this as well, which needs to be developed, but all revolves around the natural communication this number has. If you make yourself less communicative in any way, your options will begin to close down.

Even if you have been a failure, when this number becomes active you will be favored and looked after in some way. Perhaps the vibration is too lucky, in this sense, for the native can easily come to rely on others, and not carve their own path to destiny. Music is a strong attraction, and unfortunately drugs can be as well. Drugs are very destructive to the natural energies, and must be avoided unless prescribed.

24... Be Self-Sufficient, not Sacrificial. Maintain a right to your own destiny and freedom. Freedom is earned with service.

As a multiple of Twelve there are definite characteristics marked here, in particular with courage and order. In this instance there is good fortune and an end to the sense of having to sacrifice everything in order to acheive. There is a strong need for self-sufficiency that can lead the person affected by the Twenty Four astray. They can become headstrong and foolish, subsequently becoming the victim of their own ideals.

There can be financial and/or emotional gain through love, marriage or inheritance, and advancement is often through superiors recognising past effort. A good number if you wish to study. The energy is methodical, and there is a lesson in patience in store for those who wish to rush things. Listen to your intuition, pay attention to details, be sure to stay true to yourself, and things will generally go well.

25... Overall the 25 is considered favourable. It indicates strength and wisdom gained through experience.

If the person here is of a strong character people will be drawn to them. Those holding this vibration in their chart often have grand notions and causes to follow, and as long as they are dedicated to a specific purpose with integrity, people will often support them. Here can be one of the tests of power, which many fail and are cursed to wander several more centuries upon this planet.

The lesson involves not letting things go to your head, and keeping your contact with the heart. This aspect can also become quite insular, forgetting to trust their inner whispers of truth, and getting itself caught in mind games as a result. Freedom and room to breath are important here, so it is important to steer clear from situations likely to cause confusion and heartache. The simple life, good food, little of no TV and Newspapers (or other time wasters) and a focus on some productive activity is the recipe for success in this instance.

26... A number with the gravest warnings for the future. It foreshadows disasters brought about by associations with others.

Ruin, by bad speculations, by partnerships, unions, and bad advice can be aspected when this vibration comes into your life. Yet if the energy is mastered there is great financial prosperity possible here. Discovering true Self Worth is highlighted, but this can cause heartache.

Very often this comes through meeting the one of their dreams, but losing them. Self Worth stops your emotions overtaking your reason, and stops the spinning out of control scenario that equals broken hearts and wallets. 26 is a number that requires the individual to stay in charge and to watch the details. Remember, weeds grow faster than flowers!

This analogy relates to many things, but in particular it applies to the negative personal habits that can sprout when personal discipline is relaxed. Vanity is the great failing here.

27... Reward will come from being smart, not physical effort.

The nature of 27 is that you solve lifes problems internally, and not with physical effort or force. 27 relates to the balance of Yin and Yang and keeping this balance is important for success. Strong creative urges, and the ability to make them happen, opens the possibility of interest from high places in your ideas, with the subsequent upliftment into social circles of political importance. This number is *excellent for writers*.

There is another aspect here, that of hidden dreams and the struggle between the differing forces inside the person. The phases of the Moon can affect these people strongly, drawing out the male and female aspects accordingly, and thus affecting their behavior. In extreme cases this leads to insanity. Simple common sense is the balancing aspect here, and simple physical fitness is important.

28... Query all that comes, otherwise this is an unfortunate number.
This is the Builders Number. A successful builder has an outer negativity, whilst remaining positive within. Doubt all, yet believe. Catch this attitude and many things will work out for you, while others will wonder how you do it. The cat has nine lives because it understands the contradiction of finding trust by not trusting.

In the positive aspect this vibration lends a tremendous vitality which allows the person affected to start and complete projects beyond the ken of most people. In the negative a deep pessimism can overrule the desire to communicate, and dark, weird beliefs can overtake the personality. Compulsive disorders are an indication of the negative aspect.

29... Deception is possible here, either self deception or hidden agendas from others.
Inner doubt here can ruin what is otherwise a promising vibration. The person affected by 29 needs to move carefully and thoughtfully in their progress through life. Belief in one's own opinions is not enough here, the querent must search their soul and discover their true inner wishes if any happiness is to be found. This can be a great "opening" energy in a chart, one that allows many new experiences into the life of the person so blessed, but because of this the person affected must be careful of their environment. They can easily pick up negative energies around them, and become destabilized as a result.

Choose friends carefully, and stay true to your word. Honesty really is the best policy here. Personal honesty with oneself and others will keep the heart directed towards constructive thoughts, and will generally keep life in a positive light.

30... Thoughtful, deductive and contemplative. These people are creative in solutions to problems and make ideal managers, but they must be careful of becoming too mental in their approach to things.
30's can starve their own emotions from too much detachment, but even so this will not affect them with relating to others. In fact, despite their often cool exterior people are generally drawn to these folk.

In the negative there can be a cold and callous attitude that cares for no-one unless there is some mileage to be gained from them. With both the positive and negative types there can be a residual anger that comes from a resentment of authority that motivates their actions. Even so, the axe of karma does not fall swiftly as a rule, and they may seem to get away with many things, for a time. It is usually in old age that the problems will show, particularly with diseases of anger, such as arthritis. In all, a good number for planning and considering the future.

Open mindedness is the lesson here, which when correctly understood leads to open heartedness, which releases you from anger.

31... ***This number can carry great power, however, it is not personal power, but the ability to communicate with others that will allow this energy through.***

By understanding the basic desires and needs of "common" people, the person affected by this vibration can come to realize the inner strengths and weaknesses that motivate us all, and it is important that this knowledge is not misused. By learning to see the obvious, the person under this influence will discover how easy it is to sort out almost any condition on Planet Earth. What then occurs is where the trouble starts: they feel they have a right to tell others what is right for them.

The first rule is: allow people to make their own way in life. In simple terms, don't break the Law of Non-Interference. If this is done the 31 is a favourable energy. In all, this is a fortunate number for finance, and the native can often achieve fame and fortune to some degree, but the cost of this is often a sense of withdrawal from life and an inability to participate in common pursuits.

32... ***A highly favourable number when you are outgoing and accepting of others. Judgement brings out the negative traits.***

This a very good number when the person aspected is working in the public arena. The 32 has a magical quality to it, and excepting the fact that the native tends to make flash judgments of others, it is generally a very carefree vibration.

Children affected by this energy will live in a fantasy world far beyond what is normal, but no-one tends to mind overmuch because of their natural affability and gregariousness. As the child matures it needs to understand the subtle power of wishing, and needs to be careful of secretly manipulating situations and people to their own purposes.

Sharing is a major lesson here, which is the ability to give freely from the heart. This aspect is strongly affected by the other aspects around it, and so it is a difficult energy to pinpoint, but we will usually see "fey" (fairy) aspects in physical features, such as long fingers, high cheek bones and distant, far seeing eyes.

33... ***This number is highly intuitive, and often overly sensitive as a result of this.***

The 33 can mean strong, magnetic vibrations will pulse through the natives inner being. The is difficulty is in allowing this. Fear of what others think, or fears or unworthiness can restrict the heart, and introvert this energy. As a result there is often an almost hysterical shyness inherent here. If the native breaks through this barrier there is little they cannot achieve on a personal level. If not they tend to get caught up in mediocre, unsatisfying employment or unhappy marriages.

The shyness that often prevents these people from speaking up when they should is often based on a secret need for recognition. Few understand this and as a result the native can become very internalized. This process begins in childhood. Often we will find this type is drawn to poetry, or arts where they can find shelter from the harsh reality of the world. If the person gets in charge with this energy, however, they blossom in all ways, and will have a tremendous capacity to love.

34... Indicates strength gained through experience.

If the person with this number is of a strong character people will be drawn to them. If they are dedicated to a specific purpose, the will and the way to achieve it must come from within because this energy will only acheive things on its own terms. Self Creation is the watchword.

Yet there is also a need here to relax and allow life to take its course. This attitude gives the mind and emotions more elbow room, and the result is greater creativity and freedom. There can be a tendency with this aspect to become insular and overly detached from family and friends. Few people understand the need these people have to be alone, and so the person under this influence tends to tune out from their environment, and tune into whatever dream they are following.

A paradox often follows the lives of these folk: they need to be creative, yet they also have a need to be secure. The two needs rarely work well together, and so they generally suffer great frustration until they can have both in some way, shape or form. A lesson in balance and diplomacy is usually contained within this vibration.

35... Excellent for money, and education but generally terrible for judgement with personal relationships.

This is a very odd energy. The individual is often brilliant in some speciality, but hopeless in personal matters. Marriage problems, sex confusion and odd quirks can mar the character here, so there is a definite need to develop an ethical base in life. There is also a need to develop compassion, for this will open many doors to new experiences and friends. But so many doors can open for these people that they can become confused as to their true inner direction. Habitual wasting of time can result. This can lead to a sense of loss later in life.

All this can be easily avoided with a sense of practicality. Buy a car you can afford, don't care what the neighbours think, paint the house yourself rather than getting in professionals. It's all about being practical in the moment to moment details. In all there is a need to focus on balancing the emotions, and this means to focus on what is necessary and needed rather than what is desired.

If you have a paranoia regarding people, it is in this cycle it will emerge. A good Number for learning about yourself, but the grind and ploughing through events can be a hard taskmaster.

36... This indicates strong character and high ideals. A very mental approach to life is the norm for these folk, and if they can sustain this, it is fine. Otherwise, Burn Out is an issue.

The natural intensity of character can create difficulties and problems behind the scenes. These folk are unusually believable and potent when it comes to an argument, and they do not like to lose. This vibration can give the individual a driven sense, which can cause interpersonal problems with loved ones. Temper must be controlled, especially when based in pride, or else communication will fail, and you lose rfriends.

Generally these folk don't mind this, and are quite happy to continue on alone in most circumstances, but if the person cannot deal with the natural tendency to cut things (and people) off this will lead to deep rifts and enmities with others being formed, and many hidden enemies.

The lesson is to tame the wild beast in such a way that the energy becomes directed to serving a useful purpose.

37... A number that is considered to be very fortunate in love and partnerships of all kinds.

Many bridges can be built here, and if the Soul wishes, a bridge to the inner worlds that will give them the certainty in life many do not have. However, for this to come about the person must be directed to a life of Contemplation and Service. By this I do not mean a passive life, but an active, considered viewpoint that recognises other peoples needs. If they develop an attitude of giving, the plans, hopes and aspiration in their life become very magnetic and positive.

Confidence plays a big role is how quickly these folk develop, and so it is important for them to have a good grounding in life, preferably with a trade or some practical means of earning an income behind them. There is often an innate ability to construct things here: objects, relationships, anything. And as a result these people can be good counsellors and planners. Developing confidence is generally the main lesson.

38... A potent energy, but one that must be directed, or all will collapse in confusion, anger and apathy. Be warned!

There is inertia present when the 38 is prevalent in a chart. It indicates the unfolding of karmic circumstances, and so the past must be balanced and all accounts paid before real progress can be made. This indicates, therefore, a long state of apprenticeship before becoming the Master of your profession or dream. Persistence and focus on the goal at hand is of essential importance, but many find it difficult to know what their goal is, let alone developing the stamina needed to complete it.

Listening is a very important step in resolving the lessons of this number. Most importantly, listening to the intuition, and the subtle hints life gives us, will help us find direction in the present.

39... This is often a greatly misunderstood number. It indicates a lot of movement in life, both emotional and physical.

There is a contrasting need for love, marriage and security when 39 is strong in a chart. It creates an ever-present need to test the limits, and discover new ground. This creates a great deal of pressure on personal relationships. It often works out that these folk simply end up testing the limits of their marriage and partnerships, and then pay for the divorce.

39 is seen as an indicator of relationship problems, and people often become what the gypsy would call the "Cliffhanger". This is when a person is neither in, nor out of, society, and proud of the fact! The truth is this energy simply is curious and questioning. Non-conformist and radical in their approach to people and things, they often carry the germ of greatness about their being. If they could only truly believe it!

There is a great need to finish what you start with this number. An understanding of the Law of Cycles will bring great benefits into the lives of these people.

40... This number indicates self-containment, and possible isolation, in order to work out their inner questions.

The number can be fortunate or otherwise, depending on the person, but if you are lucky you will be VERY lucky, and vice versa. The number has great power, and a Soul strong in this energy has an ability to influence others. Yet the person affected can just as easily grow entirely indifferent and disinterested in life outside of their small circle.

This sense of cutting people and situations off can be habitual, and this will often result in bitterness late in life if it is unchecked. There is a bit of a social rebel in here, and yet also the arch conservatist. It can be a puzzling energy, not only for the person involved, but for those around them as well. These people do best when in a creative environment, and are happiest when creating something.

41... The Muse. Practical, rebellious, strongly sexual, adventurous and extremely lucky.

The 41 is a creative catalyst and we call it "The Muse". If the person with a strong 41 in their chart has a worthy cause, they can readily attract others to their banner. If well organised this is not a problem, even though they tend not to like the limelight overmuch. If disorganised, clutter and hoarding can become an issue. These folk excel with 'hands on' sort of work, and have an ability to soldier on regardless of difficulty.

There is a specific need with this number to develop communicative skills, and negative introversion can be a danger if the person affected becomes closed to outside influences. This number is often associated with writers, but they are often the partners or business associates who organise things in the background.

42... Luck and Opportunity. The Answer to the Quetion of Life?

This vibration embraces creativity in action. These folk must take care to remain ocused on their goals or else their life will go off the rails, and be wasted. 42 indicates good fortune and the ability to start again. People with this vibration may find that though their dreams may collapse, from the rubble of loss a better dream and a fuller life will emerge.

Peace, despite failures and difficulties, is often the end result of the action of this number in our lives, but only if the heart has remained true. The Multiples of this number are Six and the Seven. This energy is very much "at Sixes and Sevens" until you clear the decks of doubt.

43... Indicates upheaval. Generally not regarded as fortunate, but often this vibration will act like a blockbuster, clearing the way for more beneficial things to come through.

Like the storm clearing the air, this number will attract the crash of thunder, but the overall result is good. Obviously, however, if the person affected is of a frail heart they will not find this energy pleasant. There is little that can be done in this instance, because one of the lessons here is in learning to be adventurous. Some will find adventure in quiet, studious pursuits such as scientific discovery, others in scaling mountains, but a general outflow of some sort is necessary for well being. The mastery of this energy requires acceptance of ourselves, even our weak points, for it is through these that we discover our shadow self.

This number denotes defeating our shadow, or the repressed part of our consciousness we fear to show in public. If the person can succeed here they realize great freedom of action and thought in their life.

It is an excellent number to have in a birth date for a writer and/or a person seeking to go past their inner boundaries. It will help those who help themselves and can bring extraordinary fortune into your life.

44... This can be a most unsettling and unpleasant energy. It indicates dealing with karma, and the breaking of new ground.

When 44 appears in your life, it tends to indicate old Karmic Patterns are emerging. Good and bad, positive and negative are very much determined by our inner attitude, and this is what is being addressed when thei vibration enters our life.

If this vibration is present, but you feel you cannot deal with it, then perhaps a change in your name will help. However, if the energy is of a permanent nature (i.e. the birth date configures to 44 into 8, etc.) then pick up your courage and just go for it. With this energy present you must either run full bore into life, or it will run into you. The former is far more enjoyable than the latter!

Seek to remove your social and sexual inhibitions by actively doing the things that you dream of. Face your demons with the questions

Book of Number: Interpretations

"Why?" and "How?" and you will be amazed how they dissipate and diminish. Clearly it is best to be outgoing with this number, but if this is not your nature, learn to be determined. The personal experience of courage and determination will transform you.

This is a very important Number, and occurs in your life at times when you are inwardly prepared to break through the boundaries and restrictions of society and upbringing. It denotes change.

45... Silent and sure, these people can continue under pressure in a way most people find astonishing.

This is a very determined, powerful energy. The problem here is that people strong in the 45 can think they are indestructable, and like the Titanic, forget to watch out for icebergs. Negative periods will often be experienced as times of ill health. This can strike quickly and without warning, but even so these folk are resilient. No-one is indestructible in a physical body, but with this energy you can come close.

Watch out for icebergs, and when they come remember that most of the problems you face will be under the water and out of sight. Take care with diet and be sure to get enough sleep. The Lessons around the 45 are connected with practicing the Law of Silence, so avoid gossip, etc.

46... Excellent for those who commit themselves to projects, but without a sense of purpose the vibration here is useless.

Anyone affected by the 46 will feel a sense of polarity. They can feel moments of intense inner emptiness inside that if they run from can result in drug problems, etc. Or they can get TOO involved, and often sprout unasked for opinions to all and sundry. Either aspect can create a background of silent animosity that can trigger an avalanche of problems from others or from authority. The secret is simply keeping things in balance as best you can, and getting on with the task at hand.

Focus is the lesson, but it is the sort of focus that recalls priorities such as family and friends before career. Always remember the Law of Gratitude in your dealings with others and things will go well.

47... Good for the most part and fortunate for love, but not necessarily marital love.

This number attracts respect and admiration. It gives the individual lots of motivation, but rarely does it work well with finding someone to share this with. This is usually because the person affected has some inner sense that drives them on in a slightly manic fashion, and few understand this. It may seem negative, but remember that the arrow of fate is not shot by cupids bow, but by Karma. The destiny of these folk is simply not tied to romantic attachment for the most part.

Those affected by 47 usually become aware of the glaring inconsistencies in life, and in particular by the extraordinary way people lie to themselves. Ignore all of this and focus on your own path and purpose. All comes to the best if you doggedly pursue your dreams.

48... This is one of the great numbers, but can you master it?.

48 is marked by destiny, but also with great tribulation and most will instinctively avoid this. Thus their true path is also avoided. Because of this the number usually represents a wasted life, but it need not be so.

There is a pulse here that is part of the flow of life itself, but unless you are really living you will not meet the challenges the number represents. It takes a good deal of inner courage to succeed when this energy is present, especially when the 48 is present in the Birth Number.

One of the lessons that evolve from this number is to understand how the answer to harmony with life is self sufficiency. From this point of awareness those affected by the 48 will be able to cooperate with others in a balanced way. This number is a Dominant Number for the years 2000, where cooperation and coordination with others is essential.

49... An odd, quirky vibration which tends to create personalities of the same type.

The 49 represents an unbalanced force, but like a dissonance in music, a person can draw great energy from this when they can master it. The doors to harmony and completion will open once you grasp the nature of this energy.

And how do we do this? It is necessary to always go one more step in career and personal matters when this number is aspected. Careers where service is required are often a good avenue for stabilizing this energy. Service and networking are the new business builders, so a person who understands the 49 will be successful in any area that needs these qualities. It is all about allowing life to flow through, and the statement for the 49 is: "Your will, not mine, oh Lord."

50... Look for the element of Surprise in your life.

The 50 has a certain mystic quality about it. When allied with the number 32 in a chart it is a definite indicator of spiritual and psychic awareness. In the immature state wicked humour, and the prodding of sacred cows is common, but as maturity comes about a desire for peace and harmony overcomes the initial need to burst bubbles. This shift into maturity happens quickly, and with the metamophosis you hardly recognise the butterfly from the catapillar it came from.

There is often an extraordinary hospitality in the nature of these people, and though they may grow out of their waspish humour, the witty and entertaining self remains. They enjoy satire, especially satire with a barb of irony. For those who do not grow out of the childish need to point out others flaws, it bodes well to remember that the scorpion usually kills itself with its own tail, eventually. To be happy, use wisdom not wit.

Book of Number: Interpretations

51... The warrior. A very potent number, indicating sudden and unexpected advancement.

When 51 is highlighted, it indicates change. A sword with two edges and opportunities presenting themselves under this influence have to be inspected carefully. Due diligence aside, remarkable things can happen in your life when you get in charge of this frequency. Life will part for you in all you do, but remember to get out before the Red Sea closes. Keep moving forward. This number indicates a sensitivity to limits is needed, and an understanding of one's own personal rights and boundaries.

Our freedom ends where the next person's begins. Grasp this, and we can master the energy of this vibration. So much is solved through simple consideration for another's feelings.

People with this number often like to help animals and work well as firemen, nurses, and areas where service and a hint of danger combine.

52... Focus your thoughts inwardly and take clear action outwardly.

Children and people with a childlike attitude work well with this number. The principle works best when a person allows the flow of life to work freely through them, which essentially means to get over the insecurity and fears that block their natural flow of life.

The basic lesson is to be a part of life, but be very sure to learn the difference between the natural state of your being, and the social animal that has been trained into you. Knowing the true self allows you to integrate your "dark side", or the shadow elements that activate the failure buttons in your psyche. The lesson is one of acceptance.

If you CANNOT meet your negative aspects and deal with them, this number is a curse. You will come to situation after situation where you will be forced to face yourself and your shortcomings. Obviously, if the 52 is aspected in the Birth Name, you can change this and ameliorate the effects. If it is a Birth Number, you must face it. It is your destiny to know yourself, and to get past your internal fears of not being good enough.

53... The Number of Harvest and Manifestation.

While we say the Composite Series only runs to 52, the "Step Beyond" invokes the energy of 53. The energy of this number is rarely awakened until the individual is strong enough to deal with it. In this, and with all the numbers above 53, they have to be 'called to action' so to speak.

The number contains a humanitarian aspect, where the person will feel a deep desire to assist others in some way. The YMCA carries this vibration when they set up the self sufficiency projects in countries, which other aid people are just sending money to.

If you find this number strongly aspected in your chart, you may need to consider joining an organization that allows you to work in the interests of others, rather than yourself.

There is another aspect to the 53. It is a number that asks a simple question: "Is this useful?" There are a lot of apparently noble causes you might like to work with, but are they really useful? You may find a project that has a benefit to others as well as yourself, but stop and ask how useful the overall effort will be. This will qualify and clarify your decision to work with or leave the project.

The Law of Cycles is strongly at work with this Number. A simple rule that describes the energy of this number is: Do not start something that you do not fully intend to complete.

Summary to Composite Numbers

There is a specific meaning to every number in existence, but as numbers are infinite, logically it is impossible to describe them all. For numbers over 53, as a rule you either reverse them, or add them down to a Composite between 13 and 52.

However, if someone has 99 strongly indicated, a way to get an understanding of this is simple as a "double Nine". If they have 67 accented, think in terms of combining the meaning of the Six and the Seven, and it will give you some insight into what it means for the person.

And as always, Numbers do not exist in a vaccum. Every other number in a chart is part of the jigsaw. Learn to build the connections between them all, and you will get the overview of what it means.

Book of Number: Interpretations

LINES in the MATRIX

Here we look at interpretations for the Eight Lines in the Matrix

Lines are really "Straight Trines" in a sense, with the very subtle difference that their energy is primary and driven by nature, while the Trine contains energy that YOU can direct.

The Line in the Matrix will always be an active energy in the person's chart. A Trine can come and go in activity, and often they are working more in the area of the unconscious, whereas the Line tends to be overt and working in the area of open consciousness.

This is not fixed, but it can be considered as a general rule. All interpretations here carry both the STATED and the BALANCED/VACANT meaning for the line. The balanced / vacant interpretations follow on from the stated.

The Lines are:

1-2-3 Line of Creativity

4-5-6 Line of Intuition

7-8-9 Line of Altruism

1-4-7 Line of the Physical

2-5-8 Line of the Emotions

3-6-9 Line of the Mind

1-5-9 Line of Success

3-5-7 Line of Compassion

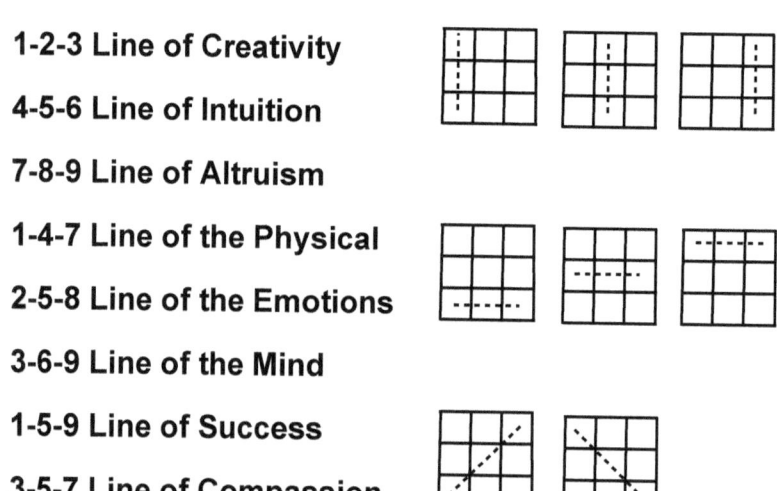

74

INTERPRETATIONS for LINES in the MATRIX

1-2-3 Line of Creation

The One-Two-Three nature almost speaks for itself. It is methodical, and does not like interference of any sort and can be quite headstrong. Yet without the imput and advice of others, the person can get lost in their plans. This is a part of the lesson of this aspect, to keep one's own counsel, yet listen to what others have to say.

The person affected by this line almost always has the desire to create something, anything, even if it's just trouble. This act of creation can follow many paths, it might be that of a builder, or simply someone who likes to follow a pattern, constructing hobby kits. We find that these folk tend to like to collect things, and then put them in some sort of order. This might be collecting items, ideas, ideals, individuals, or whatever, and then re-arrange them into new forms. Building and reshaping "stuff" is essential to the well being of this type, for if they are not involved in creating something they will weaken, both physically and mentally.

There tends to be somewhat of a panic consciousness inherent here. While the native wants to succeed in their ventures, they often have poor communication skills, and as a direct result of this, failure strikes. The problem is not failure itself, but the fear of failure, After a few problems of this sort, the individual can become so scared of loss that they become insulated, and thus reduce their ability to communicate. A very circular problem, which materializes as a fear of not being 'good enough'. Such a state is ruinous for our ability to realize our dreams. Good communication solves most problems, but especially so when this Aspect is present.

We can also find a person with a somewhat frivolous nature here. This is invariably frustrating for loved ones, but we should understand that, for those with this Aspect strong in their chart, this frivolity is simply a way of avoiding inner fears. The answer is inner confidence, which in this case is approached through the virtue of courage. Just DO it!

The 1-2-3 Line in the negative shows a sense of pettiness and procrastination. This will undermine relationships. Both of these negative influences stem from the Fear of Failure. A person trapped in the negative values can become quite miserly.

Socially, however, these people can be marvellous. They are the last to leave the party if they are having a good time, the first to leave if not! They like cliques, forming clubs and organizations for all sorts of reasons, but really this is because the 1-2-3 type hates being alone for too long. Paradoxically, they also crave solitude! You may think this odd, but this push-pull sense inside them is what activates and fires their creative instinct. We generally either love them or hate them.

There is a lesson here that requires the individual to learn to grasp things as a whole, and to need details less. In order to grasp this whole picture, the 1-2-3 person needs balance, and generally this means they have to learn to take life less seriously internally, and more seriously externally. This will differ from person to person, however, and in many cases the reverse will be true. Either way, there is a lesson in developing a more rounded viewpoint.

The major lesson is to learn to give, for the creative instinct of itself tends to be a selfish one. The acts of giving, sharing and loving are all intricately intertwined and the querent may have difficulty understanding the difference. By giving we mean to extend oneself on the behalf of another. Doing this with no thought of reward will greatly clarify the often muddy thinking of this Line, and thus improve the value and quality of life generally.

ACCENT ON THE ONE: This gives a stronger and more flamboyant sense to the personality. It also tends to increase the need for outer stimulants, therefore drugs and other diversions can become problems. This aspect can make the querent moody, yet drive them on to greater heights as a result of this introspection. Generally indicates an obsessive nature.

ACCENT ON THE TWO: Beauty become the focus, and these people may well become entirely impractical in their quest for it. The Two vibration here tends to make the querent edgy, often given to sarcasm and usually nervous in disposition. This is simply an outward reaction to a negative view from others regarding their childlike enthusiasms, even when these views are unspoken... Yet this sharp mind and nervous nature can also make the querent devoted to spiritual matters.

ACCENT ON THE THREE: This, being the creative number on the creative line, is not what one might expect. A Three in this position can acutely increase the degree of business acumen, and we find such people make excellent executives. In the negative, it can also indicate a blatant wilfulness and lack of regard for another's feelings.

As a Line of Balance or Vacant Line

1-2-3 Line of Creation:

The One-Two-Three aspect in the Vacant or Balanced position is like an empty well calling out to be filled. The person yearns for the heavens to release the rain it needs to fill itself, yet does not realise the water of life is constantly trickling in to feed it from subteranian sources. The sub-conscious forces are powerful here, and continually supply the individual with ideas and concepts. Yet so often they refuse to accept that what is inside is good enough, and there is a sort of panic and fear that appears to drive their actions.

Book of Number: Interpretations

All this outer fear and tension is really their internal motor warming up. When the person gets moving, all the stress becomes a wave that they surf. Intuitively, they know this, and we often find the 1-2-3 Type create problems and issues in their lives as a way to generate motivation. It may seem like madness, and on one level it is, but it works.

The Balanced Line of this type has a tremendous will to create. This is a will that can be strong enough to break all boundaries imposed, or conversely, a will strong enough to imprison their need to live and to express the inner feelings. Self denial can be a real issue here. Emotions can be firmly held down under the iron glove of convention, and te heart can be ignored for sake of the ideal. If this denial aspect rules, the person will often go overboard in their endeavours to keep people around them similarly imprisoned. (Such as you see with religious types)

With the 1-2-3 as a Vacant Line we find that, in the negative, the querent is unable to decide on a course of action, even with apparently simple things. They are often possessed with a wishy-washy sense of confusion, and are unable to complete anything they start. There can be a deep uncertainty of their worth, or the value of any creative effort on their part. However, if they can silence their mind, the bubbling brook of inspiration will surface and refresh them with a great and deep appreciation of life and its wonders. But sadly, rarely do the natives of this type find the inner strength to let their fears go and relax.

When they do they can become quite off-worldly and disconnected, appearing to have cast aside society. There is a definite need to not judge these people, for they are often working on other levels of existence, and many with religious or spiritual desires will only consider their physical body as a temporary residence. Which indeed it is!

In the balanced aspect this type makes wonderful and compelling teachers, who manage to find way to make learning interesting. They also make excellent writers, and have a deep appreciation of all artistic endeavour. In all, a difficult Aspect in eithe rthe Balanced or Vacant position, but one that has enormous potential for inner and outer growth.

4-5-6 Line of Intuition and Will:

This is a curious line, for it crosses many boundaries. It indicates business, but also the home life, and yet also the sense of intuition we all possess, but rarely utilize. Most with this as a Line of Force have a strong will to persevere. Because of this, the independant person with this Aspect develops a strong sense of his/her own worth. The opposite is true if the Soul is stuck on a dead end job, or living off welfare. It is also very unlikely that this Soul will realise they are in this position because of the sense of being unworthy.

A sense of personal value is necessary for happy outcomes when this energy is active. The native of this Aspect will usually have an inflated opinion of their worth, or the exact opposite. In early childhood these folk tend to parade themselves like a merit badge, thus earning the ire of their peers, or they hide in a shell waiting for someone to reach in and pull them out. The upshot of all this is that generally life's difficulties often result in a battle to prove your own negative belief about yourself wrong. This type is resilient, however, and they manage to survive despite themselves. You will find there is often an overcompensation of clownish and/or unmanageable behaviour when self-worth is lowered.

In the negative this Line can be very destructive, carrying great anger (often disguised as self-righteousness). Naturally, in society these feelings are usually repressed, and so these feelings can surface in hidden forms, such as a tendency towards emotional blackmail, and other hidden aggressions. Actions of this type will internalize the gentle nature of this individual, potentially making them bitter and judgmental in later life. Curiously, the native of the 4-5-6 Line often keeps slightly exotic pets, and will lavish unwarranted attention on them.

The positive aspect is very strong as well, with a need to assist those less fortunate being a predominate urge. There is a strong maternal instinct associated with this Line, sometimes being possessive, and always protective. Humour is one of their best assets, and it will be used to make a point that is seen as important. Many times the best traders, politicians (Should this profession be listed as positive? It can be with this aspect.) and business people will have this Line present.

Overall, the line is marked by an ability to make dreams a reality, yet few reach their true potential here. However, those that do achieve great results. The major lesson for this group is to loosen up their social inhibitions, becoming more spiritually and emotionally free, whilst still being able to live in society. They must learn to be themselves completely, while remaining aware of the limitations of life and being able to accept these. Dignity is very important with this Line, and natives will never be happy if they have to compromise their personal integrity.

Those who fail to do so usually seek to drown their sorrows in drink or sympathy, either being a poison in too large a dose.

Book of Number: Interpretations

ACCENT ON THE FOUR: This gives a solidarity to the querent's actions, sometimes a paranoia as well. There is an indication of karma to be worked off when the Four is in a dominant position in any aspect, and this is no exception. In this regard it is to do with aligning the human will with the divine. It is generally considered a difficult aspect to master.

ACCENT ON THE FIVE: Communication is highlighted, making the will more accessible to change and evolution. This can also lead to a degree of vacillation on behalf of the querent as they consider too many options, particularly if other Lines of Force cross through at this point. Understanding of inner motivations is what is called for, thus internal honesty is essential.

ACCENT ON THE SIX: Usually this indicates an intuitive gift, allowing the querent to make astonishingly accurate guesses in regard business and home life. It can also give a sort of number crunching, methodical approach to matters that many would view as being impersonal. It is, but the natives of this Line need a sense of detachment to feel content. Peaceful surroundings are essential for health and mental balance.

As a Balanced or Vacant Line

4-5-6 Line of Resolve:

A Balanced Line in this aspect makes this individual impossible to resist, and often they are very subtle, almost cunning in the way they go about their lives. They can be found as pillars of society, doctors and professional types, yet also as the housewife who knows how to get the best things in life for her children, and how to get the best from her children as well.

If a sports-person has this line they are very likely to rise to the top of their profession for there is an attitude beyond competition at work here... We often find here an attitude of clear expectancy where the native truly believes it is their right to win. This makes them difficult adversaries, because they are not intimidated by others or by adverse circumstances.

This attitude of clear expectancy keeps them focused in the present and unconcerned about the past or future. This attitude gets results. The opposite here, of course, is that the Soul becomes obsessed with appearance, and worries what everyone thinks. This makes for a very unpleasant existence, and deep, abiding insecurities.

In the Neutral aspect this type simply come to accept themselves as they are, and allow others to be as they choose. By not mentally or physically intruding on another's space, the Balance 4-5-6 learns to rise above their own shortcomings.

In the Vacant aspect the querent faces a dilemma. They know they can get what they want, but is this what they want? Getting clear on a sense of purpose is the main task here, and if this is achieved nothing can keep this Soul from its goal. There can be a considerable amount of time spent in limbo before this is understood, however. Sadly, often this individual never gets out of their nether-world of self-doubt, and perpetually create problems for themselves and others.

When balanced, the individual comes to understand the principle "When the Student is ready, the Master appears." What this means is that when our inner mind is in balance, the next thing we are to work with turns up naturally. Things don't have to be forced.

The truly negative aspect of the Vacant 4-5-6 Line is the desire to control others. We often see these people practicing with the Occult, and doing so in order to find some lever to control external situations, and people. And yeteven this negative can be a positive, because once a sense of compassion enters the heart, people with this Aspect can truly understand the inner workings of man.

22/8/1922	Ray Bradbury	Vacant 4-5-6 Line
11/12/1931	Bagwan Rajneesh	Vacant 4-5-6 Line
20/12/1917	David Bohm	Vacant 4-5-6 Line
12/08/1831	Helena Blavatski	Vacant 4-5-6 Line
15/12/1872	Sri Aurobindo	Vacant 4-5-6 Line

These are just some examples of people who have powerfully affected consciousness in the Western mind. All share the Vacant 4-5-6 Line.

7-8-9 Line of Altruism and Wisdom:

There is a fatherly nature here, which desires to direct and shape the lives of those under their care. The influence of the Line makes the native appear solitary and somewhat aloof, but this is usually merely an aspect of the querent looking within. There is a danger here of becoming too internal, and not growing out of the introspective phase (that usually comes with this aspect) can leave the person unable to form personal relationships, and suffering deep depression.

We will often see altruistic behavior in this native, sometimes to the point where a person of this aspect will jeopardize their own future for an individual or an ideal they strongly believe in. It has a certain madness that throws the person affected into the flames of desire, yet also a genius for escaping the worst of the burn.

There are two distinct modes of action here, one inward and the other outward. In some this develops as two distinct personalities, but this is due more to social conditioning than the effect of the Line itself. Indeed, the major lesson these people learn is to rise above their fear of what others might think.

There is a strong sense of individualism here, married with a swift grasp of new concepts and ideas, and thus people who work under this line make fine leaders. They need to temper their natural impatience with those less able to connect with the swift turning of events. This can aggravate others, but in reality the native has high expectations, and cannot understand people who want to be ordinary. In time, as youth matures, a cynical, impatient edge can definitely form. If you want to impress this person, be direct and to the point.

Because the native does not mind criticism, they feel that others should feel the same. Of course, it causes waves and hidden enemies. Because of this, there is a need to learn silence, as well as a calculating ability to know when the time is right to speak. This is quite important.

In some respects this is the line of nobility, and it is not uncommon for natives of this aspect to use the royal 'WE' when deep in thought about some item of discussion. This is because the native truly feels the divine self is beside/within them, and guiding their thoughts. This can create an inner tension, as this sense of the higher "divinity" and lower "self" is one of their greatest sources of frustration, for they are rarely able to marry these together in harmony.

This makes for, in a round-a-bout sort of way, the major lesson of this line: Humility. This is the ability to be both common yet divine. Humility is actually derived from HU-Man-Ability, or the ability to be both God and Man. (HU - Ancient name of God; Man - Common nature) This lesson is only learned through Silence, and by recognizing and observing the light of Soul in all we meet.

Book of Number: Interpretations

ACCENT OF THE SEVEN: Introversion is often highlighted when the Seven is accented. Spiritually speaking, this can be quite useful, but the querent must eventually learn to cast this aside in order to allow their inner light to shine.

This type is strongly draw to humanitarian projects, and willingly volunteer their time and energy for any number of worthy causes. This is one of the best way to circumnavigate the negative aspects of the Seven vibration. An attitude of sacrifice is needed before the higher teaching role comes into play, a role to which these people are destined in some way or other.

ACCENT OF THE EIGHT: Extroversion is the aspect of the Eight, and sometimes to the point of extravagance and waste in order to impress. There is a good deal of money, worldliness and world-weariness that goes with this energy, and yet the person rarely is interested in any of these. They often secretly dream of distant beaches and writing the great novel.

The problem is, however, that when these people turn inwardly, all their karma quickly comes on top of them, and instinctively they generally seek to avoid this situation. This usually means the native will practice avoidance in some manner or form. A classic example of avoidance is to promise ourselves that we will do what we truly want to when we are older, and when the money, family, etc. are secure. But who is ever "secure enough" to actually hop off the wheel and follow their dream? And is the dream what you really want anyway? These questions and more can be answered with this vibration.

ACCENT ON THE NINE: Power, Silence and Altruism are strong energies here, but there is also a fatalism, a sense of all things having their endings already fated. When faced with statements of plans and dreams from others, the native can easily shrug the shoulders and go "If God wills" that really means, "you got no chance". There can give a strong edge of cynicism that interpreted by some as being derisive.

On the contrary, this type would love to see everyone's dreams come true, but their sense of realism holds them in check. There is also a sense of identity crisis here, for these people have no great ego that is apparent to themselves (even though it may well be to others) and as a result they are easily confused by things that are not in their correct place.

They like to be tidy, and expect others to be the same, but invariably find themselves under a pile of papers, and things to be sorted out come the end of the week. What the real lesson here is comes down to a sense of mastery, of taking charge of the present and getting things in order NOW.

In the Balanced or Vacant Position

7-8-9 Line of Giving:

In the Balanced aspect, altruistic thought is strong here, to the point where the native might live in a dream world, unable to relate to life about them. Because of this they can become insular and unable to share or give Love on a human level, but will generally compensate for this by giving on an intellectual level.

The essence of Giving is an act of kindness, but many are incapable of even acting for themselves, let alone with kindness because they are pre-programmed to re-act. This is the result of social conditioning that convinces us that we are a certain "role". Recognition of ourselves as Soul is the only way to break these chains society ties around us.

Even when the native breaks out of this "waking dream" state, they must then find someone capable of receiving the gift they have to give, which is not as simple as it might sound. Try and give Twenty dollars to a stranger and watch how suspicious they grow! Therefore a part of the lesson here is to be strong enough to Give.

The Balanced Line aspect has a strong energy, and can dominate an audience, and thus this type can be very good at creating a "market" for themselves. There is an ability to hypnotize that comes with this, and the querent must be careful here, or else they will tie themselves into the karma of those they affect. In the finer aspect this quality is used to paint pictures before people that allow them to understand themselves better, in the negative it is a form of mental control.

Peter Sellers, the famous English actor born 8th Sept 1925, had this Balance Line, and well as a Balanced 3-6-9 Line. His Infamous depression and equally famous antics are typical of the "push-pull" energy of this Aspect in a person's life.

In the Vacant position this line has a hint of mystery about it, and many with occult interests are drawn to people with this aspect. Behind this apparently simple series of "invisible" numbers many secrets are held, but these are useless to the average man, until they have developed the spiritual stamina to hold and make use of them.

This Line therefore is essentially occult in nature, and represents the bringing of the invisible forces from the higher worlds into the lower, and vice versa.

It is worthwhile noting that the Vacant Aspect has not been possible in a Birth date for 1000 years, but with the coming of the years 2000 this aspect will become quite common. This indicates a great stirring of psychic activity during this period. It is also a certainty that power systems will be developed that will draw energy from sources other than burning physical fuels.

1-4-7 Line of the Physical

This is the Line of physicality, practicality and directness. The physical world represents many things: Human Love, finance, gravity, etc. Yet most of all it represents the here and now. Certainly it is where we all are right at the present moment.

Those who share this line have an ability to get things going, and to keep them going, because of their earthy nature. The energy has a certain toughness and resilience to it. There is often a good, practical view of what works and what doesn't. This Aspect seems to give people a good, clear perspective on things.

There is also a good, inherent understanding of both the best and worst of the human nature. They are perceptive and practical. This is ideally suited to working in the personnel department, or the position of a loans adviser. However, this very useful perceptive ability often goes by the way when selecting a mate, not always, but often.

These people can be stubborn and pugnacious, yet as a result get what they want, and so consider these traits as benefits. They can be willful in the extreme, often having some form of obsession that motivates their actions. This makes them poor leaders, yet so often they will want to run things because they are convinced things can be done better.

The positive aspect is that they have a great ability to get things done, and to make sure that others do the jobs they have been given.

The major lesson here is to be patient with other people and their circumstances, allowing things to fall into place at the correct time, rather than trying to force square pegs into round holes. This naturally indicates a subsequent need for the native to get a feel for the rhythm of their personal life, and life in general.

Self doubt ruins all the positive energy of this Aspect, and cripples all sense of confidence. Perserverance and courage will light the way. Cleverness and glib comments will annoy these people. They like action. And they like organising activities. Get out of the office and stop watching TV, it is time to go paragliding!

This Line, more than any other, will have increasing difficulty in the Years 2000. The "Just do it" mentality will run headlong into the increasingly petty rules mentality of government, and it is likely that many types of resistance to this will start up. In the extreme, small militias and private, politically motivated cores of secret rebels will form. If this is to be so, these are the people who will run them.

Book of Number: Interpretations

ACCENT ON THE ONE: This increases the sense of individuality, sometimes to the point of weirdness. The person with this aspect will often enjoy prodding others, and will actually use their index finger to really "point" out their argument. They have a great urge and desire to win, sometimes to the point of stupidity, for these folk will cut off their nose to spite their face, especially if someone is around to watch.

What's the difference between focused achievement of a worthy goal and sheer madness where absolutely nothing is gained? Very little, it seems, as far as this type is concerned. They can share both of these traits in different parts of their lives, and have both labeled as "ideals".

This, of course, removes any need to consider things reasonably, and thus it also removes the need to compromise. This inability to compromise often costs these folk financially and emotionally, and it creates enemies in the process.

ACCENT ON THE FOUR: This can give a sense of stoicism, but this can become quite pedantic is the querent's humor is heavy. There is a great desire to travel here, but rarely is this achieved for the native likes home comforts too much. There is a need for the extraordinary, but generally this desire for the obtuse and different comes out in hobbies and/or sexual deviations rather than actual adventure. The Four here can give a twisted energy to the mind. They can be quite devious, but will make sure it is wrapped in a guise of respectability. These people enjoy putting on a respectable front, and few would suspect what thoughts might be running through their minds.

Many dream of freedom, but most rarely do anything towards really obtaining it. The native of this Aspect tend to finds positions of sole responsibility, rather then starting their own business, as one example. They are good and reliable souls, as a rule, but with an odd bend somewhere in the character that can make them quite ideocentric.

ACCENT ON THE SEVEN: This aspect draws brings great sense of compassion for others into play. Accordingly the Soul with a strong seven will find life here on planet Earth quite difficult until they learn to harden themselves. As a rule they are often used by people, and this will continue until the querent becomes more grounded in a practical understanding of the negative nature of this world.

At this point the fine, analytical aspect of the Seven allows them to see through others like they were thin paper, and the native is rarely caught out. There is an ability to express inner thoughts here, and one of the best roles for this type would be in the teaching profession. They also make good writers and engineers. The term "Dark Horse" applies to this specific Aspect: hidden and secretive, they will surprise.

In the Balanced or Vacant Position

1-4-7 Line of Freedom:

This is one of those exceedingy rare patterns that come to prominaence at specific times in human history. All through the last 1000 years, this Line has not been possible in a Birth Date, because every date had a ONE in it. Now, in the Years 2000 this is not so. What this tells us is that the energy of this Line will come to the fore in many and varied ways during the next 1000 years.

And so what is the core element to the Vacant 1-4-7 Line? Political expediency and a ruthless sense of organisation. It is a hard, physical energy that is good for building, and laying the foundations for any form of new endeavour.

Natives with this Line generally make enough money to live in physical comfort, though often they must go through considerable struggle. The difficulty is internal, and because they do not marry well with other peoples ideas of doing things. Freedom is the goal here, and all who carry the 1-4-7 vibration are affected by this.

The danger here is when the freedom is dangled before them like a carrot on a stick by some powerful figure, they will do whatever is asked of them. In this instance these people can be led by their ambition to do what would otherwise have been unthinkable.

This is the main thing that these people need to be careful of, that they are not manipulated by unscrupulous types, or led by their own ambitions into blindness.

In the Balanced aspect there is a "Salt of the Earth" quality here that makes for endearing and long lasting friendships. There is a roguish quality as well, well suited to shady business deals and the like. However, at heart these people are essentially honest, with themselves and with loved ones, and are well loved because of it. In the negative aspect there can be a deep cynicism that can develop over time into a state of compulsive anger.

With the Vacant Aspect of this Line an individual can become dark and uncompromising towards others, with rigorous, unbending protocols and officious behavior being a commonly observed character trait. Yet quite the opposite can also be true when dealing with the family! Daddy will pamper and spoil the girls, and mommy can buy whatever she wants. This is not necessarily a form of schizophrenia, but it does create a conflict within.

There is often an inner battle over the questions of right and wrong, priorities, and ways to advance oneself here. But once the mind is set, there is little that will change it.

2-5-8 Line of the Emotions

This is a Line of surging forces, and it is very important. It is through the emotional element that our minds and bodies are empowered. This is a difficult energy to master, and health must be carefully considered by the querent, for those so affected are prone to disease caused by anxiety and stress.

Many artists share this line, but this is because of the feeling element required by creative souls, rather than any creative impulse itself. There is invariably a great need for self-expression, and those with this aspect who do not know how to speak their minds can suffer terrible inhibitions, sometimes to the point of madness.

Clear thinking is essential if one would master the emotional element, yet there must be a balance. Western man, as a rule, has over emphasized the need for thought and reason, whereby feelings have been consigned and isolated under the "effeminate" category. The subsequent non-involvement of the feeling aspect in decision-making has been the cause of many major failures in ecology and commerce.

To qualify this statement, the feeling element has little to do with what we see as emotionalism. Emotionalism is merely a bottled up reaction to fexternal stimuli, which distorts perspective and clarity. The feeling element is really a form of intuition, and so confusion within our feelings blocks off our natural instincts, leaving us with a sense of isolation. But when properly understood, our inner feelings are clear signpost our minds can read. They give us the correct direction is any circumstance. True feelings become a sure sense of knowing that cannot be shaken.

This KNOWING, then, is the still, certain point that the Ancient Greek philosophers talked so much about. (The Omphalos) Attaining this sense of certainty should be the goal of all who share this Line of Force in their natal chart, because for these people it is possible for instinct to come into accord with reason. (NOTE: Such a combination cannot be stopped in this present cycle, and this is the basic reason why Aryan Man has attained ascendancy over the other races on Earth. This process will change with the ascendancy of the next root race.)

The major lesson here is Balance, which of itself requires an ability to Trust. The marriage of these two elements (Balance and Trust) will bring about the new human, the Soul who can walk with the grace of life about them. This concept of walking in grace is a powerful image to hold for those wishing to balance the emotional side of their nature.

Many with this Aspect will be drawn to security rather than adventure, but in truth, the real journey happens inside. No matter what path you take, this energy always ask you to clarify your feelings, and be clear in your position with others.

Book of Number: Interpretations

ACCENT ON THE TWO: This will lead to a period of indecision, which the native will either rise above, or drown in. Self pity is a real danger here, and drug abuse (as a result) can result either in slow or fast suicide. Slow suicide is the most common, with self-denigration, self-contempt, and self-analysis being the common tools of execution.

The positive aspect is a deep and abiding appreciation for beauty and the aesthetic things of life, yet matched with an awareness of the dark side of the human nature. There is a great need to preserve this positive aspect, for as a result the individual learns to be both caring and careful, with relationships and with life in general.

ACCENT ON THE FIVE: This can lead to either useless frivolity or a deep, abiding depth of communication. The Five energy can take people into the depths of their unconscious, and in the journey you can break through many of the hypnotic suggestions put in place by parents and society. This is a difficult path, often with the native finding it hard to support themselves, and many times there will be a need for solitude. In the past these people would have ended up in monasteries and the like, but now-a-days it is more likely you will find them on the late shift, or in some occupation that allows them room to breath.

The Five always plays a pivotal role, and the native should be aware that this is a volatile aspect, prone to mood-swings and depression. Because of this, diet must be kept fairly simple with plenty of fresh food. If this is done there will be far fewer complications in life.

ACCENT ON THE EIGHT: This is an unwieldy aspect. Tthe positive side has a great appreciation of another's rights and privileges, but the negative can exude greed and naked lust. Discipline is essential for this type, or else noble aspirations will turn to dust and corruption shall eat into the vital essence of the self. In this aspect the Soul can do the most vile things, with the black arts of control and manipulation taking over the etical part of their nature.

This aspect does not sit well with worldly men. This Soul is of a giving and compassionate nature, and so the money they accrue will seem worthless, and its responsibilities tie you down, They prefer discovering the next rainbow. The problem is that though this aspect is lucky in regards money, an addiction to risk will often cause gains to be lost. Even though one of the Eight's characteristics is wealth, the money will be worthless unless it is being put to some worthwhile purpose.

Philanthropy, then, is the best solution against greed. Overall this aspect needs to learn to share, and appreciate the joy this gives.

The aspect of the Eight tends to create over-responsibility or carelessness. Both attitudes must be carefully pruned, for the fruits of this emotion can break the bough that grows them.

In the Balanced or Vacant Position
2-5-8 Line of Detachment:

The intriguing aspect of this Line is the cool and calculating manner on one hand, and the slightly disinterested on the other. But few come to understand how these two aspects can be developed in a positive manner. The key to this is to recognize the rich, burning heart behind the outer coolness, and if either the individual themselves or their partner can see and recognize this aspect, then tremendous growth can, and does, occur.

With the positive aspect in the Balanced Position, these people rarely see any point to getting upset by things, rather they would prefer to do something about it. Action comes easily to this type, mostly because they are not cluttered by emotionalism. If the native does get caught in emotive situations, however, life tends to fall apart around them, and they will fall deeply into the negative aspects of this Line. The solution is always to get out there and do something useful. This is something that must be remembered whenever life seems to unravel. A sense of purpose brings your direction back to the center of awareness.

It is worth noting that this aspect is not related to the astrological sign of Aquarius, though many attribute these qualities to this sign. In point of fact I have generally found Aquarians to be highly charged with emotions, but they often act detached in order to contain these.

The Line of Balanced Detachment is a clear pathway, but usually the Souls affected must pass through an ordeal of fire, and often have lives that are associated with alcohol and abuse in some shape or form. This tempers the steel with which they are made.

In the Vacant mode this aspect can give the querent a longing sadness that reaches out to others, not in a despairing way, but in a quizzical sense. They are true poets, though they may never write a line of verse. This type is only rarely understood by others, for they seem to pursue madness and pain in their quest for answers, sometimes without even knowing that they are asking a question.

In the end these people develop an extraordinary insight into the human condition, which at times depresses them, and at other uplifts them into celestial heights. They often miss the boat as far as society is concerned, and end up either mad or living like hermits. Some survive and develop a deep creativity and adaptability in their dealing with life.

Overall we can see quite fascinating Souls develop here, yet most with this aspect avoid the energy latent herein, and seek to live a life of conformity rather than danger. Soul is free to choose, but a question to ask ourselves if we have this aspect present in our chart is "What will I think of my life on my deathbed?"

Such a question often tempts us to dare to go that extra mile, and it is always in those extra steps that the real joy of life is found.

3-6-9 Line of the Mind

This is a curious line. Most persons who possess it are utterly unconscious of their potential, which is perhaps a good thing lest they abuse the power with which they have been (potentially) invested. It is known as the Dragon, or the focused mind power.

Personal power is universally based on our ability to contact and utilise the gifts we have attained in past times. When we can reconnect the string of our past lives, or at least the energy running through them, then we find that we are empowered to act in a way few could imagine.

Quite literally, all we have to do is think, imagine, believe and work towards the goal. Life will then come into accord with our belief, and what we dream of will come to pass. Of course, we still have to pay any consequences arising from this. Many people forget this.

Naturally, all people have this ability of manifestation latent within them, but those with the Line of the Mind prevalent in their chart find it easier. And yet some innate reflex seems to keep most persons from discovering it. This is possibly because the individual is simply too lazy or too attached to their present world view to act on their inner potential.

It is worth noting at this point that anyone can develop any Line of Force within themselves by simply imagining it at work. It is further worth noting that it is better to work out your present circumstances before trying to move onto the next. In other words, understand what you have before you go seeking mountains to climb.

The negative aspect of this line is the use of hypnotic commands to take control over others. This can be as subtle as a woman using a flick of an eyelash to gain control over a man, or as blatant as the events in Nazi Germany, but the results are always the search for personal power. The positive aspect is an internal learning process and not an outward form of aggregation or aggression. In this manner the native will come to recognize their role in life, and as a result find great contentment.

It is a given that in Western Society, the mind is considered the ruling force. Control, power and influence are what define a strong ruler, and it is fair to say that there is a worship akin to a religious zeal that follows strong, mind controlled leaders. One of the lessons this Aspect needs to learn is that the heart energy is far more powerful than the mind, and that unifying the energy of our emotions with clear direction from the mind is the true unstoppable force.

The real lesson is one of learning to trust the heart. In the positive aspect, and person with the 3-6-9 in their chart works easily with those around them by defining targets, making clear goals, and understanding where the heart of each person is at in the process.

Book of Number: Interpretations

ACCENT OF THE THREE: The Three gives a warmth to the thoughts, and a good humour in general. It makes the "mind" aspect more appealing, and such things as wit, charm and social graces will be considered important. These folk are the modern harlequins.

The Three also gives this Line a real business acumen, and these people often make both highly successful merchants and conmen. Generally, this type craves family life, yet it is the one thing that often seems to elude them. This is usually because they have a great show of outward warmth towards friends, but their partner is often treated as an add-on accessory. Again, work with the heart, and all will be well.

ACCENT OF THE SIX: This aspect is much cooler and outwardly detached than the Three, and relies more on Intuitive hunches for guidance. Oddly, though, the family life which avoids the Three aspect comes quite easily to the Six, which is usually because the Six aspect can allow others to love it more easily. It might seem curious to some, but there are many people who find it difficult to accept love, but easy to give it. A marriage of such a person to a 3-6-9 Line with the Six accented satisfies this type immensely, and usually works well for both.

There is an agility of mind here that makes this Soul marvellous at changing horses in mid-stream, and also good at making it work to their advantage. They like randomness, and will often take holidays by simply piling everyone into the family into the car and driving off. Because of this the Six can be good fun, and yet there is a sombre side to their nature, especially with religious and spiritual matters. In this respect these people can be extremely devotional. They make good Jesuites.

ACCENT OF THE NINE: Here there can be many changes in store, for the Nine energy has a tendency to end things. There can be many jobs, many partners, many dreams, but in the end there is usually only one goal: to understand the inner workings of the mind.

There is a also tendency towards anger, which is very unsettling for all around them, but the anger is not vengeful or consuming, merely a statement of frustration. Even so, it breaks down the inner peace, and this peace is essential for the balance the Nine needs.

The Nine is rarely interested in money, and works merely to survive, but it can become very ambitious with scientific and written work, specifically non-fictional essays.

These people love to read and/or write in detail about history, being often fascinated with the pivotal events of man's existence, hoping to find the deep psychological motivations of the human psyche therein.

Curiosity is somewhat of a hallmark for this type.

In the Balanced or Vacant Position

3-6-9 Line of Clarity:

This Aspect can be gifted by nature, or it can be grafted on by circumstance. It is most powerful when in the natural birth date of the querent, and depreciates when present only in the name vibrations. Still, if by a change of name someone picks up this pattern, it will change their view of life radically. It is one of those rare Aspects that can be trained into a person through upbringing.

In the Balanced Aspect the Soul affected will often have an overriding sense of superiority, yet often shifting between this and an attitude of abject inferiority! It is known as the trap of the mind, however, the core problem is with unresolved emotional issues. Depending on how these folk react to authority, this will determine the pursuit of profession, pastimes and relationships.

A negative authority relationship with parents, etc. will create a need for power over others, which is dangerous for these people have the mental strength to attain this. The positive aspect gives serenity of mind, and a curious sense of in definability that others find most attractive. In this instance these people will look to attain power over themselves, and as they find this, they also find that they can rule their lives through postulates. (Utilizing affirmations, images and concepts to direct life) In particular they develop the ability to imagine and create a greater value of themselves, which leads to true freedom.

In the Vacant Aspect these Soul's are drawn to helping others, sometimes dying for the cause they espouse. Hidden in this we often find the ego-self, expressing its urges in the negative value by attracting attention through self-sacrifice. These people are the notorious do-gooders who interfere in other's lives, under the guise of good intention.

The positive aspect is genuinely concerned over the plight of those less fortunate than themselves. We find both the positive and negative aspects of this person in many of the charities that abound today, as the two tend to roll into each other. This can make the querent's inner life difficult to sort out, and the only real solution here is life experience and honesty with oneself.

1-5-9 (Success) Line:

This aspect indicates a need for success. It does not determine actual success, merely the need for it, often combined with the subsequent fear of failure that this might not be so.

The Nine rules this line, no matter where the accent is, and so there is a definite requirement for silence and inner containment for these people if they are to make their dreams reality. Sadly, though, it is rarely the case, and great intentions are often end in idle speculation on what might have been.

The 20th Century has seen many of this type of dreamer, as the 1900's already have the One and Nine present throughout its cycle. It is curious that the extravagance of the Eighties (the eight connects with money and karma) came at the time those born during the 1950's were becoming financially viable adults. It was a predestined circumstance that brought the Line of Success [so prevalent in this time] within the influence of the Eight, and for many the results have been ruinous.

The Nineties were a consolidation period, but one of inherent confusion as the new energy of the coming millennium is thrown into the pot as well. Now in the years 2000 there is no natural "grounding" as the One and Nine are absent from the permanent backdrop of energy. Those who have the 1-5-9 Line must connect themselves with Earth if they are to prosper in this period. By Earth I mean all things to do with the concept of being grounded, as well as such issues as conservation, soil management and the like. Clearly, the Financial Crisis of the Years 2000 is directly related to the "success justifies everything" mentality that came from the 1980's and 1990's

The negative aspect is one of wasted hours and vacant dreams that have little hope of seeing the light of day. Ambition without drive is also a characteristic, and all that is started never seems to get finished. A very difficult cycle to break out of.

The positive aspect carries a flamboyant enthusiasm that defies depression or pessimism. This boyish sense of belief gives the bearer a sort of emotional invulnerability that allows them to walk through problems and concerns that would shatter lesser mortals. (This is often because the querent simply does not see the problem!) These people can be great fun, and much of the overall influence of the positive aspect of the 1-5-9 Line is to eradicate the lingering guilts and inhibitions of the religious influence.

Both aspects have the need to understand the Law of Completion, and must learn to finish what they start. For the negative aspect this is difficult because they fall into the "Nothing Trap" where everything appears worthless, and not even worth starting let alone completing. For the positive aspect the difficulty is because the initial enthusiasm fades, and the fun becomes plain hard work. (And thus possibly boring!)

Book of Number: Interpretations

Please note that the original course predicted the financial crash on the Years 2000, based on the prevalence of the 1-5-9 Line leading up to it.

ACCENT ON THE ONE: This gives an ego-centricity to the individuals actions, but also a greater drive to achieve. This is the most successful combination for this Line because the energy of the One can take the Nine and Five and shape them into the dream desired.

There is a slight sense of self-destruction here, and the native will often seem hell bent of some goal regardless of risk to life or limb. Sometimes this disregard will be for another's as well as their own!

ACCENT OF THE FIVE: This can make this Line even more intractable, with the querent oscillating between phobias and commitment. It makes them wonderful social animals, but they tend to be untrustworthy with a confidence, or a loan. When they learn responsibility these people make excellent communicators and motivators.

This is one Aspect that is almost entirely governed by the influences around it. The individual affected by a strong Three, for instance, will think of success in terms of what a successful Three energy represents. So here it is very much a case of what surrounds this Aspect being what defines it.

There can be a sense of cruelty here, like the cat that toys with the mouse, and these people can be very manipulative. In the positive aspect, however, the native can display a great and genuine warmth to those around them. Often we might see this type employing some unfortunate Soul, simply because they need a job.

ACCENT OF THE NINE: If the person with this Aspect has a high self-esteem factor, they can achieve a great deal. If not their life will be a series of miscalculations that end up in difficulty and possibly ruin. This is a powerful aspect, and the native possessing it should take care with their thoughts and actions, for such things as cynical and judgmental attitudes will always return quickly to roost.

Generally a sharp mind needs some sort of outlet, and curiously pets are wonderful in this respect for these people. If not pets, then a hobby or pastime which holds a high degree of interest for the querent will suffice. (Some interest which allows them to meet others similarly interested is ideal.) They have to be careful of becoming perfectionists, however, as this will lead to an overriding sense of disaffection with life. Why? Because perfection by its own design is not attainable, and the core value here is of attaining the goal.

In the Balanced or Vacant Position

1-5-9 Line of Confidence

Attainment is core to this energy, but does the individual have the drive to achieve? If not the Ego will be accented, and professions will be sought that fulfill the need for recognition, and not necessarily personal satisfaction. If so, it sets the scene for a deep dissatisfaction that will result late in life.

In the Balanced aspect the person may find either a stable acceptance of themselves, or a driving, pursuing need to influence those around them. The balance is in realizing that all people are just this, people, and that our private self is exactly as every other private self. Private!

Understanding what is simple and common to all is the doorway to acceptance, so part of the journey of this Line is to grasp our shared commonality. *It's just me, it's just you, it's just us.*

After the acceptance of self is embedded in the Soul, then the development of personal specialty can be highlighted in a balanced way. Unfortunately most get this exactly wrong, trying to make themselves special before they recognize they are common. Thus we find in this native the negative habit of trying to influence others before their own private self is understood. Success, or at least lasting success, always eludes this negative aspect.

The positive aspect is very dynamic, and loves to beat the drum for some purpose or cause, often with real success. Laughter is the lesson to learn, as this type tends to get a little obsessive and compulsive. We find that the easiest way for these people to find themselves and make friends is with humour.

In the Vacant Aspect this Soul is drawn to develop their inner senses. They try to peer into their inner worlds, often seeking to accent their occult powers. At first this is "through the glass darkly" and is often a chasing of sensationalism, but if the lower nature is allowed to fade into the background, the higher self will step forward. Sometimes this happens with a brilliance that can astound those about them, as well as the individual themselves.

In both Aspects there is a tendency towards pessimism, and to be fair, there is great difficulty in mastering these influences. What is needed here is more than persistence, it is an attitude of determination, or more succinctly, an attitude that knows with an unshakeable zeal that the goal can be achieved.

With this attitude the querent will discover that life is a discovery, and many things will seem to magically appear before them! Thus we might say that a sense of expecting the unexpected would be of use here.

3-5-7 (Service) Line:

The Line of Service indicates just this, a need to be of service. These people find selfish or insular occupations impossible to bear, and seek out ideologically satisfying ways to make their hours seem worthwhile. Among the natural professions for this Aspect are nursing, doctors, and curiously enough farming. Farmers are close to earth, and convert soil into food that feeds the masses. Indeed, a great service.

This line can be quite religious, and as such liable to a sense of bigotry, but the initial spark is because they have a liking for ritual. Conversely the person so affected might abhor religion and ceremony, yet they will still want to rise at a set time, have dinner at a set time, etc. Almost all people with this Aspect seek to be humanitarian in outlook.

In all, they like to help out in some crusade. For some they will pursue this to the point of becoming zealots in the name of the chosen cause. At this point they become utterly blind to criticism, and are the proverbial bulls in the china shop when dealing with any form of contrary argument.

This is also called the Line of Compassion, as these people feel deeply for others in distress, and they will go out of their way to assist those less fortunate than themselves. There is a problem with attachment here, and the major lesson is simply being able to let go of a cherished belief, or whatever, when reality shows that it is no longer of value.

The blindness of the person affected by this Aspect is often that they simply refuse to see the obvious. Many in the Catholic Church simply could not see the harm they were doing by protecting abusve priests, as one example.

The Negative aspect is to do with ignoring the inner guidance, and stubbornly picking a path that invariably leads to thorns and hurt. The Positive aspect is one where attunement to a higher ideal is indicated, but the native must be careful not to lose their sense of self in the process.

Overall, the influence of this energy cultivates a deep appreciation of family, friends and the simple things of life. The native will be utterly faithful to any ideal or individual they hold in high esteem, and in many ways are natural patriots. We see many in the healing professions with this Line prominent in the name or birthdate.

The main lessons are to do with freedom. Only when the person is useful do they feel they are worthwhile, and this means they feel idle time to be somewhat a waste. Work sets you free, is the unwritten motto, and while this is true, it is important to be able to do nothing but sit appreciate a sunset, and similar. You cannot be free if you are chained to a millstone, so in essence just spending the odd day reading a book and doodling away hours is essential for inner happiness here.

Book of Number: Interpretations

ACCENT OF THE THREE: Too much imagination is a dangerous thing, and this type can have plenty of imagination. More to the point they sometimes apply this imagination to influence others against their natural will, especially in the case of missionaries, and those of that ilk.

These people can also be TOO helpful. They invariably show up when you are moving in to the new house, staying for a cup of tea, and then talking long into the night when all you want to do is read a book and sleep. They are often shocked with the rudeness of those more defined people who tell them to get lost. After all, they were only trying to be friendly!

This aspect often suffers a frailty of reason, like the delusion that God will solve all their problems for them if they just continue helping everyone. Common sense and a respect for another's psychic space is a major lesson for this type.

ACCENT OF THE FIVE: Here emotionalism can get out of hand, ruling the native's mind until they become physically and mentally worn out. Untamed emotions are like wild horses pulling a cart in all directions at once, and strict discipline with inner focus and imagination are needed here. Often learning a key word, such as "relax" when you start to feel tense is a simple and effective circuit breaker for the emotional charge they hold.

If the positive attributes of discipline and focus are in place, these people can attain a great deal in this lifetime, and be beacons of inspiration for many around them. The Five aspect will then give a warmth to all their actions, and a sense of grace that will touch the heart of those they meet.

ACCENT OF THE SEVEN: This can give a feeling of morbidity and a lack of purpose to the querent, and this must be carefully watched. In extreme cases it becomes a suicidal tendency, otherwise the effect is to depress the atmosphere of the home and office. These people are usually aware of this, and as a result often choose a solitary profession where the only person that has to suffer their own natures are themselves.

If the querent can rise above this self-inflicted morbidity they can achieve a remarkable clarity of insight into how others tick, and become marvellous counsellors and advisors. There is a tremendous urge towards freedom here, and the throwing off of social restrictions is an important part of the learning curve for this aspect.

In the Balanced or Vacant Position:
3-5-7 Line of Perception:

Here we find a person who is often at odds with themselves. They like to help others, but they must also look after themselves. This can be difficult in this world, until one chooses a profession of service. An attitude of Service will open the heart, which in turn will open the pages of their inner truth.

Once the understanding and compassionate self (which is that part of us that truly perceives) is accepted as valid, then success will come more easily. In fact, with compassion and focus a whole new world of perception arises, and the native quickly finds the entire universe now wants to come into agreements with their goals and aspirations.

The ability to perceive is the gift of this line, but negative aspects can override perception with bigotry, bias, and even apparently good intentions! So called "Good Samaritans", as one example, have done vastly more harm than good in this world, not because they intended to, but because they were oblivious to the effects of their actions. WHY? Social conditioning blinds Soul to its true perception, and until we see through social lies and role models, we cannot see ourselves clearly.

The major aspect to learn here is to observe clearly the results of personal actions, and to accept responsibility for these.

In the Balanced aspect the individual is often beset with doubt and frustration as they wallow in a lack of comprehension about anything. Here it is important to understand the saying that goes "All great men are clouds until they condense their wisdom to pour down upon the earth."

Patience will bring the clarity needed to make correct actions, but in the meantime these people can have a hard time supporting themselves, let alone a family, and so tend to end up in some degree of privation. However, when this Soul comes to understand that this world is both gentle and cruel it learns to protect itself, and find a harmonious place within. Then it can make progress in this material world.

The Vacant Aspect often leads men and women into noble causes, though again there needs to be a careful assessment of the validity of the cause. The road to hell, after all, is paved with good intentions. If self-centred, these people will suffer a terrible emptiness within, and this can drive them to cruelty and/or suicide.

This negative aspect sees the native lost in some imaginary world where they believe the world is against them. (Now this attitude is termed Acute Paranoia) In the positive there is often a mechanical genius that allows these people to make or find almost miraculous solutions to problems, and as engineers, farmers, or any profession where the hands and intellect are needed to work together, they excel.

And excellent Aspect for the Healer and the person interested in helping other.

TRINES in the MATRIX

Following are the basic interpretations for the Seventy-Six Trines in the Matrix. (Not counting the 16 Trines that are in effect repeated with the unique Vacant Right Angle Trines)

This is the core area of Pythagorean Numerology, and the lack of this important facet in most current publications became the basic motivation for recording the initial course in 1991.

I had resolved these aspects decades ago, but it was not until the mid 1980's that I met a Rosicrucian who was also familiar with this work. He was genuinely surprised I was not a member of his order, as he said the books that this information came from was restricted to a very few members of his society.

In 1993 a Temple to Pythagoras was unearthed in Rome, and there on the walls were the patterns and symbols for the Trines in the Matrix. Years of experience teaches me how important and accurate the Trines are in a chart, but these small snippets were the first historical antecedent to prove to me that the Pythagoreans themselves used and practiced with them.

Overall, it is not surprising, because there is little evidence of any of the secret teaching other than what Guthrie collected in the "Pythagorean Sourcebook" in the the early 1900's.

The logic is simple: Any combination of THREE is important in Numerology, therefore any combination of Three has importance. The rules about how to determine a Trine are in the Practical Course and we will not be re-covering out tracks, yet there is still so much that could covered if we had the space.

If someone is motivated to become a practitioner, however, they can email us for more information about advanced study. Details are at the **www.bookofnumber.com.au** website.

GREAT TRINES:

1-6-7 Great Trine

1-3-8 Great Trine

3-4-9 Great Trine

2-7-9 Great Trine

1/6/7   1/3/8   3/4/9   2/7/9

Trines are drawn graphically in the above manner. A dot or a stroke for the position of each number represented.

All Great Trines create an embracing, fortunate energy that a person can collect and use in the same way a gardener will collect water in a bucket. The energy crosses over the boundaries between people, and leaders strongly aspected with a Great Trine have little difficulty inspiring others to greater deeds and higher service.

In the negative, the influence can aggravate latent attitudes of arrogance and self-absorption. So often you find great leaders have this contrary external warmth and courage, but internal conflicts in the personal sphere. It is really about finding a deeper self-confidence that is based in self-acceptance. When you have a Great Trine in your chart, it is really telling you to accept yourself, both the positive and negative, and strive to make your being an example of One-ness.

Overall, a very fortuitous energy that will encourage others to greater heights, but only if you develop the "well" within. By digging into your own being, and finding the inner truth of self, you form the bucket that carries the water of truth to others.

1-6-7 Great Trine:

FOCUS: Six: Allow yourself the freedom to dream.

This Trine is like a mountain, implying height and majesty, yet also the climb to the top. In this case the "top" is the number Six, and this numeral has both business and spiritual aspects. We may well see the individual so affected as having a burning desire to achieve recognition in both or either of these areas.

There is a religious impulse associated with this Trine (sometimes the person affected likes to preach to others) and here there is a certain need for isolation. The Number Six deals with intuition, and this Trine is often highly intuitive, to the point where the native suffers stress and nervous problems if they do not have a period of privacy each day. A half hour period of contemplation daily is recommended for all who wish to rise out of the social consciousness, but for these people it is essential.

Eccentrics can often have this Trine accented. As the need to be "uncommon" is often what drives us to extreme behavior, we find the eccentric under this Trine actually is suffering from a lack of Self Esteem, and simply needs to be noticed. Some become social outcasts, most feel that they don't "fit in", but in reality it is because the individual has shut down their ability to love and be loved. This is because the emotional energy has not been stabilised.

Balancing out the emotions is a difficult task, and those affected with this aspect are advised to seek out the company of emotionally secure individuals, and especially elderly people.

Such a meeting will be beneficial to both parties, because those who have emotional balance often find the fire and flamboyance of the 1-6-7 Trine enlivening, while the native of this Trine finds the more stable presence comforting. Partnerships with those who have a 2-5-8 Line of Balance can be most rewarding if common goals are shared. Even so, the Six-Seven combination of this Trine always tends to put others on edge. They are literally "At Sixes and Sevens".

As a note: The numbers Three, Nine and Five are somewhat intrusive for these people, and care should be taken when dealing with these. (Even if these happen to be in the street number of where they live) This is one of the rare cases where a Pattern or Trine is not in harmony with specific numbers. (It is a general rule that those affected by the numbers Eight or Four should avoid too much association with these numbers in relationships, business and home circumstances, but rarely are Patterns and Trines affected like this, as their influence is broader.)

In all, this Trine augers well for spiritual and inner enlightenment, but generally at great cost. Seeking to combine Individuality (One), Freedom (Seven) and Intuition and/or Family (Six) is quite a task, but one that will bring huge rewards if successful. Things will go easier if these people obey the Master Principle, which is to simply seek out someone who is greatly experienced in the field they are interested in, and follow closely their instructions.

From the difficulties of obedience to your ideals (In the final result this is obedience to your higher self) comes the true freedom of Soul that the Vedas call Jivan Mukti. In essence, when you see this Trine configured prominently in a chart, the indivation is that the individual is looking for spiritual freedom.

1-3-8 Great Trine:

FOCUS: Eight: *Be wary of Gifts and Promises with a Hidden Cost.*

This is a powerful aspect for developing a penetrating insight into the ways of mankind, for it combines the essence of the "Law of Three's" with the concept of Harvest, or of reaping what you sow. However, this Trine is as easily availed towards the negative as it is the positive, and so the native must take great care with their thoughts and deeds.

This will evidence itself as either moral or immoral behavior for the most part. However, with the individual attuned to their own natural rhythms, there will develop a quiet observance of the ways of people, often with an interpretation of this into some creative endeavor, usually art or fabric design. As a Note: To be amoral is more of our natural state. Children are neither moral or immoral, they simply live as they are. If we can emulate this, but add a depth of observance about human nature, we will go far into an understanding of Truth.

All the Great Trines are centred around the Five, and so communication will always be essential for these so affected... But in the case of this Trine the Five does best when allied with the Six and the Four, which will give a strong rationality to the somewhat obtuse personality this specific Trine often engenders. As a result of this, people with this aspect should look for those with an aspected Line on the 4-5-6 Axis. They are recognisable as very achievement orientated people.

It is a moot point that any Equilateral Triangle is equally "pointed" at any juncture, but the point where we would consider the main thrust of the energy to be directed in this Trine is the Eight. This indicates financial ability, and the acceptance of responsibility.

There is a tendency to want to control things here, which is rarely in balance, and rarely helps the native of this aspect overall. Control breeds control, and defeats naturalness, which is the overall goal of this aspect. I recommend people with this Trine to leave Mind Control techniques well enough alone, learning instead to listen to and rely on their instinctual senses when dealing with life.

This Trine could be said to allow great progress, but few will rise above the difficulties presented because they have not learned to work in a non-judgemental way with their fellows. This is because there is a lack of Trust... But then again, sometimes you have to look a gift horse in the mouth! Ask the Trojans!!! All the Great Trines influence the individual with a sense of being superior in some way, and in particular with this aspect the native must be careful of becoming vain and spiteful.

3-4-9 Great Trine:

FOCUS: Four: *Move with the Current, Flow with the Tide.*

This is a noble, resonant Trine that encourages the person affected to overlook the details, yet stay focussed on the end goal. This, though many will say otherwise, is the easiest way to succeed in life. The details will come, of course, but if we keep the overview uppermost in our minds details will remain as details, and not become obstacles.

This Trine indicates a great down pouring of energy into the Four. Between creativity (Three) and silence (Nine) the person must find that way to make the intuitive guesses work out in some sort of solid, useful reality (the Four energy at the base represents this)

For these people there is often an internal argument. They may suffer apparently unanswerable questions, such as: "If we are the children of God, why do we suffer so? Why does God allow his children this agony?" The answer is so simple most overlook it, which is that we are in training to be co-workers with the Divine Force, and that as we learn to align ourselves with Spirit's direction for us, life becomes less abrasive. The pain and trial, therefore, are merely instructive signposts similar to how the body signals pain when we are doing it harm in some manner.

We create our own destiny. The real question is more do we create useful and beneficial circumstances, or otherwise. For a positive result in life, learn to build. We must learn to constantly take all that is offered us, and to improve on it in some manner before passing it on. If we do, it improves our inherent value, including such intangibles as our sense of self esteem and our confidence.

On the opposite end, the negative effects of this Trine are to swamp a person with seemingly insurmountable obstacles. This is to encourage them to give up the fight, and by stepping aside to see things in a new light. Unfortunately for some this is misconstrued, and suicide is the result. Suicide is the failure to come to an agreement with your circumstances, and worse, we are recycled into the very same patterns in our next life. It simply offers no solutions.

The Spiritual Law at work here is, "Much gathers more. Less gathers loss." When this is understood by the native they tend to forge ahead with life at a pace that others can only gasp at, for there is a tremendous dynamic at work between the Three, Nine and Four, as well as a hint of mystery.

Things can come these people's way with no apparent effort on their part, but this is like the duck on the pond, who seems effortless but his legs are working hard under the water. This then is the art of succeeding with this Trine, the art of Silent Pursuit of the objective goal. This is actually the true art of surrender.

2-7-9 Great Trine:

FOCUS: Two: *See through the Illusion of Pleasure and Pain.*

This Trine can have difficulty with balance, for with the focus on the Two there can be an inherent sense of duality, or double vision if you will, with everything that is undertaken. Part of the life lesson from this Trine is to resolve the various Paradoxi. IE: Pain and Pleasure, High and Low, Rich and Poor, etc. Of course, there is no paradox when one considers the ancient truth: *All present circumstances are earned by the individual as a result of Karma.*

The resolution of these circumstance are part of the learning process of life. However, this is the higher viewpoint, and as such it must be earned through experience and understanding.

Two considerations are the keys to this Trine, Experience and Learning. The Prevalent Nine has the effect of making the native want to speak out. And so persons with this Trine are often very socially conscious and active, but time teaches that words spoken create the need for action, and so with maturity the native becomes quieter and more selective in the causes they choose to support. Their actions then become far more effective.

There is both a political side and an apolitical nature within these people, a caring heart and a cynical mind, a deeply thoughtful nature that can often act very selfishly, an open mind, yet a strong set of fixed opinions. As you can see, full of paradoxi. Because of this marital bliss is rare. Political partners, marriages of convenience, and arranged combinations are generally best for this type... and oddly genuine love can grow from these apparently "cold" relationships.

On the brighter side, these people are rarely poor. They are good at generating money when they put their focus on finance, however, there can be a problem with this in youth because the Two's sense of division may come to the fore. Then their mind will say things like "I shouldn't have money while my brother goes hungry" or "Money is the cause of all pain in this world".

There is a love for beautiful things, and for a comfortable life that tends to override this in time, but the soul so affected must be careful about how they resolve these inner questions. They may end up rich in cash, but as paupers spiritually, or just as easily poor in cash, but rich in spirit. The second appears noble until the rent has to be paid.

There is a tendency here to cut off options rather than resolve differences, and while this works and brings worldly success, it tends to leave the person at a loose end as far as friendship goes. This can lead to a lonely life, but even so these folk tend to be pragmatic about such things.

Much of their sense of paradox can be avoided by dedication to an ideal set by another, and so we find many devotees of varied paths to be affected by this Trine, or a similar combination of numerals. The Two, Nine and Seven are the "loner" numbers, yet the Two can become exceedingly co-operative with others when it is polarized to a common goal shared by all.

At this point the Two brings the energy of the Nine and Seven together, and these people make great leaders who can inspire others to heights of achievement and culture. They will remain in this position of strength as long as the common goal is held by the majority, but if the heart weakens the Two will become indecisive once more, and the dream will collapse.

In all this is a Trine that leads one through many varied experiences, the best result of which will cause the individual to choose the type of person they wish to be. The Trine gives an energy that likes to challenge sacred cows and beat the drum for social change, but so often when this is done the native is restless once more. We find that the real lesson of this Trine is not an outward one, but to turn the Soul inwards in order to resolve the differences inside.

There is a simple Motto that applies to this Trine. *"If we all swept our own doorsteps, we would have a clean street."*

The Major Trines:

1-3-7 Trine

3-7-9 Trine

1-7-9 Trine

1-3-9 Trine

1/3/7   3/7/9   1/7/9   1/3/9

Trines are drawn graphically in the above manner. A dot or a stroke for the position of each number represented.

The Major Trines are cornerstones to a building. Of themselves, they do little, but without them the structure has no basis. When a Major Trine appears in your chart, it is saying you have something to build in this life. This means you must know the basics of your profession or trade, and move in slow, certain steps.

Confidence, certainty and a deep sense of self worth are the goal posts, but until you find these within yourself, you are the ball life kicks about trying to find it.

1-3-7 Major Trine: Alone but not Lonely.

This Trine aspects the goal and the achievement of artistic endeavor. There is an indication of a period of sorrow and difficulty, and perhaps isolation when bringing this about. Because of this there is an ever present sense of failure looming about this Trine, haunting the native so affected.

This is the test of the Social Consciousness, and as a part of the Lesson of this aspect an individual must learn to stand alone.
When the fear of failure is mastered it becomes a yardstick for success, and doubt becomes a way to test if there are leaks in the boat. Via introspection, this Soul is always looking to refine their outflow, and in time this shapes and qualifies whatever they offer into a very high standard. Naturally, there is the problem of seeking too much perfection here, and so these natives need to learn when to leave things well enough alone.

It is also a good aspect for business, but not for group activity or work that requires fitting in with another's schedule. These people will pursue a task to the end, but in their own way, and their own time. Exacting and demanding, they expect results from others, and often are disappointed when the enthusiasm and commitment is not there with partners and/or employees. Good communication will prevent much of this, but here the communication is based on understanding the motivations of the other people involved, and especially the concept of "The Child Within".

This is a good Trine for work orientated souls, but naturally the opposite will often arise, and we will find those affected by this vibration who are bone lazy, and expect the world to support them. This type will always be on the lookout for some grant or scholarship, and curiously enough, they often get them! There is an overall intensity about this Pattern, which is only resolved through output and action, and so in the end the lazy ones really suffer a strong negative inertia in their lives. We often see this evidenced as frustration and anger in later life.

In time, these people become intensely practical, sometimes quite cynical, but even so with a very strong sense of who they are and where they are going... This can create an inconsiderate and obnoxious nature if the communication skills are not developed.

3-7-9 Major Trine: *A Secure Foundation makes a Secure House.*

A creative intensity is present here, with a conceptual and flamboyant tendency. It is a very structural energy, and suited to the likes of architects and those who like to design and create rather than those who just "create". These people do not work well on their own, and though they hate to admit it, generally need an audience of followers to feel truly satisfied. Of course, this can lead to a sense of megalomania which can generate problems, but others will still be drawn to the grand ideas produced by these natives. If the individual is balanced, the tower will stay upright, otherwise it collapses in confusion eventually.

Respect is very important to these people. It is needed in their lives as much as water, and without it they can become quite erratic. They often tread a fine line between what is acceptable and what their adventurous nature would like to do, and so we often find this type living on two planes. This can mean a definite public persona quite different from the private person. However, they are rarely two faced, but rightly reason that the public needs to see a face that is "acceptable". Thus we find this Trine is good for all those in the public eye.

The fact remains, though, that few achieve public recognition. Very often the inherent need for respect will be demanded rather than earned, and therefore all true communication will be strangled. Curiously, many people are happy to be bullied, and go along with what a strong personality commands. Even so this will leave the native of this type unsatisfied. Their only abiding satisfaction comes from the open recognition and respect of their peers. (Such as is represented by an Oscar or similar peer based award)

Many with this aspect work long hours in private and often remain single until their theory or goal is recognized and applied. The lesson here is to be able to carry on alone if needs be. Patience is the essential element for those with this Trine affecting their chart.

1-7-9 Major Trine: It is Only the Heart that Sees Rightly

This is a dangerous Trine, for it can lead a person into abuse of power, friends, and situations unless they get in charge of their need to achieve and be recognized.

The essential element of their personality is a dynamic, forthright nature that works hard to get others to support their particular banner, which could be anything from a political party to a school room table tennis team. These people are often patriots, sometimes fanatic in their zeal, and often forgetful of other people's feelings and emotions. Those with this aspect will often try to demand service, results and personal priorities from all they encounter, and can demonstrate aggressive behavior if thwarted... Yet they often have an intense spiritual aspect at work as well.

Often the task at hand will take on a higher value, like the patriot with his cause, and because of this many will be attracted to them. This is usually where the problems start for these folk, for generally as a race we do not handle power all that well, and the attention of others gives us one of the greatest powers in this world.

Often literate, and being able express their opinions in a structured, almost irresistible manner, they wholly enjoy the limelight that comes as a result of their efforts. However, as stressed earlier, this can often be at the expense of another's sensibilities. This is fine if their position calls for it, but not everyone wants a sergeant of arms in their life. As a result, these natives can be shunned at the workplace and in time in their home, which is a slow crucifixion for them.

If a balance can be achieved, and this is difficult here, the native will learn the art of negotiation, often developing a high level of competence in time. However, true negotiation requires an understanding of a situation BEFORE action is undertaken. Too often blind impulse rules this aspect, and it is the ruin of everything for those under its influence. As a result, there is a need to learn to qualify words and actions with a refined, overall perception of a subject, which will lead to correct action in most situations.

1-3-9 Major Trine: The Journey to Freedom begins with Integrity.

The focus here is on individuality. Be aware that the essential elements for attaining and maintaining our individuality are a sense of Identity (One), an ability to Create (Three), and the Power to Realize this (Nine).

Few can understand those affected with this Trine. They often seem to recklessly pursue dangerous situations, either physically or emotionally, and often find little stability or balance in their lives. In reality this is because they are looking for themselves, but seek this in external events, rather than sitting still long enough for the obvious to emerge.

This is the major lesson here, the Art of Patient Observance. We need to understand that without patience, understanding simply will not take root in our consciousness, but patience comes slowly, and for some not at all.

Without inner stillness these people will either be the rolling stone or the stoic rock who cannot be moved. Neither is overly desirable, for with one the creative force is uncontrolled, and with the second it becomes trapped and imprisoned in social and familial conditioning.

The positive aspects are that these people generally have a sunny disposition, and are rarely moody for long periods. Of course, depending on the other circumstances in their chart, there may be a Karmic Runoff indicated, and this will tend to create an atmosphere of introversion with this type.

A search for individuality, and in particular the need for spontaneity and naturalness, should be focused on and encouraged ... especially in children with this Trine. Be aware that children with this aspect will be very energetic as a rule, so give them lots to do. This applies to adults as well, and if the spouse recognizes this aspect in her mate, he or she should endeavor to get them focused on specific activities where they will meet new people, as this will encourage outflow.

Outflow is essential to the health and well being of everyone, but especially this type, and so inactivity is to be avoided. If there is an interest in a particular field, these people will delve very deeply into all aspects, and often come up with a surprisingly clear and simple understanding that will help others comprehend what might otherwise seem extremely complicated details. And so we find these people are good at structuring frameworks, be it computer programs, books, tools that make life easier, whatever. This Trine has very Creative energies, and the systems and concepts they generate will often appeal to the common person.

Because of this these people should ally themselves with those who have a good commercial sense, and those who are practical. This will greatly help their ability to focus, as they tend to get scattered and vague without supportive and practical outside assistance.

MINOR TRINES

1-2-4 Trine	**1-4-5 Trine**
2-3-6 Trine	**4-5-7 Trine**
6-8-9 Trine	**5-7-8 Trine**
4-7-8 Trine	**5-8-9 Trine**
4-5-8 Trine	**5-6-9 Trine**
2-4-5 Trine	**3-5-6 Trine**
2-5-6 Trine	**2-3-5 Trine**
5-6-8 Trine	**1-2-5 Trine**

Only Four Minor Trines do not possess a Five. This is significant, and indicates a general connection with the need to communicate. When a Minor Trine is present without a five represented, the people will either be chatterboxes, or sullen and silent.

When there is a Vacant Trine in this Minor Aspect, the lesson usually involves drawing energy from the creative flow, and converting it into some form of useful understanding here on Earth. Vacant Trines of this nature can be particularly difficult, and they can be exceptionally subtle, thus often hard to grasp.

We find many such Trines in charts, often there can be over five Minor Trines in any given chart. It is important not to get confused, and just go through them them slowly, and draw a general idea of how they combine for the individual. Sometimes it is as simple as a multi-faceted personality, other times the person themselves are fractured and dsconnected from reality. And still other times, the person intergrates them all well, without problem.

There is no fixed rule, other than we simply move through and assemble the most likely meaning. It is similar to the way you would piece a jigsaw puzzle together.

1-2-4 Trine: One coin spent is worth a thousand dreamed.

This is the first of the Minor Trine group that does not contain the Five. These Trines are more insular as a result of this, and if in the Vacant position this can indicate someone being closed to new ideas and/or an interaction with others.

The 1-4-2 Trine is significant in that the native so affected will usually have a deep, craving need for comfort, but little desire to work for this. In its deeper aspect this is the need for parental love, but if the native of this aspect learns to rise above their own needs, they will find the aspect reverses and they will be capable of much caring and sharing.

Sadly, this is rarely the case, and these people tend to wander around with beer pockets and champagne tastes. Note that if there is a Three strongly represented in the querent's chart there will be greater balance in the personality. This aspect will increase the ability to outflow thoughts and feelings, as well as increasing the ability to look after themselves.

Generally this Trine is considered an unfortunate aspect with the selfish nature of the One, the indecision of the Two, and the need for security of the Four... However in its positive aspect we would see strength of character (One), appreciation of art and beauty (Two), and a solid, methodical approach to things (Four). For the positive nature to emerge the individual would need to be genuinely confident within themselves. If so the Trine augurs well.

2-3-6 Trine: The Mind May See, but Does It Know the Heart?

A powerful aspect, but one where the native tends to get caught in their own dream. In the negative value, this indicates scheming and manipulation, and a peculiar ability to "lie the truth". This can go further, with the native feeling as if the world has done them wrong, especially if they do not get their own way with things.

The positive aspect gives a strong ability to both lead and serve in the same breath, for the Two, Three and Six are all good numbers that can deal well with groups and the hidden group consciousness. These are people who can perceive and understand the "secret" side of things, and who often innately know how to talk about it in ways that are understandable. More than this, the native tends to convey their message through small actions. This is one of the marks of true leadership.

These natives are very subtle individuals, and get confused and irritated around the loud and ignorant. They forever seek higher ground, and are never content amongst the valley dwellers, so if you want the company of this type don't get bogged down into conventions and social "role" playing. They will often simply leave you behind, and without a moments thought to the contrary.

6-8-9 Trine: A Moment with the Divine Rests between the Hurdles.

A great and noble combination, but one which often falls into apathy, for the dreams and aspirations often seem so impossible here that the native does not even want to try. As such, the sense of failure that lurks behind this Trine is often the great hurdle these people need to overcome.

The tendency is to find "Would be if could be's" with this pattern. However, the positive aspect shines with a strong light that attracts many to it, and so we also often find the teacher with an aspect like this. The relationship between the Six, Eight and Nine combines Intuition, Finance and Power which, when balanced, form an unstoppable energy. When imbalanced, this aspect is vague and weak with both their attention and attitude.

We will find that natives of this Trine will tend to be all or nothing types of individuals. As a result, even in the positive aspect they need patient partners who know how to keep their inner peace, especially through the often "loud" silences that stem from this Trine. Anyone who is truly negative in this aspect can cause a great deal of pain and disruption to others, but this is rare to find. One must be careful of this Trine, even so, for they will consciously ignore your feelings in order to convey whatever message they think you need. (Of course, the message is often for themselves as well, but you are expected to realize this.)

Failure, or itself, is usually the result of breaking the Law of Non-interference in some manner, and though all people must pay attention to this Law, people with this aspect are exceedingly susceptible to ignoring it. They often indulge in either do-gooding or do-badding, which eventually makes a mess of many people's lives, including their own.

This effect can leave the querent racked with a sense of personal worthlessness and failure in old age.

4-7-8 Trine: The Herald of Karma (Extremely Difficult Aspect)

This is a hard Trine to analyze. For some it is fortunate, especially if the individual is mindful of others and willing to serve life in some way. But it can be a very hard Trine, with almost impossible lessons at times as well. If this is in the vacant position of an individual's chart, it speaks of hard learning and no running away from responsibility.

This is a Minor Trine without the Five represented, one that is surprisingly fortuitous if the person affected is diligent and hard working. The others Minor Trines that lack the Five are very prone to moods, but this aspect is fairly stable. However, as mentioned, in its Vacant aspect it can be quite the opposite, and is the known as the Herald of Karma.

In the Vacant Aspect the sense of karma can be overwhelming. To break this and individual must specifically focus on moving away from established thought patterns and social moulds. The ending of a blind acceptance of stereotypes is keyed into this energy, and as such it can be both difficult and trying. Until we learn to see through the charades and posturing of the social consciousness, this Trine brings only pain.

The best way to breakup the prevalent aura generated by this Vacant Trine is through service to others, or through service to a higher cause. We will find many healers, artists and musicians affected by this aspect. It is a difficult Trine to categorize, as it works differently with each individual, but we can say with certainty that the Vacant aspect of this Trine can be a very potent teacher. When one shares some higher viewpoint on the purpose of life, and the need for spiritual growth and understanding, then the lessons are less harsh.

The Eight and the Four are somewhat Karmic by nature, but tied with the Seven there is a learning process involved, and so long as the individual keeps their tail up and nose down, life will proceed in an orderly and interesting fashion. If laziness creeps in, though, life will degenerate into a confusing series of happenings marked more by their apparent haphazardness than any message to be garnered from them.

As a rule, the individual affected by this Trine will have a need for order, and this can occasionally make them somewhat pedantic and mechanical. The focus will be on the mind, and an aesthetic appreciation of concepts will govern thought, along with a need to express this in some form. This often turns these people into inventors and innovators, though in the negative aspect they will become critical, fussy and incapable of clear decisions, other than cutting things off in a negative manner.

4-5-8 Trine: Are we Soul with a Body, or a Body with a Soul?

Again we experience the aspect of the Four and the Eight together. If the person with this aspect is of a higher mind and not needing so much in the way of material goods, this aspect is good. However, if they are materially minded with their goals and aspirations, bad luck may well seem to dog their every move. Spiritual Purpose must be found if peace is to settle in the heart.

There is a desire for emotional balance, and material well being that is often frustrated by endless problems, but if the native looks deeply into themselves they will find that this is because at heart they have little interest in worldly matters. When this is accepted, oddly enough things work out much better for them in the financial sense.

It is an excellent combination for those who would be of service in the spiritual orders, as faithfulness and persistence are hallmarks of the higher mind involved here. Naturally, the reverse can be true and this Soul can be afflicted with such traits as pessimism and selfishness. Sadly, this is often the case, but through service the effects can be reversed.

The negative attitude of materialism is more predominate because altruistic natures generally suffer in this world. However, part of learning to have an attitude of Service is to develop an attitude of inner strength as well, and so difficulty and/or ignorance is not an excuse.

In the upcoming century the energy shift will be such that the Eight vibration will be purified. This will mean a Karmic runoff of unprecedented proportions at the start of the 21st Century for many, many people. This will provide an opportunity, in the end, for a sense of inner freedom and strength. Hopefully it will be enough to help many Souls break through into the secret place inside themselves, the place which those with this Trine accented in their chart yearn for. This "Secret Place" is simply the inner self in its pure form. The discovery of self (Soul) allows a being to express itself more clearly in this outer world.

2-4-5 Trine: Grasp the Plow. Till the Earth Within. Bear Fruit.

This aspect is generally difficult unless the individual affected has a clear sense of who and what they are. If the individual affected by this Trine is strong with a clear vision, this will activate the One vibration, and draw this Trine into the fortunate Minor Square of 1-2-4-5.

The 2-4-5 Minor Trine has the awkward combination of Two and Four to contend with. The Two; seeking yet insecure, the Four; secure yet unwilling to look outside its own fence. The Five is the bridge with this combination, for it can develop a communication that allows the positive aspects of both to grow. As a result, if the person so affected can take the view that life is a series of educational lessons, this Trine can be most beneficial. A business-like approach of accepting losses and getting on with the job is needed here.

In the negative aspect, the FIVE has a frivolous energy to it, which brings out the bigotry and two faced characteristics of the Four and the Two. As such this can create a very power conscious individual. In the Positive aspect, the FIVE is generous and giving, looking to listen to and hear what others have to say. Then the higher nature of the Two and Four are activated, and we would find this type to make excellent counselors and diplomats.

These people will always be attracted to those whose light shines, and can make wonderful supporters of innovative teachers and ideas, but may also use this belief in others as a crutch to avoid dealing with the lack of self esteem inside themselves.

There is a need to develop independence if they would wish to feel free. It is a fact, however, that most people consider life as a burden, and constantly look for someone else to shoulder their problems. A person with this view would find living a problem, and suicide is generally considered, even if not acted upon.

2-5-6 Trine: Be Inspired by Life, Be Simple. Life is as it is.

A most harmonious aspect, generally considered fortunate. A wealth of good and useful ideas will flow from these people, and depending on the other aspects of the chart this will determine how effectively they can actually put them into practice. In any case the tendency is for the individual to be able to communicate their concepts and dreams, and so positions as trainers, in PR, and as business advisers might be considered ideal.

Activity is highlighted here. These people like to just get up and go when a new project arises, but can be shackled by a need for approval, procrastination, or a fear of failure. What is worse, they will be aware of these shortcomings, thus focusing undue attention of the problems, rather than the solutions. Attachment to the past must be shaken off in order for any degree of peace and contentment to be found... But to truly shake off a concern we need to be able to see it clearly.

Clarity, therefore, should be the goal to aim for when this Trine is highlighted in one's life. When we can see things clearly problems tend to percolate to their essence, and understanding takes hold, lighting up a path for resolution. Without a true understanding of a subject, it is impossible to act clearly on it.

5-6-8 Trine: A Curse can turn to a Blessing, and Vice-Versa.

A fortunate aspect for finance, though it may be dealing with others people's money at first. Experience and time will bring about an accumulation of life's necessities and luxuries, and the native with this aspect must be careful of the temptation to do things too quickly. Stability comes through slow growth as a rule, though there are exceptions.

Notably here, the person affected may be working for years with little seeming progress, and then suddenly all falls into place. In reality the growth had been happening over a long period of time, these are the roots that cannot be seen, but which took this time to establish.

If spiritually minded life will go well, with a philosophical turn of mind being needed as the Eight brings the seeds of the past to harvest, and inevitably we all have some excess baggage of unpleasant habits and ideas we will need to cast off. This will often appear to cost the person financially for a time, but as these karma's are sorted out, finance and emotions will all come into balance.

The worst scenario here is that this Soul will refuse to recognize the need for patience, and barge on regardless, never finding any pivot or base in their lives, therefore accomplishing little. The sense of frustration from this can be crushing. Sometimes the very need for results that these people feel is the very thing that prevents results from occurring.

Overall we can see this Trine in a chart as a warning. It speaks of change, and comfortable situations being turned upside down. The secret message of this Aspect is learning to CHOOSE. Just choose the path you want to go in, and many things will simply fall into place.

1-4-5 Trine: Be not so Practical that Ye cannot Love.

This type is perceptive and angular, often finding a side to an argument that is quite lateral. They like to "deal" and will be found buying and selling all sorts of things. As a rule they will make a passable living from this, but the reason they do it is often not so much for the money, but simply because they like the thrill of the chase.

This is a good aspect for the sales person, the secretary, and anyone who is up front dealing with the public, but there is a tendency for impatience and/or disdain with both their employers and fellow employees that can make these folk somewhat abrasive. Above all there is the desire for things to happen quickly, but they rarely do, with the effect of stifling this souls sense of independence.

These people do well in a self employed category, and generally are happiest focusing on business and life's little pleasures. They have little time for philosophy, and do not bear fools gladly. The major lesson is learning to be more generous, especially with allowing another room to breath. In relationships these folk tend to be obsessive, even though this Trine appears detached. The apparent detachment is often just a mask for deeper feelings they are afraid to show because of insecurity.

4-5-7 Trine: There is a Freedom in the Darkness

Few people will ever really understand this Trine. This can be a difficult and somber vibration to work through, and a great deal of perseverance might be called upon before any successful outcome appears. However, as the individual works through the sense of mental complication that often arises here, things will go easier.

In time the querent may gain an innate understanding of the human condition, and an instinctive sense of who is trustworthy and who is not.

Because of this, wisdom will become an important factor later in life, (But with the subsequent danger of becoming "Too" wise and wanting to let everyone know... Often in the form of the dreaded dreadful autobiography!) These people are not self indulgent as a rule, but can become so when dispensing "pearls of wisdom".

They make better grandparents than parents, because in the mid part of life there are often too many details and things to finish for any time to be dedicated to children.

These persons are often very career minded, and appear obsessive about things, often at the expense of health and partners. The Seven carries a certain loneliness with it, and always the lesson here is to know how to be alone, but not lonely.

A certain poetic streak is latent here, and we occasionally find truly exceptional writers who speak deeply about the human condition aspected with this Trine.

5-7-8 Trine: Be Open... Accept that Life Loves You.

This Trine can be dangerous for overall development, for it tends to create a somewhat manic personality. If not manic, then probably obsessive and fussy over unnecessary detail. They carry a certain angst with them wherever they go, and cast a black mood over the party as they try to explain the dangers of global warming to those of us who prefer to just get drunk.

However, if these people simply focus of helping others instead of trying to solve the problems of the world from their TV lounge, then everything will fall into place. In other words, the problem with this Trine is selfishness, often to the point of being self-obsessed. When these people stop complaining and start doing something useful all the internalizing energy expands outwards, and they feel really good about themselves and life in general.

So the lesson here is giving equal attention to others as we might otherwise give to ourselves, though, of course this energy can easily reverse, and we find that we give other too much attention, and none for ourselves. The balance is found with focused service to a higher ideal, but not martyrdom.

Paradoxically, when this Trine is in the VACANT aspect the Native is often highly capable of expressing their true emotions, and they can become quite excellent teachers, with a deep perception of human nature. This can occur in the Stated aspect as well, if the Soul has developed to this point. It is all about allowing yourself to be loved, and being worthy of respect.

5-8-9 Trine: If Wishes were Horses, Beggars would Ride.

Altruistic ideals are highlighted, however, these are often doomed to a lesser role than what we might have dreamed. These people have good intentions and noble ideals, but their own inability to recognize and deal with the negative aspects of their personal life all too often causes the great plans to flounder. The impact from this often sets the individual affected by this Trine adrift from their mooring, and they wonder why life has treated them so badly.

The saying "If wishes were horses. Beggars would ride" is a 15th Century English quip about how dreams are easy, reality is the hard part. Accepting the hard realities equals success for this Trine.

Essentially these folk needs develop a Negative Mental Attitude in order to succeed. Does this sound odd? It should not, for so often in life we succeed because we had doubts and reservations, which effectively forced us to look more closely at a project before we got underway. This is not an attitude that says things cannot be done, merely that things are never accomplished as easily as we might dream. Good intentions are not enough, and Murphy's Law applies: If it can go wrong, it will.

On the positive aspect, the native with this Trine is enthusiastic and responsive, and is excellent for the person who is second in charge. They will work long hours to ensure that a project succeeds. But these folk usually need a tough boss who will always keep the bottom line, and thus the profit margin, firmly in view.

Spiritually this type needs to realize that the true overview of life is only found by dealing with all the details. If attention to detail is held paramount they will find great peace later in life.

5-6-9 Trine: Limitations and Obstacles are Life's Ladders.

The Six represented in this particular Trine is often in focus, as it deals with both business and the home, as well as an inner spiritual aspect. On the higher levels the Six focuses on receiving the gifts of heaven. This Trine can represent a highly inspirational lifetime where the native so affected will find themselves lifted far above the morass of the Social Consciousness. The Five and Nine are suited to this as well, but of course many will try and pull the Soul back who dares leave. This can create a state of "Push - Pull" where aspirations drive the person to leave social inhibitions, while others move in the background to keep the person contained. Breaking attitudes like "What willt he neighbours think" are what need to be broken here.

On the common level, this Trine is good for business and general associations with people. It offers the native clarity of thought and good perceptive, though of course the reverse is always true. With any Trine,

Pattern or single Number in the Noumenal Order we ALWAYS have two sides to the coin. Remember that life presents, like Numerology, States of Consciousness and likely conditions, not specific end results. The end result is always in the hands of the individual.

With this particular Trine the native must be careful of attempting too much, and must learn the limits of their own capabilities. We often find we have a battle between the attainment of the Goal and the NEED for the Goal with this aspect. Often this comes out as a sort of "I want this, but do I REALLY want this?" question. Discrimination and self-discipline are therefore highlighted here.

3-5-6 Trine: I can create, given the Will. What is the Will?

This is the artists Trine, though the art might be expressed in numerous ways, and not necessarily in painting. In everything these people do in life they will try to add that little extra flair, and because of this, moneyed people will be attracted to them. Thus, one of the lessons is how to deal with the money consciousness, and in particular how not to be abused and confused by the worldly power that inevitably comes with the "money" people.

Another association that comes with this Trine is Fame, though many times it is unwanted once it arrives. This is because the need for Fame is generally based upon the need for love, but the native soon learns (if he or she is at all wise) that the adoration of the masses is a greater prison than a gift.

Fame is a drug, of course, and alongside this more "Up" characteristic there can be the negative trait of drug addiction, which often follows this Trine. This is a habitual, compulsive "thing" that is based within the insecurity of the individual affected, and generally this cannot be removed until a true sense of worth is established in the heart and mind. This is best done by developing a sense of purpose, but if the native goes one step further and seeks to do something useful for others, they will find a real sense of completion and satisfaction arising in their lives. Laughter is the best medicine in the meantime.

A general lesson with this Trine is in learning how to overlook the frailties and weaknesses of others, yet not fall prey to them in ourselves. It is to do with rising above the inner criticism that invariably cripples the natural responsiveness of this type when they are caught in negative mindsets.

In the final picture, the Trine is here to help us to learn STRUCTURE, and so if a person affected by this influence simply learns to find a rhythm and order in their life, things go much smoother.

Book of Number: Interpretations

2-3-5 Trine: A Shadow Lives in Balance with the Light.

Achievement seems to come easily to people with this Trine, but is there persistence to continue? Here is a hidden peril, for when things get difficult this type can often fold under the pressure. Theirs is the desire to succeed on talent alone, which, of course, is never enough in the long term.

What this is in the deeper reaches of the unconscious is an inability to face the shadow self, the part of us where repressed thoughts and emotions have taken root. Often this creates a need to propagate the EGO value of the personality, which in turn breaks down their natural sense of communication with family, partners and others. Thus we find that for some this Trine can lead to a sense of intense isolation, and severe internalization of the inner person.

How is this avoided? Goal setting, and a view towards the long term reality rather than the short term dreams, this is what must be achieved for peace to enter the heart here. Naturally the Goal needs to be one which should set some sort of stability place, otherwise this type runs the risk of losing everything in mid life. This is often the death knell for these bright, fluent and effervescent people, and the result can be a personality collapse.

Alcoholism is a real danger. This and other convenient retreats from reality must be watched out for, and this type must also learn to enjoy their own company. Curiously, when they reach this point, other useful persons will seek them out, people who will prove invaluable in helping to achieve chosen goals.

As a rule, these people have a light, almost fragrant air about them, and may even have a slight appearance of the Fay (fairy) folk. IE: Extended ears with tips, long, thin noses, eyes that seem in the distance and sharp chins. There is often a sort of "Otherworld" appearance as well, and we find some of the better clairvoyants have this Trine represented somewhere in their chart.

1-2-5 Trine: Success = Grace + Communication + Beauty.

This is a very practical combination, with the people affected by this Aspect generally being able to make great intuitive jumps when looking for solutions to problems. In their maturing phase they need a lot of time alone, resenting interruptions to their train of thought, and often seeming to be difficult simply because they like to think an lot!

This is one of the problems with this aspect, that there can be so much consideration of things, that nothing ever actually gets completed. There is a need to focus on finishing what is started for by not completing their natural cycles these people will lose track of their sense of self, and become very confused. Inattention to diet can also cause great concern, as these folk need to be careful with their health as a rule.

There is an old saying: Moods and Tempest follow the Moon's Shadow. As these folk seek out the darker, hidden side to their nature, many odd things can, and do, erupt into their lives. These storms of emotion and strange quirks of fate are the result of the individual breaking through their inner barriers, and yet ithe person is rarely aware of this process. They can be so wrapped up in their state of discovery that the world for all accounts barely exists. They won't even realise how moody and temperamental they appear to others. A difficult aspect for successful marital arrangements until this blind spot is balanced out.

We also have an energy here that is rather good at inventing and improvisation. These folk will often like to do their own repairs to the house, rather than call in a tradesman. In their view this would be simply giving money away. These folk will often have little desire for success or recognition from others, but generate a great sense of satisfaction from seeing a job well done.

Complacency is a danger on all levels here, and so the native with this aspect must always be sure to have goals. And they must be sure to complete them! Otherwise they will fiddle their lives away on small details, and wonder why little was achieved as they leave their body at death. In all, though, a favorable Trine for a good outcome.

It is especially fortunate if this Trine is present in the formation date of a Company or creative venture. When combined with the 4-6-8 Vacant Trine is is almost a guarantee of success for new ventures, given that the necessary hard work is provided.

BASE TRINES:

2-6-7 Base Trine

1-6-8 Base Trine

3-4-8 Base Trine

2-4-9 Base Trine

2-6-7   1-6-8   3-4-8   2-4-9

The Base Trines are also known as "Rebel Trines". People with these Aspects seem prone to rebel against authority, and in the final aspect, desire to BE authority themselves. Children will be unruly, wives will not pay attention to the budget, husbands will like to stray into places where fun is the priority, not responsibility. And yet, these Trines also seem to carry with them a distinct and unique level of awareness that acts as a shield and protection to the individual.

It is very much a case of fools going where angels fear to tread, yet it seems to work out fine for people under the influence of a Base Trine. You find this aspect with adventurers, missionaries and those who love to live outside of social convention. As a general rule, people under this influence tend towards impatience with authority, and a curiosity for anything that is different and strange.

You will find people in social movements and organisations trying to change the social order are often affected by a Base Trine. Three of the founders of Greenpeace all have Base Trines affecting them. Robert Hunter, born Oct 13 1941 has a 2-6-7 Base Trine. Dorothy Stowe, born Dec 22 1920 has a 3-4-8 Base Trine. Irving Stowe July 25 1915 has a 3-4-8 Base Trine.

The "Make a Wave" group is accepted as the core for Greenpeace. The only main player in the initial group of people without a Base Trine is David McTaggart, the man with the boat who responded to the initial call from the above three, and the only one wounded in the initial protests off Muaroa Atoll. It is so typical, the people with the Base Trines sail through the protests and difficulty and seem to duck the bullets.

As a curious note, Aldous Huxley, born 26th Sept 1894 has THREE Base Trines persent in his Birthdate. He was an incredibly influencial writer, but more importantly, he is the unrecognised father of modern spirituality, as he is also the one who encouraged Krishnamurti to write.

2-6-7 Base Trine: True Freedom is Mind and Heart in Balance.

Uncompromising attitudes and plain pigheadedness are often exhibited here, and this can make for a sense of being a "rebel without a cause". People with this Trine active generally have a natural aversion to following anything, yet they generally also prefer to avoid argument. This tends to make them very silent, to the point of being sullen. This trait can be mistaken for a deep inner knowing, by bothtje person affected and those they deal with. (Many semi-lost souls will chase after this type, thinking they have found their Guru.) While the natives of this Trine often possess a deep understanding of human nature, they are equally as often confused about themselves. By itself, this is a poor Trine for a Guru. It tends to suit the hermit, however.

Early on the native tends to appear unapproachable, for a number of reasons, but as maturity develops and the desire to communicate increases, these people can offer some quite revolutionary insights into the working of the human psyche. This is because they have had to survive their own inner darkness and by doing so they now have decided to express this experience, even as they contain it. *This is a good Aspect for a writer and/or social observer.*

At heart these people can be deeply concerned about humanity, even though they may (paradoxically) be indifferent to individuals. There is often to be found a burning need to learn and grow here, and the worst possible punishment for a child with this aspect would be to make them sit and do nothing for a few hours. If the native with this energy feels imprisoned in any way, they will quickly become sullen and resentful, even if the imprisonment is simply in their own minds: And it often is!

Because of this sense of resentment, the person under this Trine may develop an outrageous sense of breaking rules purely for the sake of it. The reasoning is that BECAUSE the rules have been broken, they are now more free to be themselves. The world and authority generally takes a dim view on this sort of attitude, and the native of this Aspect will often appear to attract trouble like a moth to a flame.

The actor, James Dean, portrayed characters that epitomise the energy present here. Live fast, die young.

All in all, though, the Aspects relating to this Trine combine to create a sensitive individual who tends to be a loner with an acute intuitive perception of the world about them. The push and pull of trying to merge the various disparate elements of their inner self together creates either very interesting Souls, or abject failures.

One of the major lessons here is understanding that true freedom starts with a gentle, and genuine, form of honesty.

1-6-8 Base Trine: Truth is found through many Storms.

An internal struggle, with an almost fervent desperation for the chance to be oneself marks this Trine. Intuition (Six), Willpower (One) and Karma (Eight) all vie for the right to rule the life of the native. There is a powerful internal question that is asked here: How can I find true inner peace and balance?

Only when the individual focuses his life on practical observations, and the fundamental principles or virtue, will this clamour come to order. There is a need to ask "What is obvious" every step of the way. In the negative value this Aspect can become a blind adherence to ritual and dogma handed down to the individual. In the positive it becomes a deep and lucid questioning of where one's priorities and beliefs truly lie.

Given this, the person blessed with this aspect has a powerful ability to see what is obvious in any given situation. This will often set them at odds with authority, which does not like its flaws being pointed out as a rule. The combination of a natural stubbornness and a deep sense of honesty means that this type cannot accept lies and deceit as acceptable practice. This means they rarely sit comfortably in social groups.

There is an ascetic martyrdom associated with this Trine. This can be based on a need for others to recognize the trials and tribulations of their growth, a sort of "Look how good I am because I am suffering" attitude." But this passes as the Soul matures. It then realizes that true happiness is based on enriching ourselves, not on suffering, and also that happiness and peace do not come with outside approval.

As the power of the One Vibration strengthens here this Soul often finds in themselves an acerbic wit, sometimes a sarcasm, which can overtake their sense of what is "correct" in a given situation. This offends some, if not many, depending on circumstance. On one hand this helps break down the barriers of the social do's and do not's, yet on the other it can make the individual feel isolated, and drive away those who care for them. However, a period of loneliness or isonlation is essential for the development of the independence that these natives crave.

Trust is a big lesson here, specifically trust in the higher power within oneself. Before this can unfold the Soul must make a conscious decision to get to understand their own inner workings. This is best done through some outer assistance. A guide or teacher is often the last thing these people want, but it often what they most need.

It is a slight paradox that the true independent thinkers often come from a strict, sometimes puritanical paths which require unwavering discipline and service. If people with this Trine can develop a strong self-discipline, and learn a little patience, the doors will open for them.

3-4-8 Base Trine: Believe in your Right to Live. Cherish Life.

This Aspect is considered to be extremely karmic. It is the classic Trine for the unsung hero, artist and trapped housewife. Such lives can be quite tragic, even if such a Soul produces great works as a result of this tragedy. However, there is also the possibility that there is good karma to be worked out here, whereupon the person so affected will have an extraordinarily fortunate life.

Many times the individual so affected will sense this karma on their horizon, and inwardly choose to secrete themselves away in some dark, cloistered environment, such as the public service, or even the priesthood. They feel that by living inside some non-descript occupation, or perhaps by living a secret, twilight existence, that they can avoid their inner fears, but their life becomes compromised because of this. Even so, karmic eruptions will still occur in their lives.

There must be developed a "carry on regardless" attitude for success here, which, if this is done in a balanced way, will unleash the power of creativity in every aspect of the person's life. This can solve almost every problem, some before they even arise.

Surprisingly, creativity is of itself a negative aspect. Few understand it. Most great symphonies and great works of art came after a period of anguish for the composer or artist. The negative energy in their life drove them to create something. This act of creating becomes our ladder into a higher viewpoint, and the force of creation pushes us out of the mud of human misery. This is where a solid emotional foundation, and a sense of humanity are the saving graces. Firm ideals and a deep sense of ethics turns the wobbly rope ladder into something more substantial, and makes the climb much easier.

We find that many with this Trine become dedicated to manifesting something, be it an ideal, a garden in the back of the house, a work of art or a common piece of pottery. In the end the energy is calling for the individual to manifest a greater value to themselves.

Live and grow! The sense of growth balances the sometimes disturbing energy that is present here. This comes down to mastering the art of BE-ing. Only then will Life come into clear focus. Only then do we understand the purpose we are here for.

This Aspect can be quite the imp as a child. Naughty, precocious and resistant to all authority, they can certainly be mother's problem child. And yet, they can also be so sweet and loving, that it is hard for anyone to understand WHY they want to challenge everything. It's the nature of the beast to push the boundaries, and if you can teach the child respect, many of the adult issues of this Aspect will be less severe.

2-4-9 Base Trine: I love to Rule, Yet I Long for Love.

These folk can be extremely power conscious, and often somewhat pedantic in manner, yet never they realize it! I nether-the-less refer to those affected by this Trine as the "James Dean's". This is not the rebel without a cause, but the actor who can mould themselves to the part, or any other role where charm and connivance can succeed.

In the negative value, these people can be intense, yet extremely fickle with their opinions, moving towards anyone who will give them the most mileage, and dropping friends like confetti. As such they are highly untrustworthy Souls, who would sell their own mothers for an ounce of their addiction. And they usually are addicted to something, be it for either pleasure or pain.

The positive aspect generally strives very hard to please, thinking this is the avenue for success, but in time the native learns that others view this as a weakness. And in many cases it is! When the native first recognizes this, they tend to go a little overboard with an attitude of abuse of either themselves (with guilt and self-recrimination) and/or others (with agressive tendencies, both verbal and non-verbal) until a balance or compromise between life and the individual is struck. Only then does the positive value emerge. This is a silent understanding of the many aspects of life, and with it comes a quiet assurance of knowing that we are, quite simply, good enough.

The lesson here is to come into accord with our own natural order, which is a sort of symphonic anarchy, like the chaotic yet orderly songs of nature. Here we accept that while we are not perfect, no-one ever is, and that this is OK. It is just how it is. Silence is key to understanding.

There is a child in this aspect, a Soul who is always looking to the heavens, but they seem so far away. This often gives a distant look to their eye, and a certain sense of disregard for the opinions of other people. (This is often mistaken as a disdain, but though this is certainly possible if the negative aspects rule, it is usually not so.) They are rarely happy in crowded conditions, and love adventuring in some way or another. In this sense, folk with this Trine tend to never quite grow up, but when they do, they often carry a hefty sword of discrimination which cuts through all the social and political rubbish. This creates hidden enemies, so care should be taken to deal with things as diplomatically as possible.

The negative reaction these people might get is often just a knee-jerk reflex from the Social Consciousness in others. Such a thing can create great difficulties, so the native with this aspect needs to take care to oil their relationships with some courtesy. A good technique, when applying the critical faculty of their often bright minds to someone they see as being wrong, is to head the comments they might utter with terms like, "With respect: I see this." (That way, when you tell people they are wrong, they tend to take it less personally.)

Book of Number: Interpretations

Augmented Trines:

(Called a Diminished Trine, when in the Vacant position)

1-4-6 Aug. Trine

1-3-4 Aug. Trine

1-3-6 Aug. Trine

1-7-8 Au. Trine

2-3-8 Au. Trine

2-8-9 Aug. Trine

2-7-8 Aug. Trine

1-2-7 Aug. Trine

1-2-8 Aug. Trine

2-3-9 Aug. Trine

3-4-6 Aug. Trine

3-8-9 Aug. Trine

4-6-9 Aug. Trine

4-6-7 Aug. Trine

4-7-9 Aug. Trine

6-7-9 Aug. Trine

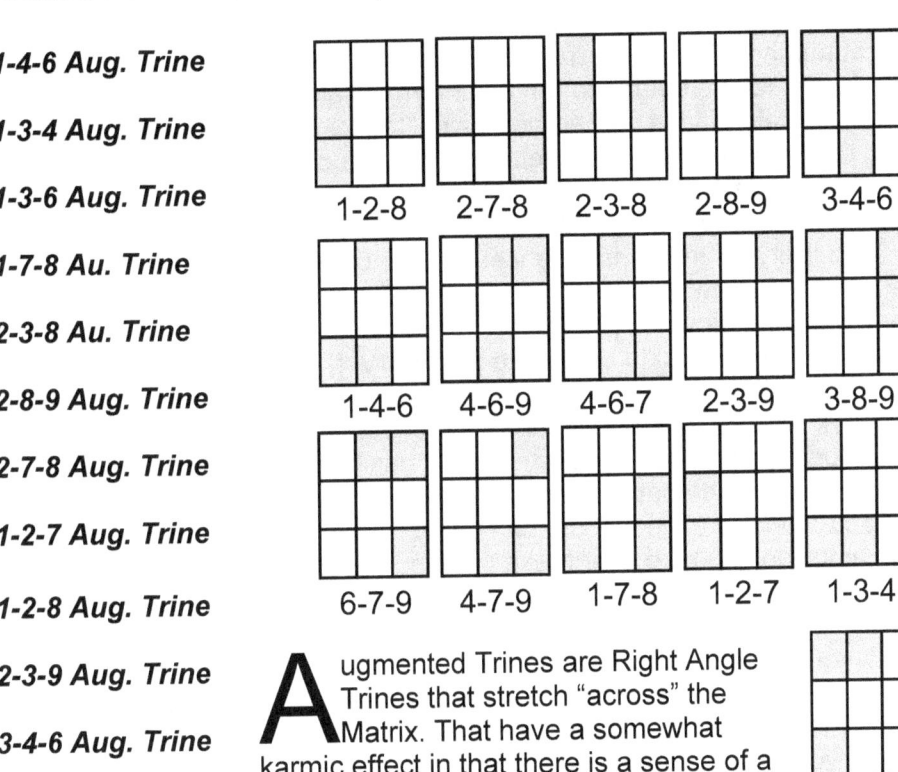

1-2-8   2-7-8   2-3-8   2-8-9   3-4-6

1-4-6   4-6-9   4-6-7   2-3-9   3-8-9

6-7-9   4-7-9   1-7-8   1-2-7   1-3-4

1-3-6

Augmented Trines are Right Angle Trines that stretch "across" the Matrix. That have a somewhat karmic effect in that there is a sense of a boomerang energy here where things return to the sender. They carry a general energy or curiousity, of something else to be known that cannot presently be seen.

In this sense, they are somewhat cat-like in nature. Angular, reflexive and needing to have an inner sense of balance to feel comfortable. Whether someone is a hunting tiger or a tame house cat, the concept of a safe haven is important, and so these are a group of Trines that generally affect the individual in a way that security is found in having a home base.

These Trines like to associate themselves to solid reliable principles or people, but rarely feel any sort of obligation of care towards another. It is a case of the strongest survive, and if you are strong, you will be loved because of it.

Diminished Trines, or VACANT Augmented Trines are on Page 145. This is a unique Trine in that the Vacant Position alters the interpretation significantly.

1-4-6 Augmented Trine: Be Open to the Truth. Test your Heart.

Auspicious and fateful, this Trine indicates great success in the field of the persons choosing. Here is one Soul who can depend on themselves to accept winning, and do so with grace. It is a strange fact of human nature that many people cannot deal with success. Why? The fear of failure seems to run the internal dialogue, and leads people down the path of loss, rather than gain. Conspiratorial thinking, excess drug usage and confusion in relationships is a clear sign this Aspect is not being mastered.

TWhen an idivudal learns to trust their instincts and accept full responsibility for the consequences of their decisions, ost of the negatives fade away. If they do not, they meet with failure and compromise their whole life long. There is a driving energy present, and it is up to the individual to choose to be the diver, or be driven.

When reasonably balanced, the person with this Trine expects that life will work out OK, and it does for the most part. The person works best when focussed on developing their own business. However, finding a partner who will be patient enough to sit at home while the native goes out and "conquers the worlds" can be difficult. Here is a warning: Greed and ambition can take over these people, and though they tend to come back to themselves later on in life, this fire or lust can burn friends and family, and they will be left alone in old age if care is not taken.

Quite often these folk literally burn up before this point. The metabolism can be so accelerated by their driving nature that their life energy fades, especially if the querent takes to eating a diet of meat and carbohydrate without the necessary trace elements and enzymes their bodies need. If the food intake includes plenty of fresh food and if they exercise lightly each day their life span will be elongated.

Drugs, especially designer drugs, are suggested to be avoided at all costs. Even casual usage is not recommended, due to the inherent drivine nature of this Trine.

We are actually working on an acceptance of self with this aspect, which is often best found through an acceptance of others, and from here gain and understanding on the varied ways of how life moves, both within and without of ourselves.

1-3-4 Augmented Trine: The Eye well trained serves you well.

This is a very creative yet practical Trine. A focus on buying things that will have more value as time passes seems natural to this type. The native here will often dabble with antiques and item of quality, things which will generally be seen to mprove in value. They have a good eye for a bargain, and are usually prepared to wait out the market, cashing their investments in as demand peaks.

Real estate investment is particularly good for this Trine, as are all matters relating to the earth. However, spiritual speaking, these folk are strongly affected by the moon, and often have the symptoms of having one foot on the ground, with another foot in the clouds. If the balance is kept this is also an ideal combination for poets and artists.

Background will determine where they end up in life, but whatever their position, high or low, these folk generally have a pretty good time of it. Yet they are forever the outsider. Authority will not not understand, friends may be amazed at their antics, acquaintances might think them vague. Yet somehow they weave like a drunk through the course and manage to come out smiling at the other end. "We thrive despite our shortcomings" was a quote someone said, and it fits well here.

It may be called luck, but really it is an odd sort of attitude which, if the querent keeps from bitterness and judgment, seems to work out in their favor. The message here is to go with the flow, and things work out well.

1-3-6 Augmented Trine: Don't spend too much time Dreaming.

Detached and distant, this Trine like to perch itself on the metaphorical rock, high in the hills of thought. These people love thinking, and they do it all the time. It is infuriating for spouses and family, for they can ask and wonder what is going on inside the querent, but he/she simply is not interested in communicating until whatever it is they are thinking of has been thought out.

Even then they might not explain! That's the way they are, and nothing can change this except falling in Love. Here they become intensely vulnerable, and suddenly realize how ill equipped they are for communication. It can be a harrowing time, and many retreat into themselves... Those who survive, however, seem to go onto to greater and greater things.

Many a genius has had the effect of this Trine in their lives in some way or another. If you are dedicated to a goal, it is wonderful, if you are not I suggest you find one because life will slowly evaporate around you. Focus is everything for the well being of this Trine, and a strong sense of purpose is the only thing that will retain this focus throughout their life.

1-7-8 Augmented Trine: Observe before you Act.

Paradox is fascinating to these people, and they like to sit and observe the flow of life, especially the peculiarities of circumstance and personality. This is important to cultivate, because in this instance a little observation can show the way to act far more clearly in any given situation. A good aspect for the researcher.

Curiosity is the most notable trait, and with this curiosity in full flight, those affect by the 1-7-8 Trine can apparently walk through fire unscathed.

These folk make excellent explorers, not just geographically but in science as well. Inner as well as outer space holds interest for them, and there is a strong bent towards philosophical matters. They are not idealists, but are pragmatic in their views on life, yet they remain dreamers of tomorrow. Few people truly understand them, but the native should not let this bother them. Their real interest is in understanding life and people, not necessarily vice versa.

They make excellent conversationalists in academic fields, and good entrepreneurs if money is their interest. Their judgments are rational and focused, and their natural ability to ask the right questions often gets them through obstacles lesser mortals would believe impossible.

To employee's, this type of boss can appear indestructible, but what they really have going for them in this sense is their persistence, and a dogmatic belief that the job can and will be done. The only real problem here is that when the worst of the obstacles are out of the way, these folk lose interest, and want to get to the next challenge. Unfortunately this is where many problems take root that have to be sorted out at a later stage, and so it is wise to learn to finalize each project before starting another.

The negative aspect is very unpleasant, however, and this is evidenced by a person without roots wandering from trial to problem and back again. This is reversed only by finding some purpose to focus their energies onto, otherwise life will continue to slowly disintegrate before them.

2-3-8 Augmented Trine: Take Care. A fox chases the chickens.

Here is the creative Soul who can really make money! However, there is a strong indication here of suffering if the native does not get out there and make things happen for themselves. When an individual with this aspect moves ahead with confidence, things fall into place very well, as a rule. Financial ability and courage are needed here. One you can learn, the other you either have it or you don't.

Incredible and tremendous leaps of faith in some concept or product can work out quite successfully. Intuitive guesses about such things as long odds in the racing, or the stock market will meet with success, but if the native begins to rely upon these, the gift usually fails them. Here there is a paradox, their inner sight can show them the way, but when the native relies on it, it often fails.

The secret to understanding this is found in the querulous nature of belief, and the human factor of seeking to get something for nothing. In other words, things can go well for a time, but the tide usually reverses and their eartwhile good fortune leaves them stranded on some barren rock. If the native moves in short, certain steps through their life, rather than the big ones they dream of, they will build up a psychic and financial foundation that will be unshakeable. This will be tested many times in the querent's life, but each time they fall down all they have to remember is to take another step.

Otherwise it will be a case of easy come, easy go. The "something for nothing" attitude can be hard to defeat, but when the querent realizes that ALL things are earned they find a new approach to life that is in balance with the universe around them. Then their prayers are answered, but only because they know all Spirit does is to provide an opportunity for us to work our dream into reality.

2-8-9 Augmented Trine: Guard your Thoughts, they can Bite!

Force flows from this Trine, but oftentimes it is too much for the person affected and they become insular. The Two and Eight work on the emotional level, where most of our energy comes from, while the Nine holds things together with Silence and Observance. So if you see you are being unduly affected by this Trine's influence, I suggest that you try to develop these specific traits.

Generally we do not find this aspect in their chart unless we are ready for it, but we are ready to accept the great responsibility that comes with the freedom it implies, this is an aspect where real and lasting progress can be made. *I have found that many people, like battery hens, get to actually like the crowded stifled conditions of life and are afraid to be individuals* ... This type is rarely able to "Seize the Day", and so much of the positive influence of a Trine such as this would simply be water under the bridge of their thought.

If this is NOT you, you will love the influence of this Trine. In the midst of conversation these natives will pick up the off word or inflection that will tell them the inner truth of the people they are dealing with, and so in such fields as counseling and business management these folk excel.

Socially they can be butterflies, and there is an indication of numerous relationships before they settle down. Marriage is not necessarily what will settle them down, but responsibilities will, and so children, positions of influence and the like will give these people a base for real expansion in this world.

2-7-8 Augmented Trine: Listen to the Silence about you.

This is a querulous Trine, where the native can feel extremely uncertain about themselves and how they fit in. They are socially conscious and nervous, but as the querent moves through his/her rather extended adolescence and into a greater confidence and self-expression, all the problems they suffered become fuel for the fire of experience.

The caterpillar becomes the butterfly, though sometimes it is a moth! The difference between the two is an attitude of Silence, an inner Silence that allows one to appreciate the natural beauty all around them. Here it is essential that the native come to the point of genuinely liking themselves, or else the Eight influence will remain karmic, and finance will be a lifelong concern.

If this point of inner acceptance can be reached these folk can go very far in understanding their inner selves, and often become excellent teachers whom assist others to do the same. They have a deep appreciation of beauty, and their natural aesthetic quality causes them to look for the finer things of life. Individually they would rather have one finely cut jacket instead of a wardrobe of cheap imitations, even if the imitations were perfect. These people need to feel quality in their lives. Very often, because this is their goal, it is exactly what arrives... In clothes, in personal relationships, in everything.

1-2-7 Augmented Trine: Cast off the Fear and Fly.

There is a creative urge here, but insecurity and many doubts tend to block it. If a person cannot personally rise above this, they wil possibly be drawn to supporting artists and writers in some way, or otherwise generally hold an interest in the arts, in whatever field appeals. It is better to cast of fears and just do what you dream to do, however, and when the person with this aspect steps forward, good things will come of it.

If the person can work through their insecurities the very difficulties they faced within themselves will be what opens up their hearts and minds to understanding life and people about them. They often make fine writers, and even though it may be in the fields of copy writing and commercial work, this should not be discreditied.

A distaste for physical work, and a sense of emotional tension often give this Trine a poor constitution. But when a person rises above their inner fears, this is reversed, with a really energetic, go-get-em personality attaching itself to this influence. A characteristic of this Trine is that it can turn on a sixpence. From being vulnerable and afraid one day, the native can make an inner decision, and the next day be ruthless and tough.

It is not a case of being double faced, but these can be very inward looking people who desire to express themselves. Usually they don't step out of their mental cage, but when they do, they really do. A part of this can be seen at a masquerade party, where invariably natives of this genre will choose garish, aggressive themes like pirate costumes. It expresses their secret wish.

There is a tendency towards a sense of anarchy here, and the native must take care to keep their personal lives in order or a carelessness will overtake their actions. The lesson involved with this Trine is to do with honesty with oneself. If the querent can take off their varied mental and emotional masks when they get home, those close to them will be able to trust, and therefore love them. If not they will suffer the fate of Vanity, aloneness.

In many ways, this Aspect encapsulates the Creative Quandry. You need to search inwardly for inspiration, yet have courage of convictions to take this and step out into the world, braving critisicim and derision.

1-2-8 Augmented Trine: Play Hard, but don't step on Toes!

These folk love to make money, and they do. On a higher level the attention might turn to seeking inner answers, but very often this area is stifled by a need for money. It is not that the money is evil, but that it takes up so much of their time and thoughts that there may be little room for anything else.

This would be a shame, for real progress can be made under this influence. It is a good aspect for the healing arts, and a natural understanding of what people need. By practicing a way of life that helps others, this Trine can influence a seeker to discover many truths about life and can in turn pass these onto to others.

The wealth created here will be the wealth of love and understanding, yet the native will usually have enough finance for all their genuine needs. However, this depends on whether they are committed to a specific course of action in their life, for otherwise their need for liquid assets tend to take a turn to the alcoholic variety. "You take the high road and I'll take the low road, or will it be vice-versa?" This is the choice for the native here.

2-3-9 Augmented Trine: A choice between Black and White.

Strong mental energies and diplomacy can combine with this Trine to form a potent statesman, diplomat or the like. Power can be used effectively by these people, and they are not afraid of consequences. Because of this these folk can literally move mountains if they have to in order to get a project underway, or they will also just as happily move themselves as Mohammed did, as long as the mountain is prepared to negotiate.

In the negative aspect, their admirable sense of diplomacy might become deceit and their bright minds used to cut rather than heal... This is invariably the case where the use of power is purely to further one's own ambitions. Another scenario of the negative energy would be that the Two energy becomes internalized and the person affected cannot express themselves at all. All that potential use of power would then become self destructive.

Most people with strong Trines such as this subconsciously avoid the possible effects by burying themselves in convention and commonality. However, the energy of this Trine will still show up in outbursts and upsets in life. This might not necessarily be from the person themselves, but it can be reflected off others in their families, and especially the children who may develop dark, negative attitudes. This may be difficult to understand, but sometimes our siblings will act out our own unconscious, repressed urges.

As with all Noumenal aspects, no one aspect is absolute, and much depends on the querent's attitude and the other influences in the chart. All in all the lesson with this aspect deals mostly with the inner person.

Creating a person of substance, having strong ideals and clear vision, is a process that really must start from birth. With this Trine the querent must learn to stand up and say "I am" and understand in the depths of their being what this means. At this point the shades of grey disappear, and all is obvious.

3-4-6 Augmented Trine: Truth needs a Peg upon which to Hang.

Angular and precise, these people do not muck about with those they see as being no-hopers. They generally are good at defining goals and organizing their life so that dreams can be achieved. Other people will often sense their innate authority, and respect them. There is little of a scramble for power or influence, here. It is more of a slow build done in small certain steps. Those who rush about looks for easy gains and short term sucess are seen as a lesser being. This Trine reflects quite statesman-like attributes in its refined qualities.

Oddly, despite the fact they dislike politics, these folk tend to end up in the middle of political manoevering, which they dislike intensely. It is the loss of dignity they fear. They usually will consider resignation from a position where their dignity is threatened, and if they do so, they generally land on their feet somewhere else. Principles must be adhered to for life to work well for them.

There is a cat-like survival nature at work here, but there is also humour and friendship, and it is important that these people find a work environment to suit their temperament. In the negative value there can be a distinct problem with relating to others, especially equals. This is often because the individual affected by this energy tends to want only mentors and people they consider able to teach them in their personal orbit. Or they want themselves as the star being adored.

In all the native must learn to be the still. certain rock. The goal is to find the inner strength of being within upon which they can build their life.

3-8-9 Augmented Trine: Take care... Altruism can Cost!

This Trine indicates a sort of mental short circuit. This is not bad, for the effect can clear cobwebs built up over lifetimes, but it is rarely a pleasant transition from the altruistic youth to the world weary/wise man. We regard these concerns as growing pains, and inevitable.

But if the querent can keep a clear focus within their life, and look at things objectively, then the Trine will assist them to put everything in order. However, very few people can look at life objectively or impersonally.

Therefore, a major lesson here is to take things less personally. It is simply said, difficult to put into practice, yet if the querent can do this life will work out extremely well for them. If not, there will be problems, emotional blowups and all sorts of negative "things" until they do.

We could say this is a GOOD Trine if you want to learn detachment and clear thinking. Otherwise, it tends to be rather painful.

4-6-9 Augmented Trine: When is Achievement not Ambition?

Go catch these people if you can, because when they get in charge of their life they won't wait for you. They just get up and go. Projects get dealt with efficiency, people are carefully instructed how and when to do things... and everything would run like clockwork, except for the human factor.

People with this energy generally have little interest in dealing with fools, and this can create social problems. These folk work best in a highly disciplined environment, such as the armed forces or police. Even so their sometimes weak interpersonal skills can aggravate others. The uncompromising insistence these people can have to "get it right" can make them appear rigid and inflexible.

Lthargy and inertia in the human consciousness are the source of most problems, and in many ways, the mission of this Trine is to combat this eberfy. Most with this Trine present will bristle at stupidity and often be quite abrasive and non-accepting of what they see as weakness in others and in self. The lesson here is not to beat the human condition, but to learn to respect ones self, and in doing so, come to an understanding that while it is only you, that this is enough. A sort of Humble Superiority.

It is best to team up with someone skilled in diplomacy, whether in marriage or business, and this will help things along. The native must be very careful not to let their ambitions rule their hearts, and to allow their family as much freedom as they expect for themselves.

4-6-7 Augmented Trine: From Darkness to Light, the Cycle Turns.

The Six and Seven in this Aspect provide a very turbulent energy, one that needs real strength to master. The Four keeps it grounded while the native seeks to do this. This Trine, more than any of the others in this group, tends to want to break down barriers rather than jump over or go around them. The goal is to learn the inner force needed to move past obstacles. Breaking down the walls of Jericho using the power of trumpets was not a direct attack, but used natural (and supernatural) forces to shake resistance until it become malleable.

Of course, in learning this the querent will find that they must practice this technique firstly on their own inner blocks and problems. This makes life in the learning stages a bit (a lot!) of a pain. This is actually an understatement, but in the highest aspect, the hard process of learning will reach in and touch the heart in such a way that it grows firm, but not hard. In the negative, the heart will be burned and the native may become cynical, biased and suffer symptoms of chronic anger. (Poor elimination, Bowel and Liver problems, Skin problems, many broken relationships, etc.)

A strong inner firmness that brings a fixed and powerful ability to focus on the goal is what the querent needs, and this is the major lesson here. With it they will rarely need to fight against an obstacle, rather they only need set their target and observe the situation that grows. Almost always an opportunity will arise for them to step in and make their goal a reality.

There can be a problem when the querent notices this effect, but attributes it to Divine Intervention. This can lead to religious phobias, and a sense of non-responsibility for one's actions. In extreme cases we will see a severe Messiah complex develop. There is a natural agitation and nervousness natives of this Trine often feel, and it is important that they do not fall into the habit of blaming others for this. It is an easy thing to do, but this action will nullify all progress.

True inner responsibility teaches us to be patient and to await the turning cycles of life. In the Spring the cold of Winter is soon forgotten.

4-7-9 Augmented Trine: Climb the Sacred Stair. A Door awaits.

This is an interesting aspect, combining the very physical combination of the Four and Seven with the Silent Strength of the Nine. In a number of cases we will see this evidence itself as actual physical prowess, such as with an athlete, but mostly we will see this as a robustness of spirit.

A well grounded energy flows through the Trine. Sometimes too much so, and people affected have a need to break out and do radical things. It is important for the native to finish what they start, and because of this it is advisable for them to choose carefully what they wish to do, and have some idea of the overall task, BEFORE they begin. Do you climb a mountain without knowing the possible dangers?

Still, there is an energy here that likes the idea of danger and risk, and so often we find the native avoids preparation, yet survives regardless.

The Four always likes to join movements, especially humanitarian causes, in its youth, but generally as it matures it becomes quite conservative. The Seven-Nine Line deals a lot with ideals, which grow into wisdom if the ideals are realized, and so we can see how the numbers can combine harmoniously. The problems here usually come when the querent fails to see the wood for the trees.

Very often the native of this Trine will have a great sense of urgency to go out there and DO something, but create so many problems for others as a result that they collect a karmic debt that can take a lifetime to eliminate. This will prevent the maturing of the energy present, and worse it can send the native into a flurry of agitation and constant anger. This anger can carry on for their entire lives, destroying friendships and communication, while also creating a huge emptiness and a sort of frustration inside. The lesson is to think twice before getting involved.

Of course, the problem here is that if you think too much, nothing gets done... Not enough and problems accrue. There is a balance in there somewhere, we call it common sense, and hopefully the native will have some.

6-7-9 Augmented Trine: At Odds with you Mind? Look into your Heart!

The Six-Seven combination can be quite successfully ruled by the Nine. The key to harmony with this aspect is Inner Silence. Though the querent with this Trine will feel a often feel a strong, stirring energy, common sense (which is the result of true Inner Silence) will always give a clear indication what to do.

The energy present here has a lot to do with humanities, and in particular with philosophical and religious thought. It is a Trine well suited to the missionary, and even the salesperson, because it is a catalyst for action. People with this aspect have an innate ability to activate others, often through the sheer force of their enthusiasm. A symbol for these folk could be a bugle calling the guard to action.

There is a natural faithfulness here, as well as a mental acuity that can pick a fault from a mile away. Yet the native may appear to others as rather vague and distant. This "vagueness" is usually a technique used by the individual to stop them judging others. After seeing so many faults in the world, the inner self decides not to look at all.

Each individual number is not particularly harmonic to each other. This is a core energy to the Trine that through disharmony, it can find function. The Seven is not overly compatible with the Six-Nine combination, nor is the Six comfortable with the Seven-Nine series, and to top it off the Six-Seven combination is pretty abrasive, but as all these energies mature, they come into accord.

This generally indicates the native will come into their own fairly late in life, but some find this maturity at an early age.

A danger here is to become too unworldly. It is fine for the professor in the protected sanctity of his mind to ignore the outside world, but others may abuse their good nature if they do not remain on guard.

SUB-DOMINANT TRINES

1-5-7 Internal Trine

5-7-9 Internal Trine

3-5-9 Internal Trine

1-3-5 Internal Trine

2-4-8 External Trine

2-6-8 External Trine

2-4-6 External Trine

4-6-8 External Trine

Here we have something quite unusual. The Sub-Dominant group has two catagories, Internal (all Odd Numbers) and External (all Even Numbers). Odd Numbers are considered a masculine aspect. Matching this with the generally introspective nature of these Trines generally creates a conflict, for the masculine energy always seeks to express itself. The development of a contemplative nature is the best answer to this concern.

The External Trines are all Even Numbers and considered Feminine. They tend towards external calculation and preparation for the future. Think of a mother who seeks to care for her children by providing a safe environment, education and practical learning. The general Lesson involves getting things moving, rather than just planning and organising.

Once more, despite the name of the Trine reflecting a chord in music, there is no direct correlation other than the mood created. In this case, the Sub-Dominante Trines carry the energy of moving towards a resolution of some sort.

1-5-7 Internal Trine: Learning to be the True Self requires a Loss of Many Selves.

This is a difficult Trine, for it takes the vibration of the One (Individualism) and the Seven (Learning through Trial) and focuses this into the Ego (The Inner aspect of the Five). The simplest way forward for the person strongly affected by this Aspect is to watch the pennies, because then the dollars look after themselves. The energy here works out quite well just by being financially careful.

With this aspect the individual will need to work through some tough times as a rule, and they will tend to do this with the feeling that they are carrying the weight of the world as they do so. In a sense they are, for we all carry the sum total of all our experiences with us, and this Trine can remind us each step of the way what these have been.

Quite simply, a person so affected must take stock of their lives to date and carefully query each piece of the internal jigsaw in order to find its missing place. These people will be drawn to studies of psychiatry and the para-normal, and in these areas they can be useful, but only if they resolve their own inner dilemmas first.

It is often the case that the priest in the pulpit never admits the dark side of himself, and therefore knows only one side to life. Thus it is so with the 1-5-7 Trine, that the person affected will tend to be one sided with their views of life, but only for fear of facing themselves.

The best symbol here is that of Saint George (of dragon fame) who freed his inner feminine aspect by beating the dragon of his reasoning mind. Learning how to accept oneself is a journey of Love, not intellect. But this can be difficult to see for this Trine, and so the path of this Aspect generally finds itself travelling the rocky road of self analysis, only finding inner freedom through the interaction of a loving partner.

5-7-9 Internal Trine: Where is the Line between WANT and NEED?

Power is the lesson here,. Even though it is an Internal Trine, the lesson will be with the use of power over others, particularly with the art of manipulation, in what we term "Lying the Truth". Think of politicians painting a story knowing it is a lie, or the advertising man selling garbage but painting it as gold. They use pieces of truth to lead you down the garden path.

Many Black Magicians suffer this aspect, for it craves influence over others. The reason WHY they do this is generally unknown to the individual, but in essence it is because they fear they will not be loved, because they are unworthy. They find it hard to accept any form of love other than twisted versions, such as lust or usury. They need power to support themselves because of a vacuum they sense within. It is this emptiness, or rther the fear of what happens if you get swucked into it, that drives them. The vacuum is actually the need to be loved and the need for the true self esteem that will attract this Love.

Unfortunately, the power person is unlovable by their own actions, at least until it is realized that there really need be no division between power and love, and that both can move together with ease. This is one of the High Spiritual Lessons, however, and not many survive Its challenge, let alone understand It.

Power can be very useful, but it must be kept balanced. This will be the major test for those affected with this Trine.

Another aspect is the so-called "White Witch". Or the so-called "good" use of mind power. Quite simple, the use of mental force to influence others is really a condition that stems from either a sense of superiority or inferiority. The person who wishes to influence others for "good" practices white magic, and does so basically because they feel superior to the person they are helping. Whereas a person serving their own ends practices black magic, resulting from an ingrained belief that they are not good enough to achieve this by other more direct means.

Both are earning karma from their actions, karma that brings us back to this world to balance it out. If bad karma represents iron chains, good karma represents gold chains. Both hold you in place.

3-5-9 Internal Trine: A Heart Married to a Purpose is Free.

This aspect is generally creative, yet often also somewhat obsessive. Because of this, the tendency is to alienate others rather than to embrace them. They snip people out of the picture when they feel misunderstood. Which is not so bad when there is a job to be done, but otherwise the habit is seen by others as socially unacceptable. The problems arise when this "cutting off" cannot be turned off, and a great deal of loneliness and misery will result if this is the case.

If the Soul here can accept others for what they are, and not hold an internal position of how or what they "should" be, life will go much easier for them However, the person with this Trine tends not to see others as they are, but how he/she THINKS they are.

Furthermore, the strong mind that generally comes with this aspect finds it difficult to let go of its own cherished perceptions, and so opinions tend to hold sway over their emotions and actions. This creates abrasion between all except those who choose to share the bias, and so the tendency here is to establish cliques.

There is a real danger of a person becoming circular in their thought process, so that in time their creative energy will stagnate inside, and frustration will be the result. Sometimes it is frustration to the point of suicide, either actual or through developing some fatal illness. The point here is to let go of opinions as needed, and to allow life to re-educate our heart by the new experiences it will bring when we open up a little bit.

1-3-5 Internal Trine: I Cherish, I Love, but I can be Fragile.

This specific Trine is awkward more than painful, for the person affected wants to get out and do things, but their sense of inadequacy and shyness prevents them from expressing themselves fully. If this is extreme the person may become chronically withdrawn, but this is exceedingly rare.

The One, Three, Five rhythm is very fortuitous as a rule, but only when the person learns to allow themselves the freedom of truly being themselves. Because this is the lesson, however, life tends to place those so affected in extremely rigid families where they are forced to grow beyond limitation, or suffer the fate of the meek: That of returning again and again to the Earth. The meek do indeed inherit the Earth, again and again and again.

Firmness, Strength, Silence in Difficulty: The quiet traits of the masculine archetype (regardless of sex) are what need to be developed here in order for inner peace to take root and grow.

2-4-8 External Trine: The Seed must break through It's Prison of Earth if it is to Grow

If you have determined enough about yourself to know the difference between your true self and what is merely your trained self, then this Trine will work very powerfully in your favor. But as the lead line indicates, the power of growth is needed if you are to succeed.

Emotional stability is highlighted here, and these souls often go through puberty without quite the drama and pain most youth experience. This is often because they have a remarkable ability to perceive a situation clearly, but without judgment. In time this matures and the Soul learns to sense what the "base line" of a person's actions might be, and thus knows how best to deal with them. This is a good survival trait.

This ability to almost instinctively know where people are coming from can also give a sense of superiority, sometimes an arrogance. More to the point, a sort of bluntness can develop that defies another's sensibilities, and which might in many cases be considered rude. It is rarely intended this way, it is just that these people simply speak out and state what is, to them, the obvious. They see no need to bottle things up or store the hurt inside.

And yet, their heart is easily hurt. People affected by this influence very much need a secure partner in whom they can trust. Many frustrating niggles and concerns will vanish with a bond of trust, and beware the soul who chooses to break this bond! Those with this Trine tend not to retreat, but lash out mercilessly. And once tipped over the edge, forget trying to tell them discretion is the greater part of valor.

It is not uncommon for orphans to have this aspect. Those suffering the negative aspects and difficulties that can arise from this Trine will want to attack society, or conversely look for some noble causes to support. Both are a mistake, because the unsettling energy the person feels comes from within, and no external influence will change this.

The real answer to the negative conditions of this Aspect is learning to hold your inner thoughts and feelings in check. Silence is an important lesson here, and the ability to still the mind and emotions.

2-6-8 External Trine: The Heart Knows.

A very upwardly mobile set of circumstances will often follow these people through their lives, sometimes seeming like a curse for things simply will not stand still. The lesson is to learn to find stillness within activity. The eye in the hurricane, so to speak.

Intuition is highlighted, and this may cause the soul so affected to seek out the quiet places where few people go, in order to find respite and harmony. Music is usually greatly loved, and these people generally also like to assist others who are creatively minded if it is at all possible to do so.

When the attention is focused inwardly, the energy of the Six will come to play, and success in life will come with relative ease... But for these individuals the focus seems to just want to keep looking out for the next challenge. One of the things needed here is the realization that the inner time in contemplation need not be separate from external activity. It is the old question asked of the Pope; "Can we contemplate while we smoke?" The answer was, No! When the Jesuits reversed this to ask, "Can we smoke while we contemplate?" the answer came back as, Yes! A question of priorities.

These folk are often good at binding things together, whatever their field of expertise, and are essentially good at protecting the interests of others. The negative side is very black, though, for these people find that reading another's mind is not too difficult. This creates an atmosphere of manipulation and arrogance, and can lead to a tremendous accumulation of Karma. Therefore, the Law of Non-Interference is highlighted as the lesson to learn.

2-4-6 External Trine: Count up the Cost of a Dream before you Spend It.

If you have determined enough about yourself to know the difference between your true self and what is merely your trained self, then this Trine will work very powerfully in your favor.

This can be a contrasting, and at first confusing aspect to be born under, where people so affected must survive the battle in their own minds before they can be of much use in this world.

Very often the inner conflict between Security, Beauty, and Inner Truth cripples this type, making them virtually unemployable, and quite eccentric. However, if they develop the breadth of vision to see above the apparent paradox of life, then this very conflict becomes the grist for the mill of inspiration.

This can develop in any number of avenues, but an appreciation of poetic justice will be prevalent as the native of this aspect learns to sit back and watch how life has a habit balancing the odds. Humor is what those affected by this influence need to learn and practice, for there is a tendency to become slightly aggressive and domineering without it.

4-6-8 External Trine: Freedom is found in the Little Things.

This is a Money Trine, so called because the individual with this aspect is very likely to make a lot of money in their lives. If it is not actual cash, it will be a wealth of some sort, even a spiritual wealth of wisdom and knowledge, which perhaps is the greatest of the riches we can earn, for this we can take with us past the grave.

There is the karmic aspect to deal with, which arises with all Eight and Four affected vibrations, but with the Four and Six combination the great direction these generate tend to draw the Karma into an active atmosphere of learning. This can be compared with the child as it is learning to walk. It stumbles but is not discouraged for it knows its goal.

If the querent has no goal, the Karma from this Trine is confusing and difficult to deal with. But given some sort of direction everything will work out quickly. Great insight into the nature of things is possible here, and these people make fine instructors and helpers because of this, but it is best not to try and do everything for themselves, as they are wont to do.

It is important for this type to involve themselves with as many people as they can, developing a broad base of contacts that they can drawn upon when and where the need arises. Because of this they should seek out positions of authority and service, where they will feel entirely comfortable, yet still be responsible to and for the welfare of others. They will invariably be drawn to running their own show, whether in business or in the home. Sharing and caring is very important for balance.

SEMI-DOMINANT TRINES
DIMINISHED or VACANT Right Angle Trines

1-2-8 Dim. Trine

2-7-8 Dim. Trine

2-3-8 Dim. Trine

2-8-9 Dim. Trine

3-4-6 Dim. Trine

1-4-6 Dim. Trine

4-6-9 Dim. Trine

4-6-7 Dim. Trine

2-3-9 Dim. Trine

3-8-9 Dim. Trine

6-7-9 Dim. Trine

4-7-9 Dim. Trine

1-7-8 Dim. Trine

1-2-7 Dim. Trine

1-3-4 Dim. Trine

1-3-6 Dim. Trine

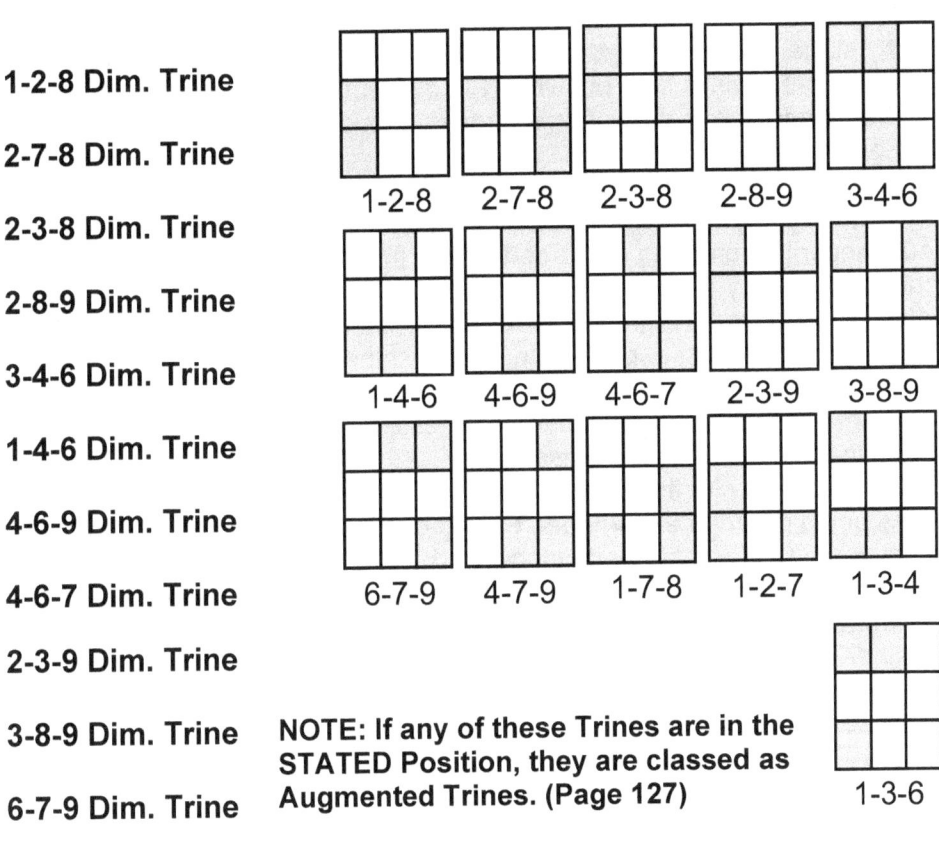

NOTE: If any of these Trines are in the STATED Position, they are classed as Augmented Trines. (Page 127)

Right angle Trines are like Boomerangs that fly through the individuals life, returning whatever energy is core to their nature. When someone is strong in these Trines, they will always have a sense that they are not going to get away with anything.

We often see people active in social and political organisations with these Aspects in the Natal Chart. They have a sense of wanting to establish order in what seems like chaos, and an essential lesson for people affected by these influences to learn is that under chaos there IS order. It is not a case of imposing order they need to learn, but of extracting it from the apparent chaotic events surrounding situations.

We find work as architects, builders, people who take a lot of random ideas and form them into a cohesive whole is very suited professions for people with these influences.

1-2-8 Trine: The King of the Ocean Rules from Below.

This is a practical, money orientated Trine, but one where the natives are generally influenced by current trends. They like fashion, the stage, the latest electronic gimmicks, and they like to be able to afford these. This is fine, but when the querent begins to want to seek higher things, the money often seems to evaporate and times can become quite difficult.

This is because when you break through into a new manifestation of individuality, it necessarily involves a subtle change of rules, and the subsequent weathering of the odd storm. Inwardly, most people know this, and so they seek to avoid change at all costs. Because of this, the effect of the Karmic Eight in this Aspect tends to keep brining up in emotional problems, especially in relationships. Rather than resolving these (By a new attitude or a different way of looking at things) the querent under this influence often blames life, their parents, their partner: anything to avoid facing themselves.

The danger with this Trine is that the person affected will spend their lives going round in an ever decreasing circle, feeling more and more confined by life and life's situations, and so the lesson here is that of what merchants call "Added Value" is completely missed. These people need to learn to build, to improve rather than consume, to plant seeds rather than envy the progress of their neighbor's crop.

As an added thought, if we envisage the Three as being present, we will see that it forms the full Dominant Trine. Imagine adding the energy of the Three (business and creativity) to this situation and we will find that this will complete the energy of this Trine. It is easy to see see how creativity and the natural flair for making money these people have can add up to an ability to make your dreams reality. Within the 1-2-8 trine the core of this ability to make things real is to be found. As such this Trine is of greater importance than most will ever realize.

2-7-8 Trine: Balance the Trials with Laughter.

The Line of between Two and Eight signifies the emotional element, and in this case it represents the energy of Soul working through an individuals feelings. This energy is being directed to the somewhat lonely Seven, and it needs to be contained within an inner state of Silence for the best results to bloom.

Silence is the aspect of the Nine, and the Nine is the "Hidden" value the native of the above Trine needs to work on continually. Often the person affected by this influence has a great perception into the nature of mankind. They could contribute much, but do they have the courage and fortitude to back this up?

The 2 - 7 energy tends to tie a person up in doubt, and this leads to a disappointing life. However, if the querent develops the Nine energy it will give them the strength to grow. This is simply developing the strength of mind to quieten the niggling voices of doubt, and find inner certainty in your own being. Without this the native becomes restless and dissatisfied with their lot, often at the bar seeking company for solace, but generally ending up alone at the end of the day.

Still, it is an excellent Trine for the artist and writer, and those whose occupation require a degree of aloneness. It is really a very depressing energy for those who want laughter and company, for the inherent Seven aspect is simply not happy on the social merry-go-round. Yet it usually wants it all the same! Naturally we can see the basis for conflict arising here, however, this generally resolves when the native gets active with a project or hobby. Anything that focusses the mind to a single purpose will work at alleviating the stress of this Trine.

Creative people with this Aspect have an ability to perceive the darker side of things, yet be able to communicate this in a light and clear manner. Humor is essential to resolve the influence of this aspect.

2-3-8 Vacant Trine: Creativity can Stalk you.

Hunt or be Hunted! This Trine has a very creative aspect, but like most creative aspects there is a double edged sword here. As you are hunting down some idea to create with, your ideas can feel like they are haunting you. Simple hard, focused work solves the dilemma and puts the attention onto external things.

The person affected by this aspect can be very complex in some ways, and yet very simple in others. It can be introverted, then reverse and become highly extrovert. This is a sort of Bi-Polar energy that lessens when financial security is found. There is often a concern over Money, and if connected with the 2-3-4 Trine this can become a sort of mania, but there is also this need to express ourselves here.

It is a difficult energy to get in charge of, but really all the person needs to do is to "earth" themselves with a good hobby or pastime that gives them a sense of personal value.

In one respect, a Soul with this aspect in their chart has the ability to make money from their creative impulses, and yet there is often a conflict here as well: Where the person just wants to "BE" and not involve themselves with the financial aspect at all.

The overall energy is one which requires you to come to terms with your creative nature. And it may well be that this will resolve itself in a creative business venture, not necessarily as an artist, or that sort of thing. People often forget that creativity takes many forms. In this case it is often linked to an ability to plan, to organize and to create a focus for others. So a consideration might be with working in some social outreach project, in an organizational role.

Take care with this energy, as it can turn to bite, however. Sometimes the people affected here want to "Plan things to Death". So allow room for the surprise in all you do, and things generally go well.

2-8-9 Trine: Acceptance is the Key. Leaving means Giving.

Not too many persons with this Trine leave the battlefield unscathed. There is a rebelliousness and resentment towards authority here, and unfortunately the authority usually wins. In time the native learns not so much of a compromise, but a wisdom that perceives how chiefs and Indians all belong to the same tribe.

"We are all in it together" should be the words at the forefront of their thoughts, and this will give them a great ability to understand the problems of their neighbors. Nether-the-less, patience is not the greatest asset of these people, and they will quickly move on from relationships and jobs that are seen as being dead wood.

This Trine is suitable for doers, as it is very active on many levels, but if the native is lazy the energy will cause great problems in their life. Procrastination is in actuality an attachment to the past and forms a potent poison in the aura, one that is fatal for spiritual growth. It is a habit with no future, and should be tossed aside or else the querent's old age shall become a burden and misery.

In relationships we find that a sense of dry wit in another attracts these people like a moth to the flame, and a quiet feeling of understatement is also regarded highly. Even so, flamboyant personalities and these folk are often drawn together, but the result is often volatile. Sometimes the flame burns the heart if there is a romantic involvement, and deep, lasting resentments can result. Other times such meetings can be explosive, but outcomes here depend on many factors.

Numerous heart-felt relationships are not uncommon, and the presence of this Trine indicates a lifetime where many things are drawn to a close. When this is realized, te querent feels they can let go of many issues and the past is left to slip away as it will, in peace and harmony. This is Soul with a mature and understanding viewpoint. If you can let go, let things be, accept that life has it's own ways it will work through, life is made so much easier.

At this point of acceptance and understanding, people of a very positive aspect will come into the orbit of the querent. In other words, these folk have to learn to shrug their shoulders and say "No big deal" before they can make any real progress.

3-4-6 Trine: An Anchor can both Hold and Imprison.

Trines that share the 4-6 Line (as this aspect does) are generally based in practicality and reasoning, yet they can also be influenced by lateral and intuitive thought. Because of this, many good leaders share an aspected Semi-Dominant Trine specifically with this axis.

The querent with a 3-4-6 Trine is often in the skies with great plans and ideals, and despite the odds they can often bring about what was thought to be impossible, specifically because of their great expansive view and the enthusiasm they can engender into others. Their ability to see what could be inspires and motivates those who are attracted to them. As a result, people with this Trine do not accomplish so much themselves, but lead and direct others to higher vision and insight.

On the negative aspect, however, the effect can be to imprison oneself in a life of convention and ritual. No real progress will be made until the natural adventuresome spirit is let free to roam, for only the bold find heaven.

Often the native finds they bear the fruits of his/her efforts late in life, yet if they persist in their goals, life will remain vital and interesting for them throughout, and this is reward enough for the most part. The great negative aspect here is to do with vagueness, which, in this case, comes from an inability to deal with reality.

If this is so, personal relationships will be poor and full of unspoken tensions. (If a relationship exists at all!) In this instance the Soul would most likely retreat into a scholarly or clerical world where there is little perceived threat or danger from outside, just the mundane "reality" of life. Still, romance will surface in the types of books read and dreams secretly held. It can also be a source of secret perversion that can greatly affect and twist the essentially kind and generous nature of this Aspect.

1-4-6 Trine: The Net you Cast, the Fish you Catch. Be Aware!

People under this influence can slip into manipulative behaviour and not realise it. The 1-4-6 Trine combines an earthy nature with Intuition, and this gives the querent a good general understanding of people and what they want. The use of Magic, or manipulation to get what you want, is not done with spells of secret rites. It is done with the mind. The Mind is the net you cast to catch the fish of though, and this Aspect can quite easily catch people with ideals and organise them into useful groups.

This Trine spells practicality as well as an acceptance of the divine, and it tends to give the querent an almost mystical force to change situations. It carries a strong warning about the misuse of psychic power, however, we often find that this misuse is practiced by ourselves against ourselves in some way shape or form.

For those with a practical nature, these Souls can seem infuriating. They are often hugely impractical where personal luxuries are involved. They tend to like comfort, style and have champagne tastes even when they don't have enough money for a beer. They often have an "all or nothing" sense when it comes to getting the good things of life, and very often succeed to some degree, even if it is only developing the appearance of money and wealth.

Or, they can go the other way entirely. A negative aspect is that this native will happily turn to theft of some sort, like tricking Social Security. They dislike authority, and are happy to steal from it, especially if this might be from an insurance company or bank. In order to have what they desire these folk can become quite proficient confidence merchants.

As a rule this type is fairly solitary, needing little but themselves to get along. They generally go through a number of marriages, often divorcing due to their general disinterest in communication on a personal, intimate level. This can be absolutely reversed, however, and if so these people will be scrupulously honest and very attracted to high profile public relations positions, which they are eminently suited for.

It is important to remember that ANY energy can polarize to a positive of negative result, and that it is the INDIVIDUAL who holds the key to this process. In particular, the key is held by our imagination and how it frames the attitudes we live by. Our attitude determines the quality of our attention towards matters that greet us, and the subtle combination of the two (attitude and attention) eventually produce life as we know it.

People with this aspect can become extremely aware of this process, and as a result can develop an ability to work with life in a way that others would see as magical. It is not, but even so an apparently undue amount of good fortune seems to come by those who have recognized the power of focused thought.

4-6-9 Trine: Whom do you Serve?

This aspect is dangerous in the hands of those who do not care for others, for there is a clear and strong current flowing here that can be used for many purposes. Attainment comes with apparent ease for these natives, sometimes giving them a derisive air towards those who appear to be struggling. This is rarely made obvious, but even so the native should be aware that non-judgment is essential for the continued well being of the heart.

There is a distain here for the social mores, and a caustic comment is often in store for anyone who seeks to put this native into some form of convention to which they do not agree. They are independent and forthright, except in matters of love, where their normally fluent conversation can falter in nerves and self doubt. This is actually good, for it attracts exactly the right partner, someone who likes to find the little child inside their adult.

People with this Trine need to be reminded that the heart is a child, and has no interest in the adult world of complication and order. When they are clear on this the order of the day will be simplicity, but there is often an awful lot of complication in the process of getting to this point.

They are quality, not quantity, people as a rule, and this stands them in good stead throughout life. They like to be selective, and as a result the finer things seem to gravitate naturally into their orbit.

Building is very important for this type. Whether it is restoring an old boat or putting together a dog house, the creative effort of building establishes deep roots of contentment in their soul, and life will proceed with a relative calm, often into a very old age. The native needs to be careful of too much carbohydrate in their diet, as this will quickly turn to fat, which generates a sense of discontent.

4-6-7 Trine: How does One reach Two? By adding Itself!

The energy of this Trine encourages careful planning. People strongly influenced by the 4-6-7 Trine tend to be meticulous in detail, and they can drive others to distraction by the way they will file their pencil down to a stubble before throwing it away. They can be open to new ideas, but you generally have to pry away the closed mindedness of their social exterior first, upon which we discover that underneath the dour exterior lurks a great adventurer and idealist.

This sort of inner and outer personality that are apparently opposite is characteristic of any combination between the Four and Seven. But with the Six highlighted this gives a more inspirational edge where the native will always dream great dreams, yet appear to be content with the small moments of life. Still, lasting satisfaction generally only comes about when the inner tensions are resolved, and in this case this is done by throwing oneself into things, and enjoying the passing moments. There is often a fear with the querent of this "boots and all" approach.

In reality this Trine is a good combination (though it might not appear like this at first) for the person affected here has a natural ability to balance themselves. Naturally imbalance can and does occur, but this is usually just one part of the learning curve, and this Soul in particular should not be judged by appearances, but by their final results.

Because of this, the lesson here is often simply to learn how to govern the emotions of failure, which are often simply fears of what others think. There is much to do, but a sense of failure will freeze us in out tracks, making a resolution of this Trine impossible. As such it is very important to understand that real progress only comes about when we throw ourselves completely into the task at hand.

All unresolved Trines have an unpleasant energy, and give the feeling that things are not right. This may result in ill health, either mental or physical. It must be noted that with this Trine, as with all Patterns and Trines that involve the Six and the Seven, that the addition of these two numerals gives the number Thirteen. This is not unlucky, but it does have a very strong energy.

For those unable to handle this energy, the combination is unlucky, but if you can go with the flow, and then go one step beyond, then this Trine is exceptionally fortuitous.

2-3-9 Trine: The Artist has no Reason for his Love of Art.

This is a wonderful Trine for the manifestation of things. The native affected by the 2-3-9 energy must learn to be very careful of their thoughts and imaginings, and most especially of their wishes and desires. Think of "Forbidden Planet" and how monsters were called up from the unconscious. Unwanted energy can easily step into our lives if we do not discipline our imagination. Diet is also highlighted, in that these people need home cooked food to be happy. It earths their energy.

Keeping silent in regards matters close to the heart is important, yet discussions with trusted friends and advisors should be entered into when contemplating business matters. These people like to have other people about as a rule, but they need to be selective as the energy here can pick up other people's problem like you might pick up a cold.

Negative energies are strong in this world, and unsavoury influences are attracted to the sort of trusting people we often find with this Aspect. Building a resistance to this is a major lesson with this Trine.

In short, these people need to toughen up and realize that there are evil souls about, as well as simply inconsiderate ones, who will use them for selfish purposes. EG: You might be a creative Soul who produces fine work, only to have some unscrupulous gallery owner or record company executive basically steal it off you. A small circle of trusted and proven advisors is essential.

Oddly, because of the natural vulnerability and inventiveness of mind, people affected by the 2-3-9 Trine can do well in the high circles of power. It is one of those curious energies that can be hermit like and gregarious all at the same time, and this is appealing to people with power and influence. Why? Because this type is rarely dull and their apparently haphazard approach to walking through life appeals to those trapped in the grips of power consciousness.

The lesson here comes down to learning to defend and protect oneself via the route of understanding the ways of the world.

Book of Number: Interpretations

3-8-9 Trine: From a Distance, All is Harmony.

The Three-Nine energy has the potential of a strong mind power, but the Eight also gives a boomerang effect on everything these people do. This means the persomn affected by this influence must take care with thoughts and action. More importantly, they need to develop a state of dedication to a higher goal, and in general this means developing an attitude of doing things for the good of the whole.

In a self-absorbed culture as we have, this takes time, and the native often goes through difficult times before they realize this for themselves. They cannot be self-seeking in their actions or dreams if they are to be genuinely happy. Here the goal must be one of service and altruism, though it is also necessary to take care of oneself in the process. The trick is balance, and not going too far in either direction. The querent with this aspect is strongly advised of the need to walk the middle path.

This can be an awkward and difficult Trine until the energy is grasped. At this point the native will experience a great desire to share and to assist those they can reach out to. Inner poise, grace and balance are necessary, and a curious ability will come about that allows you to recognize those who can, and want, to be assisted. Do not cast pearls before swine, as they say.

An important lesson here in rising above the self-conscious state, and viewing things from the level of Soul. Gaining the deeper perspective means the native begins to work through his, or her, own inner guidance, rather than the constrictions and rules of society.

There is a sense of service necessary here, for without this harmony will be rare. Self-serving attitudes will create a "sense of chasing one's own tail, while imagining it is a rainbow with a pot of gold waiting for you.

6-7-9 Trine: Is there a Heart to guide this Mind?

We have a contrary combination of the Seven and the Six, and this will tend to rule the immature soul affected by this Trine. However, when governed by the Nine the sense of being at odds with oneself fades and turns into a very powerful force.

This apparently insignificant Trine is one of the most powerful in the Noumenal Chart, for the energy of the Six-Seven combination comes into conjunction with the Silent Nine gives a pervasive aura that can penetrate the darkness of man's superstition.

Curiously, there is an association with Friday the Thirteenth here. If the Soul affected by this Trine is in charge of their emotions and mind, then this day will always be one of great importance to them. If not, they should stay in bed and certainly not try new projects on this day.

This combination is also strongly affected by the full moon. The Six, Seven and Nine work together, and are considered to have a feminine aspect. Associated with the moon, it indicaes the hidden power of the unconscious working through the darkness. The energy running through this Trine appears hidden and mysterious, but it works! However, the native must train themselves to focus and imagine their inner wishes coming to fruition if they are to master the energy here. Of Note: It is important that all wishes, prayers, spells (or whatever) be for the good of the whole, or carry a tag in the thoughts of "as Spirit desires".

The native must also learn to allow a more subdued nature, or what we might call an older head, be the role model for their actions. The person affected by this Trine will tend to go through a variety of occupations before finding one that works for them. They are on a journey to find out. The experiences gained will build up to a form of gestalt that can be of great benefit to others, and in this regard there is a tremendous healing potential within this aspect. Naturally this can only be if the Soul is focused onto the positive aspects of life.

The problem is simple. Many people who use psychic current sto obtain external goals often believe they are in charge of the forces flowing through them. You cannot own that which is freedom itself. The energy of life is intelligent, and should you try to own it, it will leave. Try to cage it, and it will break the prison.

When you have this Trine in your life, a core lesson is in ALLOWING life to move as it will around you. The Law of Non-Resistance is extremely important here. There is a quality to this Trine that, though it can be bent, it can't be broken. It can be held, but it cannot be possessed. I have witnessed people, who believe they control the energy flowing through them, have their minds break into numerous personalities before its energy is done.

However, if you simply hold an attitude of working with life for the good of the whole, then only good comes of this energy in your life.

4-7-9 Trine: To Breath is to Touch the Atoms of Life.

This is a very trying and difficult Trine if the Soul affected wants convention and security. The 4-7-9 Trine offers many spiritual benefits, but not many financial ones. Even so, great benefit can accrue if the person so affected remains open to the experience of life, rather than closing off because of the knocks and bumps.

Here we are trying to match a spiritual aspect, the Seven, with a physical aspect, the Four, and have this contolled with the internal silence of the Nine. It is a broad field that the native must cross, and in doing so they will learn much of life and humanity. But if you try to stop and dig that field, you will find storm and tempest will keep pushing you on.

There is much to learn, but you have to keep moving with this Trine active in your life. It is all about finding the NOW. Once you are anchored into the present, the energy stops pushing you, and you can set down roots. In the end the person recognizes that Heaven and Earth are all here and now, and that the future and the past are only dreams to shape the present. But this can take some time to realize.

How long does this take? How long is a piece of string? Unfortunately, this Trine tends to have an ongoing energy that never seems quite resolved. If the native will practice the art of observation and practice the principle of mindfullness, this "push" will not seem so important. The process of unfolding will preoccupy their thoughts and actions, leaving little room to worry about the lack of security.

There is a great pioneering spirit embodied in this particular Trine, and it is well suited for discoverers of any type. Be it so humble as a child discovering the joys of fishing, or the scientist discovering a new moon around Saturn, the thrill of the new will always conquer the difficulty of getting there.

In all a highly Spiritual trine, but not one that could be considered beneficial for the common man, who would find the never ending aspect of discovery a burden rather than a freedom. Patience is the great lesson, but it is an odd sort of patience that is triggered by curiosity.

1-7-8 Trine: Is Someone Knocking on your Door?

To some this may seem a very internal energy. 1-7-8 is a highly personal Trine where the soul will generally spend a great deal of time working on their inner world rather than outer appearances. To others they might appear insular, but the native of this Trine is generally preoccupied with their inner thoughts, and has little desire to communicate, as a rule.

Communication with others is an essential aspect of life, yet this energy is looking to communicate internally, and may well take on a certain hermit-like stance towards the outer world. The native often gets so intrigued by their own circumstances that they run the risk of becoming quite neurotic, possibly becoming schizophrenic as a long term result of this introverted way of living.

When this introverted stage is dealt with, usually by the natural process of maturity, the person so affected often wakes up and becomes very good at fending for themselves. Because of this they then find it easy to attract a partner, whereas before it seemed impossible. Nothing is more attractive to others than independence, but because of this inherent independence the native finds it hard to play the roles and games others tend to expect, both in love and in the workplace. This can cause marriage breakdowns.

Their natural survival instinct will push these people into management roles and private business, where they will have little need for one to one relationships, and where their freedom is maximized, and so it is often best that they find a partner who can accept this about them.

They will often possess a general hatred of having to work for others, and will, after a time, seek to run their own small business, which they will usually be very good at. There is a definite need to relax here, and the native needs to spend some time each day in contemplation, otherwise their minds will get crowded out with the day to day, and there will grow a work-a-holic habit that is really an excuse not to face the quiet moments.

1-2-7 Trine: Between the Future and the Past, there is NOW.

This is a somewhat perilous energy, for the person so affected can easily find themselves lost in a dream world and unable to fend for themselves in this world. They become what used to be termed "Moonstruck", and indeed the Moon has a strong influence in the life of this Trine. The 2-7 part of the Trine is always seeking to find a balance between the male and female aspects of the persona, while the One just wants to get things done and dusted.

The One is the point of Identity. In this case it is tugged between the feminine appreciation of beauty (the Two) and the masculine sense of observation of the facts (the Seven). It is particularly difficult because of the apparently incompatible nature of the Seven and Two. They tend to work in opposite phase with each other. In simple terms, when the Two wants to look at the sunset, the Seven is saying "There is work to do", but the next day when the Seven wants to contemplate the sunset, the Two is saying "But what about the bills". It is the contrary energy of the masculine versus the feminine.

Combine this with the naturally indecisive nature of the Two and we can find ourselves in a state of virtual immobility. Usually the person tries to change this by being either the Two aspect or the Seven, but this only submerges the other energy, and it keeps cropping up. The real secret to resolving this Trine is to strengthen the sense of Individuality and develop direction in one's life, and then the apparent opposites of the Two and Seven come into a harmonious rhythm, like the Sun and Moon.

It is all about choosing a direction, and walking there. The lesson here is a little surprising, however. It is to be yourself, completely, and to relax about your sense of worth. It is not important to be important, it is only important to be USEFUL. If the native can grasp this, the energy of this Trine will allow them to overcome virtually any obstacle, because they will be able to see all sides of the story. It is one of the Noumenal Influences that train one to reach a 360 degree viewpoint, or the viewpoint of the true self without the influence of the mind or emotions interfering.

1-3-4 Trine: Lift your Heart with a Love for your Journey.

The energy of this Trine alters dramatically as the native ages. This is one of the very few influences that does this. Though all the Patterns and Trines change with the deepening perspective of the native so affected, this Trine moves in accordance with the rhythm of Time and Space, as well as with the person's own sense of creativity.

Creative endeavor has the unique ability of bending the fabric of time and space. Look at the child completely absorbed in its play, forgetting the passing of hours and the outside world, delving totally into the world of its imagination. This is Freedom, but to retain it, you need to practice having this childlike creativity of absorption into the task at hand.

This training of the Imaginative faculty, which is best done through a form of creative application, is very important. The nature of this creativity can take of many forms and is not necessarily limited to the traditional ideas of the arts. Great success can come to people with this Trine if they succeed in harnessing the power of Imagination.

One of the major lessons involved here is how to make creativity pay, either financially of emotionally and thus, by finding this reward, we learn to give credence to our own beingness. Belief in ourselves is the most powerful tool we can develop on the road to self mastery, for when we believe in ourselves it is easy to love life and those about us, and this Love lifts our hearts and makes the journey far easier.

1-3-6 Trine: Do you Hear the Harmony about you?

Here the energy of One, Three and the Six combine to form one of the most attractive Trines in the Noumenal Order. This Aspect is exceptionally harmonious, and those so blessed with this Trine often have charm and wit, as well as attractive natures. However, this can make for a devil as easily as it does a saint, and so those with this Trine must always be careful to look at their motivations.

A strong intuition and a gifted manner can make things so easy that these folk forget that actual mastery only comes with patience. They often think they have gotten in charge of things when they really haven't. This will lead to a form of vanity called "Bluff" where the individual is constantly kept on the move trying to impress people, but never digging in roots.

It is a gypsy existence, which though romantic is generally not very pleasing in the long term, for things rarely get themselves to a state of completion. The innate frustration of one's good intentions never quite coming to fruit challenges one's sense of personal value. These people need to strike a bargain with themselves, a bargain of patience to finish what they are doing, in order to get to the point where they KNOW what their next action or task might be.

Book of Number: Interpretations

  This is rarely done, however, and these people usually live out a sort of twilight life, on the razors edge of their natural talent and pitting this against an ever changing world. Some like this, and thrive of the sense of danger it produces, but eventually we all yearn for a place to settle down.

  When this mood becomes strong enough, you will know it is time to stop and begin building. What we build does not matter, it could be a family, a business, a freindship. What the thing that your heart desires most is what you must build. The lesson is "Build, and the Law of Life will never repay you in negative way." A worthy motto for us all.

VARIANT TRINES

1-2-6 Short Variant Trine	1-5-8 Short Variant Trine
2-6-9 Short Variant Trine	3-5-8 Short Variant Trine
2-4-7 Short Variant Trine	2-5-7 Short Variant Trine
2-3-4 Short Variant Trine	2-5-9 Short Variant Trine
1-4-8 Short Variant Trine	1-8-9 Long Variant Trine
3-6-8 Short Variant Trine	1-6-9 Long Variant Trine
6-7-8 Short Variant Trine	3-6-7 Long Variant Trine
4-8-9 Short Variant Trine	2-3-7 Long Variant Trine
1-5-6 Short Variant Trine	1-2-9 Long Variant Trine
5-6-7 Short Variant Trine	3-4-7 Long Variant Trine
3-4-5 Short Variant Trine	3-7-8 Long Variant Trine
4-5-9 Short Variant Trine	1-4-9 Long Variant Trine

1-2-6

The Variant Trines come in short or long varieties. The all tend to have the effect of cutting through things. Picture them as the broken fragments of a mirror, scattered across time and space.

As you pick up each one, you get a glimpse of something, an insight into a deeper mystery. But never the whole thing. That's the nature of the energy here, to give you a clue, a sense of direction, but never an answer. The overall message when a person has a number of these Trines is that they are on the "Road to Find Out".

You see a lot of actors with these, and they often occur with people who play many roles in life.

1-2-6 Short Variant Trine: Strike a Match and See Light.

Intuition and practicality combine to make this a very fortunate Trine. As long as the individual affected keeps themselves in balance, all is well. If there is a tendency towards extremes in anything, then their luck will turn, and life will go amiss.

Many under this influence will sense this, and keep things on an even keel, however to others it may appear that their lives are colorless. But, like the Cypress tree, this influence keeps you growing steadily no matter the season and in the end this will prove itself by a secure old age.

Unlike many of the Variant group, these people are quite friendly as a rule, and unobtrusive. Still, they can be quite clair-ordiant or clairvoyant, and if you are married to a woman with this Trine it bodes well to listen to their thoughts and wisdoms. The One Two combination is creative, and the Six ruling it is intuitive, and so it is an excellent energy for problem solving, etc.

Men tend to use this faculty for understanding themselves, whereas women will tend to use it to tune into the rhythms of life. Be warned about becoming too self obsessed. Always staring at your bellybutton can make you a bit of a Guru, but not necessarily someone who is useful. As a rule these folk could use some fire in their bellies, as they tend to become too passive, but regardless they generally get by very well.

2-6-9 Short Variant Trine: Mind your own Business, Keep Gossip from your Door

The Two and the Six are highlighted here, and these have a clairvoyant sense. Usually this is fragile, but in this case the Nine can make it extremely robust. If you understand the principles of silence, this Trine has much more force behind it. People with this aspect may well become practicing psychics, though they will often disguise this behind their work in some healing profession. Many masseurs for instance work through their intuition, but these folk will work with a surety and a certainty that goes beyond mere guesswork.

Inner vision, combined with intuition and strength are a powerful coimbination in any field of endeavour. If you have this Trine aspected, the indication is for a good deal of study to master your art or craft, and that at the end of this you will be recognised in your chosen field.

If the person affected are confident in themselves, the confidence that comes from this will stand them in good stead for making a living, but if they are hesitant and unsure of their presence, the reverse will happen. They will be plunged into difficulty, often to the point of despair. However they rise like the Phoenix when the least opportunity is offered.

An important lesson here is to trust the inner guidance as it comes through, even as we challenge it. This idea of trust yet challenge is little understood! How do we trust yet challenge at the same time? It is really like breathing. We have to breath in, the positive, and yet we have to breath out, the negative. The two go hand in hand. This is the querent's major lesson, understanding the balance between the positive and negative energies in their life.

2-4-7 Short Variant Trine: Be Strong. Cut yourself Free.

For many this will be a difficult and wearing Trine to master. The Two and the Seven have a natural affinity, but like the Moon and the Sun they have difficulty meeting on common ground. As the Four has a very grounding energy to it, this makes for an inharmonious relationship until the querent matures enough to accept the apparent paradoxi of life, and learns to carry on regardless.

The tendency is to see wonderful things about, and to want to tell everyone about these, but to feel too insecure to do so. Also, because of this inner tension, when the querent does open up, they tend to gush sentimentality many find repulsive. This causes them to retreat even deeper into their homespun cocoon.

Eventually the butterfly emerges, but it can take a lot of time. If the person affected by this Trine seeks to break out of their shell they will suffer great confusion, but if they persist a real and genuine confidence will be theirs. There is difficulty in accepting oneself here, but by following the beat of their own drum the querent can find that they succeed beyond their wildest expectations.

A danger here is to run off and do lots of courses that apparently open up doors, but with this aspect the only things that will really work are time and patience. These will bring a deep, impenetrable understanding to their heart, and will bring about a permanent transformation within.

2-3-4 Short Variant Trine: If in Doubt... Do It! Find out!

Strong current of energy are generated by sequential numbers. The 2-3-4 Trine is no exception to this rule. People affected by this Aspect can be progressive and forthright, and creative solutions are always at hand for them. The sense of clear direction can be interfered with by the Two energy, however, with the classic problems of double mindedness and double standards arising that plague this energy.

The lessons here involve setting goals, setting standards, and sticking to them. If the native does this, their life moves like water running down the hill. When they are caught up with something you can be sure that if there's a crack in the problem, they'll find it and squeeze through. As a curious result, these folk make good thieves, spin doctors and salemen.

On the highest levels they can realize their inner wishes, and direct them into outward, productive results. On the negative side the opposite happens: Big dreams, but no result.

If the querent works with the natural, forward moving dynamic in their lives things work out. If they are inhibited with guilts and repressions they often will still succeed, but may find that they suffer personal difficulties and serious health afflictions.

One of the lessons involved is simply to learn to get involved with a situation, but divorce themselves from an attachment to the circumstance that arise as a result. This is not a lack of responsibility (response-ability), but a way in which they INCREASE their ability to respond to the changing tides.

1-4-8 Short Variant Trine: Be dedicated to a Higher Goal.

This can be a very unpleasant Trine on a personal level, but it can be very good for business. Ideally the native should learn to have the very basic and uncompromising attitude of this Trine when they go to work, but to turn it off when they come home. It can be done, but grasping this "Off-On" attitude can be very difficult.

The Four and the Eight resonate to money and karma, with the One being in this case the driving force. People with this aspect can drive through many difficulties unscathed if they keep their spirits up and their confidence intact. It is when life gets them down that the full weight of what they carry comes crashing in. It is therefore wise that people with this Trine should endeavor to avoid high levels of debt.

The tendency is to do the opposite, however, because they are always looking for an opportunity to invest and increase their capital. Remember that cycles of economic and psychic activity come and go. It is essential they people form a safe haven, a base where they cannot be touched, or else ruin will stalk them like the cat in the night. In short, avoid such things as Negative Gearing and the Futures Market.

On a higher level, people with this Trine can be utterly dedicated to some higher purpose. This is more in accord with their overall destiny, and with this sort of goal the native will find life moves far more simply for them. You will find a natural religious impulse when this Trine is at work. This type make wonderful workers in religious orders, and are not the complaining type as a rule.

this is also a building energy. If you are a person who enjoys hard work the energy is extremely fortuitous and almost always very positive. So if there's a big project that is good for all, take it by the horns.

3-6-8 Short Variant Trine: Hare-brained Schemes or Brilliant Work?

The Soul affected by this Trine has a tendency to live in a world of theory and unreality. Insanity is only a hairsbreadth from genius, and these folk may well walk the fine line between both. The Eight is in the background, pulling away, but the Native tends to not want to deal with its influence, and tries to stay in the Three-Six combination, or the mental state. It cannot be done, and a major lesson here is to learn how best to live in this world. This generally means learning practicality.

Dreams and goals will never come to fruition until the querent can deal with the negative aspects of their lives. It is from dealing and mastering the negative influences within that they will attain the necessary strength to master their lives outwardly. If they do not deal with their hidden face, as the negative is often termed, there will be a tendency towards (perhaps) psychotic behavior and an obsession with details.

The positive aspect is equally powerful, a peculiar aspect of which is the fact that it can slash and burn through traditional thought. Like a brushfire starting from a small spark on a hot day, these people can be the trigger that sets off enormous changes about them. Sometimes this will be deep resentments and frustrations that have been bottled up inside others, but if the native persists with their line of thought, things generally work out for the best. In this aspect they are a catalyst, setting off a chemical reaction that cannot be reversed.

The balanced aspect is where the native comes to terms with his/her own inner fears and inadequacies, and makes steady progress in life. Here the change is within, more of an evolution than a brushfire, with effects that last long after this present life is finished.

Do not expect others to understand what motivates the person under this influence. Close family will generally be puzzled by some of their actions,. But if the native of this Trine continues to follow the beat of their own drum long enough, then those around them will come to accept the odd rhythm. And maybe even join in!

6-7-8 Short Variant Trine; Patience is Needed.

Here we see another sequential order, one where the person affected by this Trine can be extremely patient and observant, garnering great knowledge and wisdom from the course of their life. Or else it is the opposite, and they can be the bull at the gate.

The problem in this instance is that the gate to life opens inwardly, and without patience this energy only smashes itself into unconsciousness. This can be indicated as being "accident prone" but in reality it is an unbalanced energy.

An understanding of the nature of the world is essential here, if the native is to avoid continual problems of their own making.

There is an indication and need for an apprenticeship, to learning a trade before setting out to challenge the world. If this is done, in what ever the field the querent will be successful. This is quite important, the idea of a profession or trade, and a person affected by this influence must realize that with such a thing behind them they will be able to move more freely in this world. In a word: Credentials!

4-8-9 Short Variant Trine: Silence before the Howling Gale.

Torment can follow these people like the hounds of hell, but from their suffering a new being will arise. The pain here is simply a stripping away process to reveal the inner self, as well as a purification... But rarely will others see this process. Rather, the querent will keep their difficulties locked away inside, afraid that if one tear shows the wall will come down.

There is a fear of appearing vulnerable as well as a need to break away from convention, and so these people will often arm themselves with a dry wit, a sharp sword of cynicism, and a hard shell of indifference. Alcohol can be a real danger, as well as aggressive behavior that will cost them friends and relationships.

What the problem actually is often avoids their comprehension, but in the meantime they are prepared to fight their phantoms and nightmares like a modern day Don Quixote. Unfortunately they are doomed to a noble defeat unless they understand the need for, and practice, inner silence. This will give them the strength and comprehension needed to understand themselves, and thus rise above the otherwise negative influence of the Trine.

The lesson is to see beyond the illusion of pleasure and pain, and begin the journey into the depths of beingness.

1-5-6 Short Variant Trine: Remember Kindness is your Virtue.

There is a tendency towards sarcasm here, and a sort of mental assault towards those weaker than the Native. But it can flip to a worship of those who are strong and powerful. This, of course, is an apparently natural human trait, but one that is almost a drug for those under the negative influence of this Trine.

With this Trine the most negative aspect is a sense of carelessness. There can be an abuse of friendships, and a desire to find a lever to control others. But the positive side can also shine. This aspect has a ferocious generosity for those who are close, with a lavish sense of love and affection being parceled out to those who are deemed worthy. In many ways, it is like the Two Faced God of the Romans: Friendly to those who share viewpoints, fierce to those opposing them.

Because of this they can obviously be construed as being two-faced, but this is not really the case. It is simply that these people see a sharp difference between those who are personal friends, those who are merely acquaintances, and those who are there to server their purposes. You often see a sharp tongue and sarcastic wit used as a device to stop people getting too close. But the native of the 1-5-6 Trine must be careful that the cat playing witht he mouse doesn't alienate them from those whom they truly love.

There is a strong intuitive sense here which, if followed, will guide the Soul throughout their life's journey. But if this guidance is misused, and the respect for another's space forgotten, much trouble will arrive on their doorstep. The worse punishment for these people is loss of face, and if they are too manipulating this seems to be the fate in store for them.

Regardless of all this, this is an ideal Trine for an executive, or for those who have a strong desire to do well in life, as there is a sense of commitment to progress that is almost zealous. However, please note that if there is no motivation for a personal ambition, then these people can make much spiritual headway in this lifetime.

The Lesson here is not about achievement, however. It is one of learning to quieten the mind, and to still the heart in order to see things clearly. Many people who feel the power of this Trine early in life, find they become deeply contemplative towards the end of it. Much progress and useful endeavour can be made under this influence. There is often a distinct tilt towards writing the biography in the later years.

5-6-7 Short Variant Trine: Humanity is You... So help yourself.

The energy here is introspective and not overly challenging towards others, but an acuteness of observation can give others the sense they are being "seen". This offers a good, natural ability as a counselor and/or therapist. There is often a period of deep introspection and difficulty faced by people with this Trine. This is a necessary step in self discovery. In doing so they come to understand every person.

The Five-Six combination is ambitious and direct, but linked to the Seven we find a leaning towards study and the humanities. This tends to channel the energy of this aspect Inwards as the seeker looks to discover the depths of his/her Soul. On the way, the person can have a desire to analyse everyone and everything, but the self holds the answer.

Naturally there is a risk of introversion, but the greater problem here is that a person can become so caught up in having everything in perfect balance, that their sense of perfection seeking borders on the masochistic. The native here tends to like things to be "just so" when it comes to work, relationships and the home, which of course never quite happens. This can leave this Soul feeling disgruntled and irritable, and thus sharp of tongue.

Marriage is unsuitable for this type, as a rule, and a permanent friend who visits is often preferred to the burden of compromise these people feel they need in order to live with another. Socially their needs are slight, but these people need to do something of social worth, and will often involve themselves in worthwhile projects and pursuits. These pursuits are often where they make their friends.

The Five, Six and Seven all working in a sequence can add a dramatic energy to the nature of these Souls, but the combination tends to be quite dominant, and is somewhat jarring to others. This is why true friendships are often only generated with those who share a specific common interest. This jarring influence tends to precede these people, regardless, and they have an extraordinary ability to get another's back up, even when they mean to be kind.

This is one of those greatly misunderstood Trines. It is not suited to the social whirl, but not quite a lone wolf type either. These Souls tend to live their lives on the fringe of acceptability, and can be quite eccentric. When the energy is mastered, the individual feels extremely comfortable in their own skin, and come to understand simply will not be ruled by external conventions. However, before this confident state arrives these people tend to feel out of sorts with the world, and to avoid this reality develop a desire for drugs or some form of addiction.

Acceptance of oneself is a big lesson here, for this frees the heart and mind, and allows contentment to grow.

3-4-5 Short Variant Trine: A Fountain waiting to Burst Forth.

This is a clear, ordered sequence with this Trine. It gives a greater focus to the activity of the individual, and stresses the need for a sense of purpose. As with all Aspects, anything can "flip" and send the person to the opposite spectrum. With no inner or outer direction, an attitude of almost total aimlessness is entirely possible here as well.

The real secret here is to have both of these qualities at work in one's life. Knowing when you need to be totally dedicated to an ideal or goal, and when to snip and completely detach yourself is a powerful energy. You will find the greatest success stories all carry this attitude. It's a sort of Manic Depression, being totally "on" then totally "off", but without the depression in between

Making goals a reality is the core driver of this Trine, or of course it flips and the person lives totally in dreams. It's a very curious energy at work here, but one that promises to make things interesting, at least.

Often those affected by this energy will be considered rude and abrasive, and it is unlikely they will have much time for social pleasantry. More to the point, they tend to scorn the social niceties and, in particular, those who associate themselves with them. THis is great if you are a military offier at war, but unwise situation in the public sphere. If you happen to be dependant on funding from some outside source, employ a public relations person .

This Trine has the goal of achievement firmly in its sights. The Three gives it a business-like creativity that allows your dreams to be obtained . This is a creative drive, but the Four also kicks in, which is the energy that knows how to count the costs. Here we often find a person who can design to a budget where necessary, but remain the wild horse, willful and unrestrained. There is an unexplained brilliance that can shine with this Trine. Others, not just competitors, find this too challenging, and as a result of resentments and jealousy the 3-4-5 Trine will have to contend with having its dreams interfered with by less creative types, simply through spite for the most part.

Dealing with another's negative emotions seems to be part of the lesson involved with this Trine. If this is learned, the querent finds that the development of diplomacy and courtesy create an environment where the inherent drive of this aspect can be properly unleashed. The lesson here is curious. It is to do with connecting with the environment, and these people will always find a great relief in nature and amongst animals.

Lyndon Johnson (President after Kennedy born 27 Aug 1908) had this Trine aspected. It was "swallowed" by the more powerful 2-3-4-5 Square but in the Vacant Position it still was a driving force. This is the sort of energy that WANTS military action, and he is the one responsible for Vietnam. This remains as the greatest US military humiliation.

4-5-9 Short Variant Trine: Intention, not Hope, Moves Mountains.

The focus of this Trine in on the Nine, which on the surface offers a much quieter nature, yet underneath lies a dynamic personality.

This native generally does not desire to create new concepts, rather he or she will seek to broaden the horizon of learning by understanding and reworking the ideas of old. Yet in doing this they often create something new as a result.

There is an element of refinement here, both in character and manner, that is pleasing and comfortable. There is also a drive to refine and clarify things, and as a general rule this includes the spouse. Choose wisely is all we can say here. There is somewhat of an historian in these people, It is mostly to do with finding precedents from the past to work out how things will go in the future. Because of this they make excellent researchers and even lawyers The natural diplomacy inherent here means they can revoice old ideas in a way that reveals the present situation more clearly.

This Trine has a certain political value. Though the native will usually have a distinct lack of interest in politics per se, they often come to understand the political process. The person with this aspect may well find that they are naturally drawn to the resolution of disputes and the governing of departments as a result. They make excellent counselors, but work best in the background with negotiation. As a rule, positions in the public eye should be avoided.

There is a lesson of learning how to simply leave things be, for the querent often has the impulse to do too much. This native must consistently practice the art of detachment in all things, as well as keeping the inner nature quiet. This inner quiet is more than a steadfastness, or a sense of the stoic. Ultimately it is a perceptive state of beingness these people must learn to rest in. All will flow to them if they can develop this.

1-5-8 Short Variant Trine: Strengthen your Inner Resolve.

Emotions and Identity are challenged with this combination, and so the early life of this individual as they come through puberty is likely to be quite difficult. There is a Karmic influence from the Eight, which brings a deep need to be above the trails and tribulations of this world, but when we tell life we want to end some trouble, all we really do is focus on it. In fact, the world generally throws more problems our way when we try to lift ourselves above them.

Thus a core lesson here is that the Native must learn to fend for themselves. Part of this process is to become quite clear on what they want and wish for. Only in this manner will the fog and confusion depart. When clarity is found within, this frequency allows you to look through the confusion in others, and see their heart. Even as children those strong in this energy will sense a lie told to them, and an atmosphere of honesty is needed for them to prosper. Otherwise the child will lose respect for parents, and become unmanageable.

Introversion is a real danger here, and the native must be careful not to fall into its clutches too deeply. Developing curiosity and a sense of adventure is the best answer for this danger of "falling inside oneself". Asking questions and getting out doors, with lots of exercise, is important to keeping a balanced perspective on things.

The sense of looking within gives this trine a softer, gentler value than most of the other Variant Trines. The native will find their greatest happiness in quiet moments by themselves. There is another common danger here, which is a cutting off of communication with others, then swinging towards sexual indulgence as a balance. This makes good, sustained relationships virtually impossible.

Acts of unspoken kindness will break this cycle. As the querent learns to consider others and not just him/herself, they learn to practice "Senseless Acts of Random Kindness. The native must recognize the value of those around them, and develop a discriminating approach to life before peace will settle in their heart.

3-5-8 Short Variant Trine: Who Understands the Poets?

Emotional impact is the desired goal with these people, and they very often achieve just this. A career on the stage, or in a position where the native can unleash their emotional energies is an ideal path to follow, and possibly a necessary one, for the force of the Trine is quite strong and will cause introversion and many subsequent health reactions if the individual cannot externalize their energy.

So often, though, the person so affected will just want to curl up in their room and write beautiful things, and think beautiful thoughts. They generally find the sadness and loneliness of life somewhat of a cosy blanket to lie under. They are invariably shaken out of this dream world.

The classical pattern here is one where life lessons must come through hard knocks. More to the point, it will appear to many that the person affected by this aspect actively pursues trouble. The Eight inherently accelerates Karma, but these people seem to actively reach out to find it. If you are sensitive to the rough and tumble this will not be a pleasant energy to master. The natives of this energy tend to be a pain to live with in a shared situation, and need a lot of compassion before they find their feet in life. They often stay home with Mum.

Otherwise they will seek to cloister themselves in some protected environment, but the inner doubts and insecurities will still plague them. Though some will say life never gives more than we can take, obviously if you walk in front of a moving train you will probably die! People with this Trine must learn to allow their lessons to come to them. There is a tendency to either get things out in the open and over and done with, or to seek to avoid reality at all costs. Patience is the cure for both extremes, but it is hard bought and harder to come by.

Acceptance is another big lesson here, but the major one is really focus. Problems often multiply in the lives of this type simply because they cannot focus on what their priorities are, let alone sort out the best way to achieve them. The gathering of focus will subdue the more extravagant whims and tendencies, which allows others to believe in them more easily. This is very important, and must not be overlooked.

Focus will bring clarity and freedom, and the best way to achieve this focus is to practice doing one thing at a time. This will clear the mind and emotions of clutter, and allow the native to get on with the things at hand.

This Trine will largely be found in the Vacant Aspect in the years 2000 and this alters the energy. If you have this Trine in the VACANT position you will do well in promotions and entertainment. Any area that requires the organisation of fun and excitement will benefit from this energy being present, and positions running amusement parks, theatres, etc. are ideal.

2-5-7 Short Variant Trine: Alone but not Lonely.

A somewhat ugly and destructive tendency pervades this aspect, though it need not be so. This frequency carries a great, but well hidden, desire for power and influence over others, and the native may well suffer few scruples to achieve this end. They are good at covering this up, however, and many times the goal and the means to reach it will be glossed over by some noble and high ideal that will fool even themselves! Covert (hidden) ambition rules many with this Trine.

If the native is not affected by this strong negative aspect, they will have a deep, and even grateful sense of the beauty with the creation energies. In particular, there is a love of music. Many of the finer musicians will have some influence that combines the Two, Five and Seven, but still the darker aspect of this trinity will trail after them. Such things as drug and alcohol abuse are a characteristic concern.

These people can be both polarized and scattered at the same time. The immediate task can carry full focus and attention, but small things like the wife's birthday or picking the kids up from school can be completely forgotten. They tend to frustrate friends and relatives who see so much wasted time and energy going into tschemes and plans which appear pointless, but all this is the round-a-bout way they travel to their secret inner dream. It remains a question throughout these peoples lives, however, whether the secret dream can be realized. And even if it can be, can it be maintained?

It is this inherent insecurity that creates a need to control their environment, but what the native really needs here is an ability to respond positively and directly to the day to day things about them. Looking after the little things matter here. Yet those under this influence have a tendency to let whatever appears to be boring or trivial fly like a kite without a tail. They just want the big dream, the big win at the casino, or that flash new car. Carelessness leads to trouble, like the employee doing a job. They will do it, but they will not care if it works or not. And in the end, they get fired, and realise how important the pay cheque was.

This habit of carelessness will bring only greater confusion and difficulty into their lives. Added to this, procrastination will also stir the pot, because the individual doesn't want to face the reality they have created.

The result is one of the most difficult of all patterns to break out of, that which is called "The Nothing Trap". This is an attitude where nothing matters, and life is just an existence to survive or die in. Take care.

Yet despite all the negatives, the inherent beauty and grace of this Trine will evidence itself. The Querent would do well to surround themselves with people who love the arts, as this will temper their vision of what makes success and increase the value of personal relationships.

2-5-9 Short Variant Trine: Friends are your Greatest Resource.

This aspect gives both a capability and a willingness to tackle difficult and unsavory tasks, but usually with a strong profit motive behind it. The influence is rarely selfless in its energy. However, it is all part of the major lesson for those with this Trine to learn: Developing an attitude of Service!

Family is important, and those close to the heart will be cherished, but others such as neighbors, business acquaintances, etc. are usually kept at a distance. These people are good at dealing with technical matters, and make excellent magistrates and legal people for they have an innate sense of detachment about them. But if this is not so, they will be emotionally fickle, and are not to be relied upon.

The Two allows an appreciation of the duality of things, the Five gives an ability to communicate this, while the Nine has the strength to rule these tendencies. Fully formed, this gives a cohesive energy that is both clear and decisive. Naturally, the cold approach these people might take to get a job done can easily upset those with emotional natures, and they are advised to avoid emotional people in personal matters.

Paradoxically, however, the tendency here is for their "opposite" to be attracted, and in a marriage situation it can work out well remarkably well. Remember though, that the native of this Trine is not overly interested in how another feels. If you marry someone with this Trine, do not expect to be pampered and listened to. The tendency is to only be interested in the way another thinks, and the feelings are unimportant. They avoid the soap opera of the emotional rollercoaster. Regardless, this Aspect tends to be too wrapped up in their personal world to notice much else beside their immediate concerns.

Nothing aggravates the emotive type more than this sort of approach, and yet the two are often found together. This is because both need what the other has to offer, of course. The ideal is simple: The native of this Trine needs to focus on accepting and balancing their inner emotions, rather than shutting them off. If this is achieved they will find interesting and stimulating company with the opposite sex, rather than the brief, exciting liaisons that are the tendency otherwise.

Living in the moment is the great lesson here, for these people need to learn to appreciate and experience the simple joys of living. To this end they are often drawn to country pursuits, and things that bring them close to nature. (Even if it is shooting foxes!?)

This Trine CANNOT appear in the Vacant Position in the years 2000. In the Vacant Aspect the energy reverses, and is incredibly "caring and sharing". It is one of those Aspects that are all one way, or the other, but either way in the end, friends are what will make life worthwhile.

1-8-9 Long Variant Trine: Do not Cherish Opinions.

Here we find a very powerful combination, though not necessarily a fortunate one. These people can easily suffer the fate of great wealth, yet dogged with private misfortune and even tragedy. This is not always so, and depends on the other combinations, but the Karmic Eight will usually crop up in some manner. The One/Nine is essential to the Line of Success. This means that the Eight can accent both the successes and failures in this natives lifetime.

The energy here is very perceptive as a rule, though somewhat inclined towards cynicism. People strong in this energy will enjoy positions of influence, but will usually find power over others to be a dry blessing. It is never the rich fruit it promises to be. If the native of this aspect forgets to take off their professional cloak of judgment at the door of their home, their personal life will be thrown into turmoil. This will happen if the native become too possessed of their own sense of pride.

Listening is the lesson for this aspect, and the native must learn to listen before they speak or act. If the native masters this, then there is little they cannot do or achieve in this world. By listening with the heart we bind others to our cause, whether we realize it or not, and by combining our energies with others we are empowered in our own endeavors.

NOTE: This Trine is one of the few where a missing number has great relevance, in this case the Five. By focusing and bringing the Five's sense of communication to the fore, many of the problems will disappear. There can be a powerful lesson involved with believing in oneself when this aspect is Vacant in a Chart.

The native here will have the opportunity to understand how one small change in our lives can and will set up a chain reaction of continuing change. If the change is for the better, the following conditions tend to work in this direction, and vice versa if it is a negative change.

The secret here is to learn how to be the Catalyst rather than the Prime Mover. If you seek to combine and coordinate, the doors to your goals will open. Try to control and direct, and the way will be difficult.

1-6-9 Long Variant Trine: Tend the Light that Shines Within.

Here we have the drive for success, or in some cases, failure, with the Six speaking to the One/Nine Success energy saying "Listen and life will lead". Of course, do you trust your instincts? If you do, it is success, if not, faileur. The energy gives a business and intuitive influence that can make this Trine supreme over weaker minded persons. By simple mental influence these people can cause others to act in accordance with their wishes, and this is a double edged sword..

We are talking about charm, which is a form of hypnotism. All forms of hypnotism run the risk of breaking of the Law of Non-Interference. If you have this aspect in your Natal Chart be certain that you are not seeking to cause others to act unduly or unfairly on your behalf, for the benefits will not outweigh the personal costs that will accrue as a result.

This might be as simple as the woman who manipulates things so that a man will wish to marry her, or the child who will say things that will mean it gets a special treat. There is a lot of charm that goes with this influence, but it can happen that the native can forget who they are, and fall into their own make believe world that they have painted for others to believe. And, falling so deeply, they cannot escape.

We will recognize the negative aspect of this Trine at work when we see we have the habit of thinking too much about ourselves.

The bottom line of the Law of Non-Interference is a very curious one most would not guess at. It is that we must all one day turn around to face ourselves, warts and all. In other words, we must one day seek to stop manufacturing stories, and accept ourselves for what we are. The inference here is that the native of this Trine needs to learn courage, but this is also a general lesson with all who share the One vibration. The main lesson is a simple acceptance of ourselves and others as we are!

We are all in it together. When you truly and deeply understand this, the energy of this Aspect will take on a powerful spiritual reality. You will be able to master almost any influence that comes into your life, and be able to travel at will into other worlds.

3-6-7 Long Variant Trine: The Wolf is happiest with a Family.

A sort of creative fatality stalks this Trine. There is a sense of "do or die" that, in the extreme, allows the native to achieve great things. But it is essential to focus on what will work and what is practical. Committing to poorly focussed goals means you will fail utterly and find yourself pursuing a hopeless dream. It all becomes a tragic drama.

Even when successful an attitude often dogs these people with a sense that things are never quite good enough. You will them checking the books after work, looking for mistakes. This native loves to shoot at long shots, and often hits them! They can do well at the races.

Oddly enough, two of the greatest creative geniuses of the current day both share this aspect. Many people see Bill Gates (28 10 1955) and Steve Jobs (24 2 1955) as polar opposites, yet they both share the 3-6-7 Variant Trine, and they were both driven in the same way to create a "perfect world" in their own image.

There is the danger of falling into the Perfection Trap here, and while we must seek to do the best we can, we must also learn that enough is enough. The push-pull energy of the Six/Seven combination will tend to pull the native to either end of this perfection idea. On one hand needing exactness to the extreme, yet on the other exhibiting a sort of carelessness. All of this combines in such a way that others may be unsure if these people can be trusted.

The Three is an agitating influence, always seeking a new way of doing something, chasing down blind alleys, looking for a scrap of information. And yet, if the individual pursues the dream they have a marvellous way of having things all work out in the end. Common sense is the basis of deciding whether a dream is worthwhile or not.

There can be a degree of personal confusion inherent with the Trine. This is where you dream great dreams, yet finding reality confounds and discredits your high flung notions. The truth here is rarely understood by the Querent. It is a curious dual principle: *Good outcomes are dependant on true inner confidence,* and yet paradoxically, at the same time: *An acceptance of personal limitations teaches us who to trust.* Without confidence these folk are their own worst enemy, and without recognising natural boundaries, they will not retain the trust of those who will help them complete their projects.

The overall lessons here are developing a practical perseverance, and by becoming efficient rather than just busy. Everything of worth takes patience and stamina. This is equally true of anyone who wishes to partner with a person strong in this influence. The native with this Trine can be quite trying to have around until they relax and trust those in their orbit. Then things work out far more smoothly.

2-3-7 Long Variant Trine: Art is Subtler than Craft.

We often find a confused sort of energy here. There seems to be a cloud around this Aspect. There is a great need for clear direction, but the Two aspect keeps cropping up with issues and contrary ideas that hold the individual in a state on indecision. There is a strong need for freedom, but without a clear sense of Identity; who you are, where you are, etc. There will be no clear answers. Yet the easy key to unlocking the energy of this Trine is found in a sense of discovery

Book of Number: Interpretations

By having a curiousity and a sense of adventure, the querelous, doubting nature of this energy is kept to the background, and the native moves quite fluidly through life. Salvador Dali, 11 May 1904, has an active 2-3-7 Trine in the Vacant Position. We think of Dali as an Artist, but he also produced Film, was an ardent photographer, and was involved with sculpture. It is a perfect example of the drive to discover getting him past the questioing, doubting aspects of this energy.

If a person is too meek, the native will make a life based onsome sort of inner argument, believing that their continual inner dialogue is actually leading them somewhere. It does not. It leads only to schizophrenia. Think of Golem from Lord of the Rings for the negative aspect.

Yet real balance is found with service and developing a sense of working to assist others. The field of humanities is often where the person under the influene of this Trine feels most at home., The Three and Seven are along the Line of Service/Compassion, and so tasks of a compassionate nature will be most suitable for this type. But be aware that if the energy of the Two is not resolved, those under this influence will often be used by others. If you are under the influence of this Trine you need to aware of others trying to abuse your good nature. When given a "Please help me" story, question it.

Oddly enough, the indecisive nature of this aspect can soften the somewhat rude tendency that the other Variant Trines all share. But if the native does not grow beyond their indecisiveness, they end up with a bigoted and biased world view. This is to stop the inner argument,

We find many artists vibrate to this aspect, some become very fine craftsmen, but the desire is for the aesthetic consciousness of what they are working on to come through. It is a very subtle thing, and until mastery of their art is achieved these folk can feel quite driven.

In the negative instance, this Soul will use politics and personal influence to manipulate others, and seek out positions of power under the guise of wanting to benefit our fellow man. They are the first to draft wonderful social reforms, but the reason is to get their hands in the till. This type will seek to capitalize on another's indecision, recognizing the vulnerability therein, as they have had to deal with it in themselves.

Yet the major lesson for this Trine is not decisiveness, but one of clarity. These might appear one and the same, but clarity is an act of perception, decisiveness is the act that emanates from this. In other words, understand what you are getting into before you jump off the bridge. Clarity brings correct action, correct action brings freedom from doubt and insecurity.

By focusing on understanding the situation, this type will be able to get off their millwheel of quandary. This is, in truth, a disguised fear of failure. By seeking to percieve more than achieve, they will overcome.

1-2-9 Long Variant Trine: Cowering Mouse or a Creative Lion?

The Two takes on different characteristics depending on what numbers it is associated with. In this instance the Two is the dreaming number, and likes to deal with concepts, especially when they are to do with beauty and form. As a result this Trine has a certain architectural sense about it. This is a Trine that like to build, to form something new from the clay of the past, yet the inherent fragility of the Two also tends to make this a little unstable.

So we find that the natives of this genre tend to have a sort of panic about them, and an urgent need to complete tasks. They sense that everything might fall apart and so they hurry to make sure the task will be finished. It is this sense of urgency that is often the activating force that counters the Two's indecisiveness, and yet it is also that impulsiveness which builds on sand.

As a result the lesson here is be more methodical, and to be more conscious of what are facts and what are dreams. However, paradoxically, the native has a tendency to view this sort of thinking as detrimental to the creative force they wish to express. They will tend to try and bluff and argue their way around the need for detailed planning with things like "Don't inhibit my spontaneity". Unfortunately this only serves to create more work in the long run, as well as heartache when the hard numbers come in and pull apart the precious dream by saying that the figures don't add up.

The weird thing is that both states, the dreaming and the practical, are all correct. But neither tends to see this! Dreams and reality are two ends of the same stick, but only the truly great beings see this and grasp it. Those who do will rise to the very top of their profession or trade. This Trine is a message that you need to bring your Drames and your Reality into alignment.

We need to understand that there are necessary, and very common sense steps, that we need to follow to make this happen.

And it is at heart an INTERNAL PROCESS, a defined form of inner communication where the individual ties together the disparate elements of their own psyche. Only when the inner forces are aligned can the individual work in accordance with the natural flow of life about them. All this requires the development of a methodical nature, or a step by step approach to problems. It's the Little Red Engine, saying "I think I can, I think I can" and finally realising, "I KNOW I can!"

The true lesson for these people is balance, which is the great prize a methodical nature brings. This Trine is one of the most powerful in the Noumenal Order. It marries disparate internal forces into a focussed, defined path of Destiny. Called "The Spear of Destiny" in ancient texts, it is really a calling to arms for Spiritual Warriors.

3-4-7 Long Variant Trine: Over the wall, beyond dreams, the sleeper awakens to a new horizon.

This can seem to be a thick and rather unpleasant Trine, with a constant push pull sort of energy about it. The individual would like to be generous, but the stoic Four will generally prefer to serve itself. The Four/Seven combination likes the things of the Earth, but the Three yearns for the sky. The Three/Seven wants Freedom, yet the Four chains it to fears of security.

All of this tends to create an edgy, confined person. But if the barriers and inner blocks can be cleared the Four transforms into humor, the Seven into wisdom, and the Three into freedom. So the mature Aspect is incredibly warm and funny, yet in the immature phase, really not much fun to have around at all.

This Trine offers a very powerful combination that can give the individual training in the most important aspects of personal mastery. These are ONE: Learning to be of service to a higher cause, and TWO: Learning to not take things personally. The message here is for the person to have perseverance until this state arises within.

The major lesson in bringing this about is one of lightness. Allow Life to work with you. Simply let things be rather than "work it out". Try and catch the moments of laughter rather than write eulogies about the tears. This is a difficult Trine with the the tendency is to internalize and dissect things but real freedom is found in EMBRACING CHANGE, not looking for what is believed to be "wrong". This trying to correct wrongness within, is like taking patent medicine for an undiagnosed illness. You are ignorant of the bigger picture, and you will tend to bury yourself in problems. The solution is to be found in ACCEPTANCE of Self, and embracing change.

As a note, the internal argument this Trince stirs up can create a poor mental balance, which in turn affects the physical health of the querent. Natives with this Trine should seek to keep their diet full of fresh fruit and vegetables, with not too much meat.

This is a Trine of awakening, but only when the argument over creativity versus stability is solved. It is really just easiest to not worry about things, and to allow life to find the solutions you need. You will never work it out on your own.

3-7-8 Long Variant Trine: What's it to Be? God or Mammon?

Three and Seven look for Freedom, yet the Eight accents a need for wealth when this Trine is active. This need can well take over as their main focus in life. If so, they generally succeed. But the cost if often suppression of the Inner Child. There is a choice to be made here.

You might think that Freedom and Wealth go hand in hand, and they do if FREEDOM is the motivation. If it is the money that drives you, everything that comes to you becomes a prison. Having money does not preclude spiritual attainment, nor does it require that the person sell their Soul, so to speak. However, the LOVE of Money can make a person forget their common humanity, and thus forget tto care for those around them. This creates a personal isolation, with Howard Hughes a perfect example of how Money can distort and imprison us. Money Addiction often results in suicide in old age, either overt, or covert through drugs or some other sort of abuse.

You might think it is a Lust, but this is not the driving force. Vanity is the frailty of this combination, yet it is a subtle vanity based on progress and attainment. This is difficult because success can prevent the individual from viewing any problems in what they see as a "Winning Combination". (IE: Themselves!)

Because they are successful the querent here often uses this as an approval from God. This is the Industrial Age thinking that makes child labour perfectly acceptable. Self justification can confirm any action, but if you are careless of others, Life will be careless of you..

If money is not the focus, it is likely that something else will become an obsession, for this is a rather obsessive Trine. The lesson here, therefore, is not what you might expect. It is to be more open minded and willing to listen to the whisper on your intuition.

If someone with this aspect becomes dedicated to a Spiritual Purpose, they can make tremendous gains in understanding themselves, and the nature of Life. There will be difficulties, to be sure, but each will become a stone in a set of stairs that lifts you to the highest of heavens.

1-4-9 Long Variant Trine: The Warrior Sharpens his Sword.

This is a bulldozing energy. These people tend to want something done, and want it NOW. They do not want excuses or rationals for failure, they want reults.. These psychic strength of thios Trine can be so strong that even bad mechanics realize it would not be worth their while doing a bad job on the car, and so the job gets done right.

The negative aspect is a complete, inner denial of this mental strength, usually replacing it with a passive, accepting demeanour. If this is so, there is usually a subsequent mental and/or physical abuse by others who know how to manipulate this type. Thus there tends to be a polarity of being either a leader or a slave here. And sometimes we will see this occur in the same person, where they might run a corporation, but at home their wife utterly rules them.

On the positive aspect, these people like power. We tend to view using Power as a negative, but that is like saying the executive of a company should obey the workers. The world works on Power flowing through a Leader, and when this Trine is active, that is the message. Be the active channel for growth and the creation of things.

People who are pro-active in creating business tend to be dismissive of bureauocracy. They have a disdain for politics and crowd mentality, thus they stay out of public office and public positions and work alone or in a focussed group for the better part. However, if this Trine is shared with a Vacant 3-5-7 Line, then public service will be an ideal vocation..

As a leader, the energy will inspire loyalty, yet also attract sycophants. Surrouding yourself with "Yes Men" will destroy the effectivness of this Trine. In a leadership position, a small, tight team is the way these people function best. The direction is up and out, yet in any organisation the natural issues of people will arise, and require someone to deal with their issues and problems. Hire someone to deal wwith it.

People with this Aspect like honesty. Often brutal in their assessment of others, they tend to create an atmosphere of ill will when they try and solve social or political issues. The greatest concern is a sense of anger these people have, for they find it impossible to accept the imperfection of this world, and especially those who seem to embrace it.

A perfect example is Clive Palmer, a highly successful buisinessman who was angry with the political stalemate in Australia, and so started his own party which had significant success in it's first run in the elections. He is born 26 March 1954. He has the 1-4-9 Trine active, but he does NOT have a Vacant 3-5-7 Trine. This takes away a sense of compassion for others that may eventually cause him to lose favour. However, his birthdate is one of perfect balance. If he can keep the energy of his Vacant Seven (The Dark Horse - that is the frequency which drew people to him) and combine with the stated 3 and 5, he will create an atmosphere of change and growth. But Vanity and impatience will be the challenge.

The world won't fall apart if we have to wait for a bit. Generally I tell most people to get on and start doing things, but these folk need to learn to the opposite. By this I don't mean to procrastinate, but to give themselves and situation they are in a little time to resolve things.

More importantly the lesson is with patience. Especially in allowing others the mental breathing space to collect their thoughts, and make internal decisions. Here the person with this Trine will discover that a little patience employed on their part will help them communicate, and this will break much of the negative aspects associated with this aspect. This Trine needs to give others (and themselves!) room, especially members of their personal family. In this way a great peace will come upon those who possess this Trine. A peace that they secretly yearn for.

Patterns in the Matrix

There are Sixty Patterns noted in these Interpretations. When a Pattern is present in a Chart, it indicates that this is either a potential energy, or one that is dominant in the person's life.

The influence of a Pattern is two fold. In the Immature Stage it effectively incubates in the Sub-Conscious. When the energy matures, it becomes a dominant force in the person's life. This does not mean the Individual affected is aware of it, but it is important for a reader to recognise the difference.

An example is a Martyrs Cross. (2-5-8 / 4-5-6) A person with this Pattern will in early stages throw themselves into causes, give money away to charities, and generally appear to waste their life. In the Mature Phase they will tend to be in charge of the charity, or stage production, or whatever it is they can throw themselves body and soul into.

It is important to recognise because if you see they are in the early stage, you can say "You need to stop and get in charge of whatever field of interest you are in." In the later stage you can suggest that they need to focus on effective effort and focus.

Simple things like this make a great deal of difference in how effective we are at reading a chart and advising people.

PATTERNS In the MATRIX:

Patterns are one of the most simple, yet evolved ways, to understand core energies surrounding a specific event or individual. When you grasp how they work within the framework of events, and in particular when Patterns come out of an Overlay Matrix, you will have one of the most powerful tools of Numerology available to you.

Many times, the readings given are so remarkably accurate that people are shocked. I cannot count the number of times I have heard words to the effect, "So if I were born in March instead of February, then this Aspect would not exist, and I would not feel these feeling?". However, this is approaching things from exactly the wrong angle.

The NUMBERS themselves have NO POWER. They are DOORWAYS through which energy flows, and the fact that you have a specific set of doorways in your chart is symbolic of the energy you are DRAWING towards yourself, whether by choice or karma. So yes, if you were born a month later, the doorways and energy fields would be different, but you weren't. You were born into the situation you incarnated in because of the exact and EXISTING FREQUENCY in your own nature.

To be born to a different time means you carried different frequencies. Your Date of Birth, your parents, your environment are REFLECTIONS of your own internal process. Further, every single thing in this process is set up for your learning and the purpose you are here to serve. Random events happen, but the larger picture carries very specific energies you NEED for your growth. THERE ARE NO COINCIDENCES! Every detail of life arrives, grows and departs according to the internal clock of frequency.

Yet there is a greater truth at work here, a secret I will share with you in the trust that by this time the seeds have been planted so you may understand it. This is that without IMAGINATION, there is ONLY FATE. However, IMAGINE a different reality, IMAGINE a greater NOW, and you change FATE to DESTINY.

To change the wheel of becoming (karma) all you need do is IMAGINE something new. This is one of the hidden powers of Numerology. Let's say you have a Pattern or Trine that is difficult. Perhaps there is a Square Pattern at work, or a karmic 4-7-8 Trine that seems to be the source of financial loss: Find an Aspect, such as the Vacant 4-6-8 Trine (self employment, self sufficiency) and see what days that are coming up THAT carry this Trine.

Then just IMAGINE you are at this day, and that the financial worries are behind you. Imagine you are generating income, and feel the sense of this Trine waking up in the background. Now, if you are really tuned in, you will HEAR the frequency of this Trine. (We also have ways of resolving specific dates and Trines into physical music that we record for people)

IMAGINE, if all is Song, as the Pythagoreans stated, and the SONG WE SING determines the LIFE WE LIVE: *Then all we need do is sing a different song to change our life.*

The true study of Number is not about understanding your FATE, but one where you learn to MASTER YOUR DESTINY. The Numbers you were born to live can be modified through simple imagination, combined with an awareness of alternatives.

But a small warning. Yes, anyone can change their present through imagination, but if you have not resolved the energies that brought you to where you are now, the rubber band effect will take hold, and you will be snapped back into the emotions/mentality that created your current world.

How do we resolve the current situation? Gratitude, kindness and a resolve to do no harm are the starting point, but in the end, it is how you serve life that opens the doors to Wind of Change. I do not mean you serve another, or some cause, but that you become dedicated to LIFE ITSELF. Have this attitude in your heart, and Life will start to show you the way to your destiny.

V Patterns

V Patterns are literally two Lines of Force that intersect. The point of Intersection is the "Pivot Point" and the Number between the two "arms" of the Pattern is the "Forming Energy". They are like a funnel that collects water, with the tap being the Forming Energy, the the point to where it flows being the Pivot Point. Obviously the name is based on the fact they look like a "V".

There are Eight possible combinations of "V" patterns in the chart:

3-5-7/7-8-9   3-2-1/1-5-9 (upright)

9-5-1/1-4-7   9-6-3/3-5-7 (right side open)

3-6-9/9-5-1   3-5-7/7-4-1 (left side open)

1-2-3/3-5-7   1-5-9/9-8-7 (upside down)

3-5-7 / 7-8-9 "V" Pattern:
Forming Energy: Six
Pivot Point: Seven

The individual affected by this Pattern needs to be of service, and will find that "Their cup shall runneth over" if they do this. This is not service in the sense of martyrdom I talk of here, but service that gives a genuine pleasure gained from assisting others. It is not easy going, for there is a contrary element in the nature of the Forming Energy and the Pivot point. This is an aspect at Sixes and Sevens with itself until it resolves the internal argument, and learns to express it's natural self.

There is often a desire for spiritual truth, and we may find many of this type strong supporters of religious institutions. If the person with this aspect is not spiritually awakened the pattern generally encourages a scathingly critical outlook on people and things.

In this instance the individual would usually have no compunction about surviving at the expense of others. In this negative aspect we may find tendencies such as prejudice, greed and prestige consciousness overruling the sense of fair play and the appreciation of humanity.

The positive aspect invokes self-sufficiency, common sense and a high degree of intuition. A good deal of how the internal compass is set with this type comes from the family upbringing, and a person under this influence who is not close to their roots will generally be unstable, moody and somewhat depressive.

The focus of this Pattern is on the Seven. This indicates a degree of internalization, contemplation and consideration. However, when the complexity of thought is worn through, the native finds a tremendous freedom to act stirring in their souls, and later in life they can become real adventurers. We could apply the principle "Through Complexity to Simplicity" with those under this influence, for while they often seem to take the longest route from point to point, when they arrive at a point of understanding it is generally with a point of great clarity and wisdom..

1-2-3 / 1-5-9 "V" Pattern:
Forming Energy: Six
Pivot Point: One

Based on the One, this Pattern often finds stupendous success, yet also stupendous failure in the process of getting there. The ups and downs are often wrapped around associates, and the Querents desire to believe in others, who let them down. A general lesson here is to take a more cautious approach in choosing people to work with you in any given project. In personal affairs, the male with this aspect will attract a woman with clear intuition. This may be as a secretary, or wife, but regardless, they should be listened to.

The female with this aspect is often possessed of second sight, and often lives the later years of here life on her own. This is generally not a burden, for these are independent Souls as a rule, who actually find great peace in their own company.

A very curious person who carries this aspect is Vincent Van Gogh. Now considerd one of the great artists of the world, his life was one of spectacular failure. Everything was wrapped around his associations, or lack of harmonious association as the case was. An Incomplete line of Balance on the 1-5-9 line and an Incomplete Line of Force on the 1-2-3 line, plus other Aspects, give his chart a distinctly disconnected energy. He desired success, and he desired to create, but he also had a -2-3 / 3-5-7 "V" Pattern at work, that gave him a compulsion to find some higher force. Everything about this chart is difficult.

Talking to him would have been like talking to a person on the other end of the phone who cannot hear you. And yet, as the right associations are made after his death, he becomes celebrated and famous. If he had married an intuitive woman, many of his personal issues would have been lessened, and yet would he have achieved fame after death?

This intensifies the argument that trying to direct nature is at best difficult, and at worst pointless. We have our nature, and it must be allowed to run it's course, yet if you see someone trying to get to Paris on a road where the sign says "New York" isn't it obvious that you might say something? Of course you do, but it doesn't mean the person has the ears to hear you.

Overall, if you have this Aspect in your chart, it is wose to remain active. This type is at their best when building something, and should always take care to have some interesting occupation or hobby to do something useful for themselves and others. Creative endeavor is highlighted, and if this is the mainstay of life things and projects will seem to naturally progress towards a satisfactory completion, provided that the native relies on their own resources. (Van Gogh didn't. He relied on help from family, which destroyed his inner confidence)

If the native falls into allowing another to subsidize them, options will begin to close down, and life will become a narrow band with few enlivening experiences to brighten it up.

There is a marked possibility that these folk will be drawn to highly spiritual organizations, or organizations that serve worthwhile purposes. In these areas they will find both a spiritual satisfaction and an outlet for their organizing abilities. Everything here is about trusting the intuition, but the real message is SELFHOOD. Discovering the natural self is the real journey this Aspect sends you on.

1-5-9 / 1-4-7 "V" Pattern:
Forming Energy: Eight
Pivot Point: One

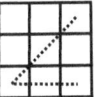

All patterns based on the One (such as this) emphasise individuality. The Forming Energy of Eight with the 1-5-9/1-4-7 Pattern creates an energy that is excellent for an understanding worldly affairs, the arrangement of finance, and the clarification of ideas into practical application. On a different level, an individual with this aspect may be draw to religious service of some sort, and thus embrace the opposite of worldy things.

The Pattern is good for research and accounting, and though often of an entrepreneurial nature, natives of this type will make sure the books balance. If the drive is there, they can also turn into the world's greatest jugglers of finance, managing to swing preposterous business deals, but only if they work in secret or with a trusted group of like minded souls.

Executives, Motivators, Prime Movers: these people are best suited to a role where they are a catalyst for growth. When financially and emotionally established they will discover a natural ability to help others achieve their goals, if they are so inclined.

The Spiritual aspect here can easily fall into a martyr like attitude, and this is one of the negative traits of this Pattern that is best avoided. The core of this attittude is actually a need for approval. This is often the seed cause of all the problems experienced under this Aspect.

The negative aspect can also create miserly attitudes, and short sighted behavior in regard personal relationships. In the positive aspect the native learns to accept and welcome input from others. They can then become less guarded and cautious socially, and in time learn to be extremely gentle, whilst remaining forthright in matters of importance.

In the Balanced aspect the fierce battle lust has cooled, and the more contemplative nature of these folk emerges, giving them a focus on the value of the heart. With the security of a true heart, their soft inner nature can now be shown, yet these people still have a warrior mentality when it comes to protecting their own, which, of course, is good.

3-6-9 /3-5-7 (or "Reversed Seven") "V" Pattern:
Forming Energy: Eight
Pivot Point: Three

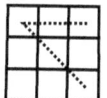

This is a somewhat somber Pattern, with the native affected being almost gray in outlook. This is not of itself negative, for it helps to build stability in life. It is a very considered and weighty aspect, and so one of the major lessons here is to do with laughter. Specifically, learning to laugh at oneself.

This pattern contrives to unite a clear mind with a humanistic tendency, which are often apparent opposites. Adolescence tends to be difficult, mostly because stress is keenly felt. Based on the Eight for its energy source, this aspect (when matured) gives an inspirational energy and an organizational capacity to any organisation the Querent is involved in. With the focus being on the Three, there is a need for creative expression, and this is generally expressed in business.

Architecture, writing, and oddly enough such things as professional dancing are suitable occupations here. In fact, anything that involves clarity of thought and a sense of unity with people is ideal for this energy type. These people can design anything, but generally it is best that they rely on another to construct it. These folk tend to construct on a mental and planning level, and generally they find things easier for them when they can allow others to carry out these plans.

The writer with this aspect will usually look to base his/her stories on actual events they have experienced or witnessed, and the writing will often have an important social message. Seldom will these people be flippant or fashionable, rather they will seek to analyze what is the stereotype or archetype behind the apparent situation before them. After this they will try to convey this understanding in some manner, and so we see quite a number of this type as writers, teachers and speakers.

The need to understand is a driving force here, and if successful in life and business these people also have a good ability to communicate their findings. As such, they can provide a good platform for others to build from. As a note, we often find this Pattern in the matriarch of a Dynastic family, which is one example how this energy might employ itself.

1-5-9 /7-8-9 "V" Pattern:
Forming Energy: Four
Pivot Point: Nine

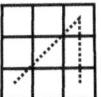

This is a very curious Pattern, often found in compulsive dreamers, yet when active in a mature individual we find great perspective and judgment present. These people are capable of wisdom, and often we might find this aspect in the charts of very powerful individuals. The positive aspect of this pattern has a habit of making things work from the ground up, paying attention to the details on the way.

Those under this influence can be very conscious of power, and there is generally a desire to achieve the heights of their profession. If the native enjoys climbing mountains, either intellectual or actual ones, they soon discover the importance of a **polarized perspective**. With this attribute in their life all things come far more easily. This, of course, can make them somewhat one sided with their views, and different problems can arise. When there is too much focus on the goal, there may be not enough enjoyment of life. In adolescence they often take a far too serious view of social issues, looking to be politically active instead of just enjoying their life, as one example.

Very individualistic by nature, these people do not take orders very well, nor are they inclined to give them. You are expected to know what to do. Yet at the same time they make excellent teachers, ones who remain extremely faithful to their ideals and to those in their charge. Of course, the flip side to this is that if the native with this Pattern does NOT have a purpose or goal, they tend to lead useless lives.

In this case, drugs and self abuse will likely fulfill a perverted sense of purpose, and rebellion will seem natural. Even so the upward current prevalent in this pattern will generally work to mature these people, and barring accidents or ill health, they often grow into a useful role later in life. Ideally, being of service in some way or another.

This Pattern makes for better grandparents than parents, so to speak, but it is important to note that ALL "V" Patterns can be balanced by strengthening the energy point they draw from. In this case it is the Four energy that the person might strengthen. Paying attention to finances. thus finding a stability, solves a good deal, and also simple laughter can shake off many of the negative concerns of this Pattern.

Book of Number: Interpretations

1-2-3 / 3-5-7 "V" Pattern:
Forming Energy: Four
Pivot Point: Three

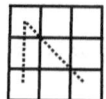

This is a Pattern that tends to have a lot of emotional and temperamental people connected to it. Campaigners for human, animal and environmental rights may well carry this in their Noumenal Chart. There is an odd creative somberness that is attracted to a cause of some sort, particularly those of the Earth, social injustice, and cruelty to unfortunates and/or innocents.

Often deep, imperious moods blow across their inner landscape, driving their actions, to the point of being a fanatic. As such, the single mindedness that develops from this Pattern can easily become blindness for this native, and it is something they need to be aware of.

This Pattern can be made far more difficult if there is also a 1-5-9 line present in the Birth Chart or Name chart, or even if the people they deal with carry this vibration. (Which is a desire to succeed and be recognized) This (unfortunately for these folk) is an extremely common Line in the 1900's. Such a pattern creates a certain messianic tendency that is ruinous for personal relationships.

These people tend to see everyone as equal, and are generally ignorant of the economic motivation of profit. When immature, their argument is usually based on emotions and not reason, and they can be prone to outbursts of accusation that are quite unrelated to the issues at hand. This almost childish way of seeing the world often puts them up to ridicule, thus they rarely see their ideals fulfilled. However, it should be noted that at heart the ideal is genuine, and based of the principle that we are all in it together. The Querent of this aspect must learn to grow with a broader viewpoint, and become more accepting of society as it is. At this point they can begin to be very effective agents for positive change.

Paradoxically, many of this type ignore their inner sense of rebellion against injustice and join large organizations. They become slavish adherents to rules and often rise to positions of importance. This is often fatal to their personal growth, for this personality is more susceptible than most to Ego imbalance. They become the worst of beaurocrats.

However, if they can keep a balance, trust that others have their role, and give them the freedom to be themsleves, then they do very well in life, and are often well regarded in their community or lodge. There is a martyr like tendency that needs to be watched, especially as the classic "do-gooder who doesn't listen" stereotype that often crops up here.

These folk can have a missionary zeal, but if a balance is kept they make excellent teachers and educators. Positions in the Public Service, in the true sense of the word, and areas of healing and humanities are the perfect avenue that natives of this type should seek to follow.

1-4-7 / 3-5-7 "V" Pattern:
Forming Energy: Two
Pivot Point: Seven

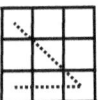

These people are the "Salt of the Earth" type. Those under this influence will do anything for a friend, and are caring and considerate to others, yet would not hesitate to shoot a troublesome dog. Is this a paradox? Not at all. This type is generally intensely practical, and the word for them is pragmatic. They tend to be faithful and persistant, and they have a spiritual side as well. It is rarely seen in public, but is often felt by the native in their quiet moments.

They are very blunt Souls, often farmers or those involved with production based on the natural seasons of life. They are the cultivators in organizations who tend to the details and make sure things are going along well. They do well in both personal and systems management, and also as the "kingpin" secretary.

In the army, they are the Sergeants, in life they are the Head Chefs and Supervisors. Only rarely are they out there on their own, for they both like and work well with others. They often give and wish to receive input and assessments on a regular basis in regard any projects they are working on. The native of this aspect generally understands the importance of communication, but there is also an inherent seed of self doubt at work with this Pattern.

We often find an odd sense in the back of the mind that things are not quite right. As a result there is a tendancy to value the opinions of others too highly. The reverse can also be true. Because of this inner doubt they ignore others opinions, and barge on recklessly into deals and business, not wanting to trust another's considerations, or look to those more experienced for advice. Neither state is fully balanced, and unless the native can come to terms with this inherent uncertainty they may find themselves driven to confidence substitutes such as drugs, obsessive behavior and/or hero worship. Alcohol is a virtual poison to these people, and they must be careful with this.

Drug abuse can stir up a tension between the internal male/female balance. Issues such as Passive Aggression can arise, and an almost schizophrenic self obsession can warp personal judgement.

These folk tend not to deal too well with entrepreneur types, sales people and/or outlandish individuals, but if an individual is seen as capable and honest their view will be listened to. In the workplace there is but one rule, which is if someone pulls their weight, they will be accepted. The negative aspect relates to insecurity, while the positive aspect relates to continuity and perseverance. The lesson overall is to develop an understanding of people and life here in the physical world, and find ways to survive in it.

3-6-9 / 1-5-9 (The Seven) "V" Pattern:
Forming Energy: Two
Pivot Point: Nine

We find this aspect can be very polarised. On one hand, the person affected sets goals in life, and generally achieves them, or they will do the complete opposite. Right association and right thinking are very important for positive outcomes. Drugs have a very negative effect on this Pattern, even prescribed drugs, so the native in need of medical help would do well to seek out natural remedies and generally focus on finding a quiet life free of overt stress.

For those with an essentially kind inner nature this Pattern can be incredibly lucky. They will go through tremendous learning experiences, but if they develop a real confidence in themselves, as well as a love for life, they will grow into a balance and poise that will bring them great contentment later in life.

This Pattern makes for natural philosophers, and it often indicates plenty of enthusiasm. As we can see, this Pattern forms the number Seven quite distinctly. This lends an air of spirituality, and also a tenancy to internalize, thus making simple things difficult. Yet vice-versa, they can also make difficult things easier! Why? Because for the Soul affected by the Seven vibration, a challenge that is seen as big and important is actually easier to meet than the mundane and provincial problems of life. They like the more complex things. Their attention focuses on complication with more natural will, and therefore they can find the solution. Simple matters, on the other hand, bore them, and can be allowed to snowball and become unmanageable.

A clear head and positive attitude is essential for harmony, and this requires an ability to sort out what is useful and what is not in one's life. Once dedicated to a task, this native will complete it, however, even when the cost seems to far outweigh the payoff. But the dedication itself gives great peace of mind, and thus proves worthwhile.

This is the crux of the Pattern, commitment to an ideal. Without this commitment the native will wander aimlessly, and life will be a failure. Even with dedication to a goal, it is a difficult Pattern, but the results far outweigh the consequences. As the native tends to forget how others feel as a rule, good marital relations are rare with these folk, and communication tends to break down through this lack of empathy.

Patience is needed, for only with patience does right understanding, and therefore right action, come into conscious awareness. The native then finds a good ability to take a concept and break it down into explainable ideas. Curiously this Pattern is a good one for those in the Political arena, but it is most commonly seen with writers, designers and those who like to build with their mind in some form or another.

"U" (or Cup) Patterns: There are Four possible "U" Patterns:

1-2-3/3-6-9/9-8-7 Downwards Cup

3-2-1/1-4-7/7-8-9 Upwards Cup

1-4-7/7-8-9/9-6-3 Left Open Cup

9-6-3/3-2-1/1-4-7 Right Open Cup

The "Cups" or "U" Patterns all tend to invoke a sense of attraction, and encourage the notion of holding on to some ideal. This easily becomes attachment to ideals and preconceptions, and these series of Patterns tend to easily show when the Soul is evolved, evolving, or simply interested in getting what they can.

When present in a Chart it indicates some higher purpose is calling that individual. It does not mean they will discover it, but often they will go on odd quests, like a modern Don Quixote, that others simply do not see as practical. It's just part of the Pattern evolving in their lives.

1-2-3 / 1-4-7 / 7-8-9 (Upwards Cup) "U" Pattern:
Forming Energy: Six
Pivot Point: Five

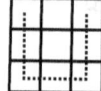

This is the Upwards Cup, and those with this in their Noumenal Chart have the ability to collect and store Spiritual Wisdom. However, they are also able to collect and store of all levels, including that of finance, affection and material goods. As a result of this, the native must be careful of what they bring into their lives (which is true of all the "U" Patterns) for in this instance hoarding and misery behavior can be common problems.

Generally this indicates a kind Soul, to the point where a person can be gullible to the extreme. But with the Forming Energy of the Six properly activated they get a sort of "cap" or filter that acts as a spiritual and physical protection. This Six is actually the intuition, but it also attracts the presence of inner and outer guardians, as well as the Spiritual Force. So really, trust your intuition is the message.

The Upwards Cup Pattern, has a desire to grasp and understand that which is beyond itself, which can lead to a wasted life if feet are not kept firmly on the ground. All of the "U" Patterns have no specific anchoring point, except that they revolve around the Five. This indicates a need for balanced communication from those who figure in their plans and aspirations. If the lines of communication are left open here, most things will work out satisfactorily in their lives.

The one great foible for the Upwards Cup Person is that they tend to love too much, and thus find great difficulty with detachment. As mothers they will be over protective, as fathers they will tend to be domineering. As employees they tend to get so enmeshed with minute details that they waste time on trivial matters, and otherwise generally forget the concept of profit. As employers they want to involve themselves too much in their employees lives, playing a father figure role that is often resented.

The main message from this Pattern is more of an understanding that all things pass. If the person is feeling pain, they only need to remember to say "This too shall pass" and this will invoke the higher energy of this Pattern. Let it go, and better things will come to you.

3-6-9 / 1-2-3 / 1-4-7 (Right Open) "U" Pattern:
Forming Energy: Eight
Pivot Point: Five

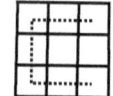

Here is a Pattern that can be incredible wasteful with finance, but if their Nine energy is strong, they will be equally capable of scooping up other people's losses. If the Querent has the NINE strogly featured in other areas of their chart, they can make wonderful market raiders, businessmen and stockbrokers, yet hey also tcan be good in counseling, and areas where they can exercise their ability to reframe peoples concepts of things.

The bottom line with this type is a need for creativity, in whatever way ikt applies to this individual. If they are denied this at work, at home or in education they will simply shrivel up inside. There is often a strong sense of jealously prevalent with this Pattern, which must be carefully watched. On the other hand their generosity (when it is based on the Ego) can be such that their own family will suffer so that a cause will succeed.

Between these two extremes, the Right Side Cup Pattern can be intoxicatingly alive and vibrant, which is suitable because their Forming Energy comes from the Eight, the number of the Harvest. We can have a Soul who is the life of the party here, yet privately there can be an almost sullen aspect that few will ever see. As with all "U" Patterns, the Five is of great importance, and again one of the great failings with this type is that they forget to tell others what they are doing, preferring to work in secret and covert ways. This can create disharmony and road blocks.

When this "secrecy mentality" works, it pays of handsomely, but when it goes wrong it goes badly wrong. As you may guess, this can be a rather extreme Pattern, but the fact is that most people affected opt for a compromise between their personal wishes and social rules. This greatly dilutes the energy of this (and all) Pattern/s. This is because the energy flows from today's individual have been greatly and outrightly interfered with by social and religious conditioning, to the point where many run on what I call "False" programs.

These are like "tape loops" in our heads that keep telling us what we should do. Rather than us taking charge and recording what we really wish to be and do in this life, we let the pre-programmed concept/s rule our hearts and minds. This reduces the natural efficiency of this Pattern.

This "tape loop" happens with just about everyone, so the effect of the Pattern is distorted, and this distortion warps the character, creating a death wish. Working then on the negative aspect of this specific Pattern, or the reducing energy within the chart, these people have emotionally unsatisfying lives and rarely keep their health beyond the age of sixty.

Many times people with this particular Pattern will be called on to confront themselves in the mirror of their personal experience, and if they feel a sense of failure as a result, few will have the courage to pick themselves up and change things. In my experience, this is a karmic Pattern, where much will be worked out.

The Law of KAMIT (Silence) needs to be strictly obeyed if the negative influences are to be kept at bay. This is really knowing what to say in any given situation, rather than not saying anything.

Even so, persistence will reap rewards, and many will find riches (both spiritual and material) later in life if they simply keep going with their chosen profession.

3-6-9 / 7-8-9 / 1-4-7 (Left Open) "U" Pattern:
Forming Energy: Two
Pivot Point: Five

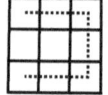

When we consider the lines used to make up this, or any, Pattern we will find the clues we need to understand it. Here we have the Line of Altruism (9-8-7) as the base line, with the Line of Mind at the top and the line of the Physical at the bottom. Clearly then, we are working in these areas.

The energy of the Two as the Forming Energy. What this indicates is that through altruistic ideals and pursuits, this individual will seek to unite the natural division between Mind and Body. Few people are truly connected within themselves. We have minds, emotions, bodies, but all of these live separate lives. For example, consider the case of when you want to go up to an attractive member of the opposite sex, but you don't!

Here your emotions said one thing, but your mind disagreed, thus your physical actions get tied up in doubt. We find with this Pattern that the person will be working on breaking through social restrictions, that which separates our mind actions from our physical actions. In other words, we have the chance to learn to become more instinctual.

However, society rejects instincts as a rule. People acting on impulse is seen as dangerous, unstable, and is frowned upon. The native will generally seek some less conflicting route to the inner freedom they seek. Often the individual will choose to do this via a sense of altruism and giving, getting involved in causes and charities. But in time we realize that only our inner instincts can lead us in the right direction, and that nothing else will suffice.

All the time the native with this Pattern will be trying to grasp the Two energy, which indicates perception of Beauty, but also duality and politics. We can see twe are attempting a difficult task. The Two is one of the most difficult energies to work with, because of its inherent instability, but if we approach things with persistence and application the energy can be mastered. Generally this is only done when the individual casts off double standards and double mindedness. Easier said than done.

In conclusion to the above we could say that the native affected with this Pattern will seek to be altruistic, but they will also need to understand the dual nature of things in this world. One example of this is the simple fact that if some one wants to give, someone else has to be able to receive. Even though the Spiritual Law states that to receive we have to give! A slight paradox for you to solve.

This Pattern encourages philosophic thought, which is fine if you are wealthy, but for those less fortunate it usually indicates a champagne taste with a beer pocket, and as a result a great deal of frustration. On the whole, a difficult and unsatisfying Pattern to work through. Most of your efforts in this direction will go unnoticed, but please consider that anonymity is the best training ground for learning true humility.

Humility is the key to working successfully through this configuration. It is the ability to be great within, yet common without. It also is the ability to recognize Soul in all you meet, or to see the greatness within another, even though you are meeting with the lowly.

As Humility is the most important of all virtues after patience, in the long run this is a crucial Pattern, but few actually complete its significance in one lifetime, often returning many times into its influence.

1-2-3 / 3-6-9 / 7-8-9 (Downwards) "U" Pattern:
Forming Energy: Four
Pivot Point: Five

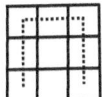

Gaining stability is what this Pattern represents, and this is what this aspect will be looking for in life. The problem is that the energy can be vaporous, and unable to come down to earth. We may find the consequences are to lose possessions, friends and employment through what appears to be an almost suicidal failure pattern. Even the attitude seems self defeating. But it just FEAR driving the bus.

This Pattern must be looked at closely, for it is crucial in understanding human nature. Much is hinged on the ability of the Querent to serve some cause. Only when the querent gets out of the self inflicted prison of fear, will the Pattern's positive aspects be realized. If you are looking to get something for nothing, the Pattern is a curse. In this immature state little happiness will ensue. If this is the case the advice is that self obsession in any form is inevitably destructive, and that any success met with will slip away until the principles and attitudes of service are firmly established in the mind and actions.

The mind is the problem with this aspect. Its own inventiveness is what defeats the Querent at every turn! As soon as we can imagine a good result, another inner part, the area of the Shadow, recognizes an equal and opposite negative outcome as being possible. As a result of this, deep, powerful moods and depressions can hold sway over the emotions, and the Querent may suffer a sense of abject powerlessness.

If so, the person affected by this Pattern can turn quite evil, especially if they have a vacant Line of Balance along the 1-5-9 Line. This would configure in this chart to a Soul needing power and recognition, which are the classic traits of the murderer and the dictator. Only a righteous heart can defeat this negative aspect.

Yet once balanced, the Pattern can be extraordinarily successful in this life, and very great wealth, be it spiritual of financial (or both) can fall upon them by what appears luck. This is not so, of course, for even the most apparent stroke of luck has been earned in some way.

Book of Number: Interpretations

As an overview, this Pattern has a tendency towards irresponsibility and evasive behavior, but this is generally because they are extremely self centered. Once an attitude of growth and expansion is realised, however, things just work out for this native, no matter what the situation.

Personality disorders are common, and hallucinogenic drugs are often sought after (rather than alcohol or barbiturates) as a way to resolve these. Of course, they only accentuate the problem.

The overall goal is Stability, in all its many aspects. But because of the fickle nature of this Pattern, the Jewish proverbof "Cash for luxuries, credit for necessities" should be applied.

"L" Patterns: There are FOUR "L" Patterns.

3-2-1/1-4-7 "L" Pattern

1-4-7/7-8-9 "L" Pattern

7-8-9/9-6-3 "L" Pattern

9-6-3/3-2-1 "L" Pattern

The "L" Patterns rarely represent an easy ride. They look like a boomerang, and they act like one. Whatever you send will come back to you. In the case of Karma, if you have worked hard, earned the respect of your peers, then these Patterns tend to indicate great success. Alternatively, they indicate a life of hardship until the individual learns to get above their petty concerns and see the bigger picture.

Think of them as Learner Plates, you are restricted until you gain the confidence of society to be set free to roam and do what you will. When combined with Vacant Squares (As they often are) there is usually an attraction fo organisations and big business. The preference is to run them, but those with this dual aspect make very good executives.

1-2-3 / 1-4-7 "L" Pattern:
Forming Energy: Any Vacant or Visible Trine
The 5-6-8-9 Minor Square in the Vacant Position.
Pivot Point: One

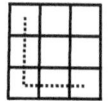

This Pattern holds a very creative urge within it. Yet there is a conflict where the individual often feels bound to the earth. This can lead to a tension where the person affected has unbridled enthusiasm and creativity, but little emotional and financial stability to go with it. The paradox is usually resolved by the person fulfilling their creative needs with a hobby, whilst still keeping a full time job. However if a person can combine inner and outer energies correctly, much financial and spiritual gain can be made.

The areas in which this Pattern works successfully are those involved in "hands on" art work, like pottery, sculpture, woodwork and the like. Also traditional crafts are a strong contender for the fulfillment stakes in this instance, and people with this aspect often find that working in these areas is not only satisfying, but that they generally produce extremely fine specimens of their craft.

The energy flows in this Pattern are focused on the One, which stresses such things as individuality, projects and single mindedness, but it also can stress the negative aspect, such as stubbornness, vanity and vagueness. However, if there is undue weight on any specific number in the Pattern, there will be an effect in accordance with the quality of that number as well. (See "Noumenal Weight")

Of course, if the Pattern is broken with a missing Number, that particular energy will also be drawn in. As an example, if there was a missing Seven the individual might be particularly short with others, for they will tend to have little connection with humanity. (and may well disregard their own as well with things like drug abuse and by attempting projects that have no reasonable chance of success) This occurs frequently with the artistic type, who often ends up poor and unrecognized because they refused, or didn't know how, to shape their work so that it was either accessible or acceptable to others.

As with all "L" Patterns, there is trial, but with the gaining of self confidence these trials become but learning curves and stepping stones. Confidence is the key, and with this specific Pattern a certain amount of breaking away from traditional values and thought is necessary for inner peace. We need confidence in ourselves to survive the isolation period this breaking away entails. Sometimes sheer persistence will do the trick. In the long run we all have to develop confidence, don't we?

Self assurance is then the watchword if you are the keeper of this aspect. Focus on your trade, master it, and discover real confidence.

Book of Number: Interpretations

1-4-7 / 7-8-9 Pattern:
Forming Energy: Any Vacant or Visible Trines
The 2-3-5-6 Minor Square.
Pivot Point: Seven

Here is a Pattern that has a very particular Karma to carry, for here the one so burdened must bear the terrible weight of Freedom. This might not seem so bad a trial, but when you think that this Soul must learn to fill their life with their own value and their own sense of purpose, we can begin to see that this can be a lonely path to travel. No-one can give ourselves the confidence to do this but ourselves.

Without the necessary belief in oneself, the Querent with this aspect tends to tread the path of compromise and doubt their whole life long, believing themselves failures and worse than this, there is the tendency of seeing others as important while they themselves are worthless. How is this problem solved? Generally this attitude is only resolved by mastering a trade or study, and thus we find professional qualifications can be very important to these people. However, this training can lead to narrow mindedness and cynicism for some.

The ability to open up and trust is always very important, but here it is even more so. It is odd, but there is a tendency to be suspicious and somewhat obsessed with personal privacy with this aspect. Mostly this only occurs when the individual is working out of the negative cycle of doubt and failure consciousness.

Doubt is fine when it is a tool of discrimination, but not when it is the scalpel that cuts others and/or ourselves. The old Simon and Garfunkel song that goes "I am a rock, an island" fits this type. But only when they are at this stage of their evolution! We must remember that all Patterns and Aspects have what appears to be a coat of many changing colours, but it is really just a reflection of the inner change. There is a natural evolutionary process here.

Every apparent negative has a simple cure. In order to move through this specific "rock" mentality we find that compassion for others will melt down the walls and allow the light of day into the terrible isolation.

Much of the problem with this Pattern, and with human relationships, comes from misunderstanding freedom. The Querent can falsely believe that loneliness and isolation gives freedom from the suffering of social interaction. This is incorrect, freedom comes from an involvement in life. True detachment, or spiritual freedom, comes from the ability to be totally involved with a situation, but detached from the circumstances.

This Pattern has both high aspirations and an appreciation of the commonness we all share. Which is good when it is balanced, yet often these aspirations push us to escape the mundane, or "Tic Tock" as Stuart Wilde calls it. As a result we often find a driving sense of ambition can overtake the sensibilities of these folk, causing them to consider others as worthless cannon fodder. People are here purely to serve their needs. This "super salesman" sort of personality can have outward charm and connivance, but at heart we will find a hermit-like tendency evidencing itself here. Too much intellectual activity is one form of this.

Trust is a major key in resolving the problems of this Pattern, but a cautious trust, if this be possible. Ideally marriage to someone with a strong Line of Compassion (3-5-7 Line) (or alternatively, through dedication to an ideal developing this Line within yourself) is a solution to the terrible burden of freedom.

Focused on the Seven, the Pattern often gives an articulate, though difficult nature, with a strong tendency towards learning and application to the noble and somewhat metaphysical sciences such as Physics, Quantum Mechanics, Philosophy, etc.

These people need to lighten up as a rule, for they tend to take themselves and life too seriously, and yet because they do take things very seriously, a great deal of understanding of the human nature can result. We see this Pattern in the chart of truly fine writers, if not in their Birth chart, often in their Name chart, or with the combination of the two.

7-8-9 / 3-6-9 Pattern:
Forming Energy: Vacant or Visible Trines
The 1-2-4-5 Minor Square
Pivot Point: Nine

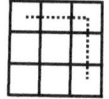

Based on the Nine, this Pattern is ruled by the Law of Silence. Without Inner Silence those affected by these vibrations will tend to have a hard time with life. They will have great and noble ideas, but somehow, and often without any apparent reason why, it will be that no avenue will open up for them to exercise their lofty aspirations.

Many things will come to a climax in this life, as the Pattern indicates a certain amount of karmic run-off. The native may experience the effect of many lifetimes in this single one. This often means several partners, changing jobs, and shifting goals throughout life, which would be fine but these natives are not gypsies and tend to prefer a more settled existence.

The person with this Pattern likes to stay at home and have a warm meal each night on the table, which can make their life quite difficult, considering all the changes that usually follow this aspect.

Things are most calm when the native works hard at keeping lines of communication open between all parties they are involved with. It is a little difficult to reconcile the need for inner silence with the idea of outer communication, but this in effect is what is called for here. Yet the combination of Altruism (7-8-9 Line) and Mental focus (3-6-9 Line) tends to keep these folk somewhat distant from others.

Few partners can understand or fully accept their odd coolness to things, and so they don't often remain partners.

Inner Silence will succeed in the long run, however, for instead of seeking to justify their actions, with simple silence the native will go about their business and find they can LISTEN to what people say. Suddenly all the coolness they have demonstrated to others will make them popular. Everything go more smoothly if others feel they are allowed to talk and have some imput, which is an essential characteristic of communication.

Keep in mind that there is a Law of Reversed Effort at work here! Don't ask me why, but as soon as this type is happy to be alone and not be bothered by anyone, people come knocking at their door. The easiest way to understand this is to imagine you are walking along a piece of wood. It is easy to do when it is on the ground, but if this same piece of wood was suspended over a thousand foot chasm, it would suddenly become difficult.

Inner Silence keeps things in perspective and in close focus. It also means that things are approached on a one to one basis. It has the mental effect of keeping the piece of wood on the ground, so to speak. This is the easy way to succeed with life, and people with this Pattern have the chance of doing just this, succeed. It is a common Pattern with scientists, statisticians, anyone who has to deal with fitting variables into appropriate holes.

3-6-9 / 1-2-3 Pattern:
Forming Energy: Vacant or Visible Trines
The 4-5-7-8 Minor Square in the Vacant Position
Pivot Point: Three

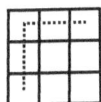

This is perhaps the easiest of the "L" Patterns, except that the native can sometimes have great difficulty relating to others on a level they understand. They are often the "professor" type, absent minded but with lofty ideals, but who tends to need the security of an institution to feel at ease. And this is fine. When they find their feet, they can be creative forces to be reckoned with.

With the focus on the Three, creativity will be highlighted. But there is another side to the Three few recognize, and this is the business aspect. If a creative Three can master their sense of perspective they can become extremely competent business people. Thus these folk are capable of generating an excellent income, but the focus must be on sharing or else they will internalize, and even exhibit miserly behaviour.

Brad Pitt has this Pattern, born 18 Dec 1963. It is a classic example of creative freedom being combined with financial success

These people often carry out valuable research work, finding discoveries that benefit the race, but often they also have the habit of getting lost in their own discoveries. Thus they need a ruling body over them in some form, to keep the direction of the project, school, or whatever moving along in a straight line. Inner discipline is essential here, otherwise the natural enthusiasm and curiosity of this aspect can take them out of the bounds of common sense.

Real and lasting balance is obtained by coming to understand, and being able to relate to the common man, so natives with this Pattern should take the time to talk to people. Not on high esoteric subjects, but about the weather, babies and who will win the next election. These type of "common" activities will ground them, and allow a greater creative input into their lives. Is this is a paradox? What I mean is that by getting both feet on the ground, this type will find it easier walking from point to point, whereas otherwise they may barely have one toe scraping the dust as they go along.

One important note, if someone with this Pattern has Higher Order numbers (10, 11, 12 or 13) strongly featured in their Birth or Name additions, they may well be inclined to devote themselves to spiritual study, and they would be well suited for this. For example: Brad Pitt's name is a 29 into 11, and so there is a distinct possibility he will undertake some sort of education or social role later in life.

"T" Patterns: There are Four "T" Patterns:

3-6-9/6-5-4 "T" Pattern

9-8-7/8-5-2 "T" Pattern

7-4-1/4-5-6 "T" Pattern

1-2-3/2-5-8 "T" Pattern

The "T" Pattern has a certain sense of "certain-T" about it. This represents the intersection of two lines of significance in a person's chart and it has a somewhat emphatic energy.

In many ways, this influence draws a line in the sand in personal and professional relationships, and people tend to know where they stand with those who are strong in this energy. Or, of course, they are very weak willed and vacillate over every decision and detail.

The natural meticulousness can invert and become pedantic, while the careful assessment of external factors can flip to an internal judgement of everyone's failings. It is very much an "all in" or "all out" energy as far as the positive or negative characteristics go.

Because it is so polarized, we tend to find people affected by this influence doing the "Duck and cover". They simply avoid things in an attempt to keep the social wheels rolling. The real secret to learn with this Aspect is COURTESY. Simple courtesy will resolve almost all the abrasive aspects of the "T" Patterns energy.

As the person begins to understand courtesy, they realize the real way forward internally and externally is with acceptance of things as they are. When the internal dialogue moves into into a point of observation and patience, these become incredibly influential and powerful aspects.

3-6-9 / 4-5-6 Upright "T" Pattern:
Drawing Energy: Six
Pivot Point: Six

The old saying goes "copied him to a Tee". The energy here has a sort of mimicry about it, so the principle of Right Association is very impotant. People with this Pattern will naturally be drawn to the higher circles, the right club, the right social crcles, etc. At an early stage they may even appear to be social climbers. It is more they like things to be right, and be around people who understand this

There is a sort of perfection found in the Pattern. A person with this aspect can put their mind wholly and solely on the business at hand. This means they can achieve great success.

The prevalent Six energy gives this Pattern a certain sense of spirituality, and we find this concept of higher thought as much in the housewife as the Guru, and so this should not be taken as a reason to join religious orders. There is a tendency towards philosophy, and in general a desire to seek a view higher than that of the common man.

The capping line (3-6-9) is the Line of the Mental power. If in the Balanced aspect this lends a particular emphasis on the strength of mind these natives possess. The 4-5-6 Line is one of willed achievement, not of luck, so the person involved must very much choose their own course of action. For example, they are unlikely to get financial windfalls unless they have worked for them in some way or another. However, results might not come directly from efforts, but from circumstances generated by their connections. Some might call it luck, but really, Right Association is the key to this Pattern.

If the individual with this aspect is clear regarding their goals, then there is not much that cannot be achieved. Conversely, if the person affected is confused (and this will happen if they are vain or pretentious) then they will constantly be seeking to "juggle" some sort of balance in their lives. But when you start int he wrong direction, the energy keeps driving you.. All the energy of achievement now degenerates into an abject fear of failure, which can only be resolved when the individual affected learns to cut away social and emotional taboos, and recognize what is obvious. How do we recognize the obvious? Simple common sense. This distills the querulous nature, and gives the querent a chance to refocus on their lives and purpose. Then all becomes clearer.

These natives must be careful of what they express, what thoughts they think, and especially with what they pray for, for they have an uncanny knack of manifesting these things. A careful consideration of any new project will reap huge rewards, but life has a tendency of testing the person with this aspect. So many times you may feel that you are being pushed to make a decision. It is important to take your time, and perhaps learn to use the word "maybe" rather than yes or no.

The person with this Pattern often needs to learn how not to feel rushed or pressured by outside circumstances. If they can do this, which is actually rising above the human emotional element that saturates this world, they can give great service to mankind simply by being pillars of achievement and balance.

This Pattern has a curious "I am a majority of one against the crowd" energy to it. One person who masters their circumstances does more for the human race than all the so-called charities could dream of doing. If one man can see another's worth clearly, then emulating this can be the inspiration for changing his entire life for the better.

Great harm can be done indulging in greed. Greed is not good for balance, and entire fortunes have been lost again and again by successful people overstepping the mark. Find your line, do not cross it, and you will do fine.

7-8-9 / 2-5-8 "T" Pattern:
Drawing Energy: Eight
Pivot Point: Eight

A powerful combination for illumination and clarity, but only when the individual so affected has a higher purpose to attain. Otherwise a person with this aspect can get caught up in a world of personality worship, money, politics and the need for power. The Energy focus is based on the Eight, and this is the ideal Pattern for the philanthropic benefactor in the years 2000. On the reverse, though, the Pattern can encourage miserly behavior and short sightedness.

The Line of Emotion (2-5-8) actually represents the ideal of combining perception (2) with practicality (8) via communication (5), while the 7-8-9 Line of Wisdom and Altruism is at its best when bringing high ideals to earth. We can easily see how this can be a powerful combination for the building of noble endeavors. However, it is ever the case that in the building of great ideals that power and influence can corrupt the original vision, as was the case in Nazi Germany.

Hitler appealed to the mass sentiment of the nation (which equates to the 2-5-8 Line in Numerology) yet also drew on the resources of psychics and other higher forces (9-8-7 Line) and raised Germany out of depression. Of course, Hitler wanted more. Fortunately he was defeated, but it was his own bad judgment and loss of focus that gave the allies the room to bring about his downfall. Russia, reknown for its powerful psychics, was his millstone. Few will note this in the history books, but Hitler was defeated psychically before his armies were.

Focus is everything with this Pattern, as it is with all the "T" Patterns. This focus is not concentration but a resting within the object of contemplation for a long enough period until all things become clear. I wrote about this in "The Three Moon Principle". This is best explained by the motto "Patience and Observation bring Understanding, which brings Right Action, which brings Successful Completion".

The 9-8-7/8-5-2 Pattern is quite difficult to master, for with its main energy being the Eight this requires the Soul affected to comprehend their inner worlds, and to be able to bring this back in some manner to the outer world of man. Generally few people can reach so far within themselves, and usually get hooked on the finance/money principle attached to the Eight vibration. If so the karmic intensity that results will destabilize them, and lessen their ability to keep both feet on the ground.

We find that the general lesson with this aspect is to realize a degree of far sighted practicality. See the stars, but realize you need a rocket to get there. This practicality should have the general principle of service to a higher cause within it, otherwise we find that the native here tends to become too power motivated. The reverse of this is when the individual simply lives in a world of their own, not bothering to develop lines of communication with others, thus living in a dream world rather than facing the harsh reality about them as a result.

1-4-7 / 4-5-6 "T" Pattern:
Forming Energy: Four
Pivot Point: Four

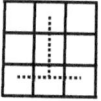

Practicality and enterprise are the hallmarks of this Pattern. It represents an ability to achieve a great measure of physical success. This is one of the most stable of Patterns, but the inherent stability itself can trap the native into dogmatic beliefs and narrow minded behavior.

Single minded, sometimes bloody minded, these people can cleave through obstacles like water. They would like to have nothing to do with the armies of bureaucrats, the lies of politicians and generally resent the moribund control of law makers. In other words, they can create a lot of friction and hidden enemies, yet somehow these people have a habit of succeeding against all odds. This type is a dying breed, unfortunately, for the grip of law and bureaucracy is becoming so vice-like that few can escape it, let alone combat it.

This Pattern represents Thor's Hammer, and those possessed with it's power can batter down the greatest of obstacles if they have a mind for it. It is very hard to defeat anyone who has a deep belief in themselves. Even if they lose they swear by the adage, "Live to fight another day".

In the negative aspect, this type cannot be advised or told when enough is enough, and will run themselves into bankruptcy over a ten dollar argument. If well balanced, however, their perception is clear enough to avoid, rather than confront, and to use subterfuge rather than

Law to win their goals. You need to learn the art of avoidance (which is actually the beginning of detachment) in order to avoid the locking of horns in situations where both combatants will die.

When these people learn to base their energy on the Six, or inspirational energy, they will discover a greater involvement with living. By doing this the energy they wield will become far more flexible, and life will take on a higher purpose. They are often involved in the movement of funds and goods for the benefit of the whole.

The most negative aspect is the tendency to gather a "clan" by manipulating the hates and fears of the followers. The Klu Klux Clan is a classic example of this, where the leaders twist noble ideals into brutish sentiment.

The positive aspect is where the individual affected becomes a ray of hope for those under the thumb of oppressive rule. We might look at Robin Hood as the role model here.

The general goal is to learn how to see and react to the obvious, and the balanced person with this aspect will have learned how to curb their temper in order to find a more effective way to deal with life situations.

1-2-3 / 2-5-8 "T" Pattern:
Forming Energy: Two
Pivot Point: Two

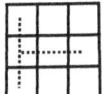

A very special Pattern for those involved with creative activity. Here the spiritual beauty of the imagination is brought to earth, usually through art work (but it could be through any medium) where people feel uplifted and inspired by the efforts of the artist.

The negative aspect is an overly emotional nature that runs rampant, ruining the finer appreciation of what is subtle and gentle, and creating a disturbing picture of anger. Anger is the characteristic difficulty with this Pattern, especially righteous anger based on the principle of "artists privilege", as similar to the poets license.

The positive aspect is where the person affected comes to understand the ebb and flow of life's moods, and learns to remain unaffected by outer circumstances whilst they go about their business.

The focus of the energy is on the Two, which gives an appreciation of beauty, but also a tendency to be double minded. This Pattern will occure a lot in the years 2000 and the curious outward creativity and inward doubt will forge some odd personalities in the Art world. This Pattern is capable of intimate sharing. It is not selfish with emotions, and so those affected have little difficulty finding a partner. Indeed the only problem is that they generally find too many, and old age catches up to find them alone. Better to have loved and lost, as they say.

Book of Number: Interpretations

Satisfaction with work is usually a better aphrodisiac for this type, and often they find enough recognition in their lives to allow sufficient remuneration for quite a comfortable retirement.

This Pattern needs to avoid conflict with power conscious individuals and overly intense Souls, but they are drawn to them all the same, and like the moth to the flame they often get their wings burnt. However, the powerful are often draw to this type as well, and so the meeting and dealing with the power consciousness is often something an individual with this vibration must work through in this lifetime.

We might sum up this odd tango by saying that Artists always need money, but money needs the artists even more. The creativity and form the artists can bring to the powerful is a far more valuable commodity than the money they hold. And in the years 2000 many artists will come to understand this.

Overall, this is a good building Pattern when the effect is harmonious, but it becomes a destroying aspect when it is not. The effect is similar to the idea of the game "Snakes and Ladders", where we find that even in apparently disastrous circumstances, things can still work through to a healthy conclusion.

The idea with this Pattern is to retain your focus in order to see yourself through the rough patches. More than anything, the native with this aspect needs to understand that the point of creativity and art is to discover and develop STRUCTURE. In simpler terms, this is a practical understanding that big things come from little things. Grand projects are the result of many small details correctly connected together. It should be noted that the "T" Patterns all share the common Five, and so everything they do will be hinged on communication in some way or another.

The Motto here is "Every big thing is made of any little things. It is what every little thing must always remember, and what every big thing must never forget."

"H" Patterning: Only two "H" Patterns exist.

1-2-3/2-5-8/7-8-9 "H" Pattern:

3-6-9/6-5-4/1-4-7 "H" Pattern

When you see an "H" Pattern in a chart you immediately look for issues with Power, Money and Deceit. These energies always flow around government and big business.

1-2-3 / 2-5-8 / 7-8-9 "H" Pattern:
Forming Energy: Six and Four

The Upright "H" Pattern is characteristic of the builder, and whether this relates to building houses or an understanding of life, or an understanding of human emotions. It still comes back to an attitude where we realize that the only way to build the house is to place this brick on top of that brick. Thus we find that the most valuable attitude these folk can develop is a step by step, methodical nature.

In the positive aspect these people are pensive and considered, and often wonder at the shallowness of the majority of people. As a rule we will not see them meandering through their lives, but walking clearly in the direction of success. Generally they like to plan, and this alone often sees them through the rough spots. Those with this Pattern in the positive aspect are draw to the energy of the Six and Four, which is Intuition and Solidarity, an odd mix that works well for this type.

Ideally, they make wonderful partners for creative types, for as a partner they are able to shape their husband/wife's creative energy into useful projects. This seems a major role for "H" people, that of building the picture from behind the scenes. And this suits them well, for they are not showy, disliking the spotlight as a rule. They are like the moon, glowing happily in the reflected glory of their mate.

As parents they are generally excellent and as teachers they excel, for they seem to have an inherent kindness and patience that endears those under their charge to them.

In the negative aspect this Pattern can be shiftless and exceedingly lazy, expecting to be supported by the world. They will use their planning ability to extract services and cash from others, never intending to produce a fair return for the efforts exerted for their sake.

In all a balanced Pattern, but remember: Too much balance can be the cause of little or no result in a lifetime, simply because there can be so little to fight against that the individual just cruises along, allowing the world to carry him or her. As such, this indicates that a sense of purpose is very necessary for these people, crucial in fact, if they are to lead productive lives.

3-6-9 / 4-5-6 / 1-4-7 "H" Pattern
Forming Energy: Two and Eight

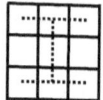

We have a Pattern that is very fiery, and those with this indicated in their Chart are very likely to burn out from exhaustion before they will give up on a project or goal. The ability to recognize the limits of oneself and the limits of a project, then, is an important attribute to develop. It is important to gather around you people you trust.

The energy from the Mental Line (3-6-9) and the Physical Line (1-4-7) meet along the achievement axis (4-5-6) giving these natives enthusiasm and oddly, a curious gullibility. It is a sort of innocent wisdom, however, and for some reason they are well looked after with their affairs as a rule. But this is only if they do not get caught up in the negative habit patterns of gossip, drugs, and small mindedness. If they do all their good fortune will reverse, creating absolute havoc in their lives.

Generally they are dynamos, often driving themselves and friends to the edge of exhaustion with the new ideas and schemes that keep coming forward. They need to learn discrimination, and focus only on one subject at a time, with the view to completion.

The Forming energies of the Two and the Eight gives a curious weight to bear, that of combining an artistic appreciation with a sense of worldly and financial success. Of course, this generally propels them into the higher echelons of society, (even if this is just as a caterer) where these people are then sustained by contacts with like minds. This contact is the thing that makes them irrevocably happy.

They will pursue the finer things in whatever form they come, and so these natives need to learn not to be ruled by fashion, but to learn to see into the depths of humanity, and to work towards the lasting traits and qualities of life. If they develop ideals and ethics worthy of a position of respect and excellence, life goes easier for them, for this type needs the genuine respect of others to feel certain about themselves.

Normally this would be a negative circumstance, but these people need to have others around them to assist with the achievement of goals, for they are not solitary persons. The display of high moral behaviour will attract the particular type of persons who are naturally attracted to them, and knit them together. Because of this trait this Pattern is suited to those in public office and community service where an active role is required.

Typically, stories of King Arthur and the Knights of the Round table fit in this category. Noble ideals, impossible goals, and a desire to lift the universe to a higher plane.

Book of Number: Interpretations

"X" Patterns: There are TWO "X" Patterns

3-5-7/1-5-9 "X" Pattern:
2-5-8 / 4-5-6 "X" Pattern:

These are extraordinarily complex energies, often associated with dire consequences, martyrdom, and a need to feel the presence of God in daily life. Unfortunately, for many this is the pretense of God as the human foibles crowd out the noble aspirations.

3-5-7 / 1-5-9 "X" Pattern:
Pivot Point: Five

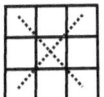

The Martyr's Cross

These two intersecting lines indicate what appears to be opposites meeting. The Line of Compassion and Service (3-5-7) and the Line of Success (1-5-9) would not at first appear to make very good bedfellows, but at their highest levels they are intrinsically comfortable with and supportive of each other. The idea is that true success is based on service and compassion, but here we are talking of inner success, and not the drive to compete with and win over your brother.

The true paradox is having the aspects of compassion and success apart from each other! Think about this. So often we see people who want to help others, but only get trodden on by the system, whereas those who are ruthless seem to be rewarded. However, when we consider that one has friends, the other enemies, we might see this as a balancing out. The fact is that neither energy is balanced until it comes to terms with its opposite, at which point we find they are in fact two ends of the same stick!!!

This can take some time for the native with this aspect to come to terms with, and generally we see quite an inner battle taking place when this Pattern appears in a chart. It is a difficult Aspect. The native tends to want to assert themselves and achieve a recognition to the point where it becomes an obsession. And yet they want to hide behind a mask of insecurity and shyness. In the end we see that either excessive self aggrandizement or self denigration are both aspects of the unstable Ego, or that which we commonly term Vanity.

The balancing out of this concept of success verses suffrage is what is indicated in this Pattern, and this can be a very challenging role to play as it requires a recognition of our true inner self worth, yet also a recognition of our inherent failings. As a note, it is because of our sense of failure that we internalize, yet this is also the spur for most of our growth.

Perhaps we should look at an ancient teaching. The old Tibetan phrase that gives a solution to the paradox of this Pattern goes "What use has God for your success or your strength? It has enough of this. What It wants are your failures and your weakness, for only through giving these to God do we discover the door to truth within us." In the end, the path here is an act of surrender into the Love within us.

Not many will grasp this. If an inner balance is achieved with this Pattern, the individual can expect to find great understanding and clarity coming into their lives, and great freedom of action. If not, the person will feel constrained and tense their entire life, blaming the world for their problems, and becoming more and more internalized as the years go by.

Naturally we would prefer to avoid this, but this Pattern just puts us through the hoops until we come to understand that our own success must not be at the expense of others. If this person deceptively sells a car with a bad motor, within a few years they will buy another with exactly the same problem, until they learn honesty and service are the best policy.

Curiously this Pattern is drawn to unconventional employment, and often find themselves shifting from profession to profession as they go through life, which only multiplies the difficulties. Yet if they persist with their inner dream, they find their problems become their greatest resource. Nietzsche said "All great men are clouds, until they form and condense their wisdom down on man."

When the Martyr's Cross appears in your chart, remember that your job is NOT to become a martyr. It is all about handing over your insecurity and weakness, and rising above fear and self-loathing.

2-5-8 / 4-5-6 "X" Pattern:
Pivot Point: Five

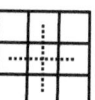

The Messiah

This is known as the Messiah Pattern, an obvious reflection on the bearing of the cross, but also because these people often seem to live a burdened life, full of self recrimination, self pity and concern, always wondering if they are good enough by worldly standards. It tends to combine to give an impulse to sacrifice self in order to save them from their own "sins".

The often answer hese inner doubts by trying to convince themselves (and as many others as they can) that they are important people who deserve to be looked up to. These natives will also associate themselves with causes and groups that appear to be doing some sort of good, but more often than not are fairly superficial in their attempts to bring about lasting change. When they get it right, however, they really do a good job, an example being the Red Cross! The symbol of the cross is a very old one indeed, and most suitable to be used by the Red Cross.

Book of Number: Interpretations

The individual must learn to lift the game, to recognise that good and evil, right and wrong, are subjective interpretations. By placing self responsibility as the core message for ethics, the energy here stops chasing it's own tail, and starts to focus. This is the only lasting "cure" for the doubts and afflictions that come with this energy.

The cross is not a specifically Christian symbol as many suppose, but one that is universal. It signifies the meeting of ways, the combining of the higher and lower, and the conflict between the individual and the group, among other possible meanings.

These can all be applied to this Pattern, for it is the cross that marks out the meeting point between achievement and the emotions, or should I say, the Balancing Point between these two.

All motivators know that to achieve, an individual needs to be EMOTIONALLY excited in some way or another, but the problem is that the emotional element is the one area where we are most fickle. Our emotional scale changes moment to moment, and cannot be relied upon, and this is what the individual is working on with this Pattern: Emotional balance. Right Discrimination is the best, and only, long term solution.

Here we learn that the only way to complete a task successfully is to balance our emotions. Balance is what preserves the strength needed to complete the course. Balance involves gaining an oversight of a task before we embark on the journey.

This Pattern tends to be somewhat painful. We tend to butt our heads against a lot of brick walls before we understand its message. The real key, even when learning to master the vibration, is to take things as they come, and to try not to rush matters through.

The other major problem with this Pattern is in the Vanity area. The focus on the Five seems to generate a need to communicate, but often we find we far prefer to talk about our own personal discoveries, or personal successes, rather than listen to another's. As a result the native pushes people away, and often suffers a growing disinterest in those around them. The result here is a tendency to cut off personal relationships rather than negotiate a settlement.

Obsessive natures run rampant with this Pattern. It must be carefully watched, especially in areas of religious obsession.

When the vibration is mastered these people can be the heart of a spiritual and/or physical organization, for they will have learned the art of balanced discrimination, which qualifies them for the management and trust of large groups, companies, and teachings.

Before this time, however, the native will find they are best employed simply learning how to best get on with others.

Book of Number: Interpretations

"Y" Patterns

"Y" Patterns are effectively an "X" Pattern with a missing numeral. Essentially, take the general interpretation for the relevant "X" Pattern, and alter it with the significance indicated by the "missing" number. There are Eight in all.

While all these "Y" Patterns are really variations to the "X" Patterns, they have very different effects. The latter tends towards karmic intensity, while the "Y" Patterns tend towards a solution for this.

These are classed as Minor Patterns, but they add a very real and specific "colour" to a chart when they occur, particularly when they appear in an Overlay Matrix.

1-5-9 / 3-5 (Missing Seven)

A "Y" Pattern tends to accent the solitary nature of the Querent, often making this Soul a lone wolf. However, it should be remembered that there can be other influences at work, such as a wife who is strong in the number Seven, or perhaps the Querent's name might have a strong Seven representation. This would modify the energy, even though the tendency to like being alone will still be there. Even so we must always understand that the full picture is only given when all the major influences taken into account.

In time the "Lone Wolf" idea modifies to a high degree of inner strength and self reliance. This type is good for initiating new projects, and seeing through the fog of details to bring clarity to a project or cause.

3-5-7 / 1-5 (Missing Nine)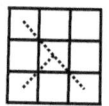

A "Y" Pattern with a missing Nine would indicate an general absence of consideration in regard actions taken. Also there is a tendency to fall into humanitarian causes that have high ideals, but little practicality. These people often to talk a lot, but say very little of note or worth. This indicates a Silica deficiency. A degree of patience is called for with this Pattern evident, for things will not fall into place easily until the person discovers the inner silence and power of the Nine force in themselves.

At this time the mental focus will sharpen, and these folk can be of great use to themselves and those around them.

Book of Number: Interpretations

1-5-9 / 5-7 (Missing Three)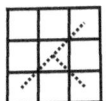

A missing Three can be quite frustrating, for the person will tend to feel driven towards projects they cannot complete, and as a result suffer a degree of doubt about their abilities. This type needs to learn persistence in the realization of their goals. They should also focus on communicating their desires and the perceived outcomes with relationships and business ventures that they would like to come about, but only to those most likely to assist them with a positive outcome.

As a result, discrimination is generally a lesson that needs to be learned here. When the individual grasps this, they also learn to adjust their expectations to fit the plausible reality they can expect to come about. In doing so, they are more able to manifest their dreams.

3-5-7 / 5-9 Missing One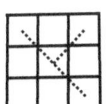

A missing One can give a sort of aimlessness to the native affected. It is very important to focus, and be able to take care of oneself. There are generally good intentions here, but often little actual application towards achieving the desired goals. The road to hell is paved with those same good intentions. FOCUS is the message, focus and act. Drugs and alcohol will only accent the negatives, giving a lack of motivation. Despite all this, these people tend to gravitate to high positions in bureaucracies.

They like to lead, but not in an external sense. It is more the power behind the throne they will covet. If the Two is prevalent in any of the other aspects within their combined name and birth charts, the individual will probably be drawn to political matters, and even move into the political service in some manner. There is an ability to look after oneself here, but the native must be careful that this is not at the cost of another's happiness.

4-5-6 / 5-8 Missing Two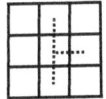

The missing Two may lead to a general disregard for things of subtlety. This can create a single minded attitude, where intolerance and racial hatred could well be a part. (if the native carries a negative value) This is especially significant if the entire 1-2-3 Plane is Vacant, for these persons' would then be plagued with an apparently unreasonable desire to create something important, but have no obvious means or ability to do so. This can make them very bad tempered.

The other aspect of the Missing Two can be a deep appreciation, and even a fanatical devotion to the arts. In the negative value this can create a sort of "collector madness" and a blindness to what is true quality. The native in this respect must look to refining their aggressive instincts, and seek a more balanced outlook in life. Physical exercise is often essential for the well being of these folk.

2-5-8 / 4-5 Missing Six

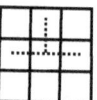

A missing Six gives a somewhat critical nature, and a "believe it when I see it" attitude. It can be useful if you are a builder. If cynicism does not rule these people, they lead very down to earth and practical lives, but are often somewhat insular. They often find themselves alone and at a loose end relationship-wise, usually because of their caustic wit and abrasive personality. If balanced and comfortable with themselves these people are invaluable do-it-yourself people who often manage to invent lots of interesting little gadgets.

These people have the possibility of the Vacant Line of the Mind, which lends them to deep philosophical thinking. This energy is usually employed seeking to relate the psychic to the physical world in some manner, either to prove or debunk its validity.

Generally we find these folk with a strong intuitive sense, but many times they will ignore it for a more "logical" way of life. They often need to loosen up and have some fun, for they are usually dour by nature.

4-5-6 / 2-5 Missing Eight

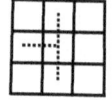

A missing Eight is probably one of the more fortunate of the "Y" Patterns, for this can indicate a life generally free of karmic debt. But of course the reverse is always true and it might mean a lifetime when a lot of Karma will have to be worked off! Either way, generally these folk rise over the obstacles, and make mileage out of misery. If there is a Vacant 7-8-9 Line the Soul will be greatly influenced by their higher thoughts, and often seek to assist others to achieve goals. They are great and practical people who do well as primary or secondary producers at whatever level they feel comfortable, but the important point is that they like to build in some manner.

There is a tendency to be pedantic, and to try and drive a point home with a sledgehammer when a gentle push was all that was required. Otherwise these folk are generally fair minded and considerate, but obstinate when resisted.

It is important to be careful about obsessions with security and money here, as these traits can pervert and distort the clarity with which these people see the world. You can get "Money Sickness" where even people and friends are seen as a value relating to the dollar.

2-5-8 / 5-6 Missing Four

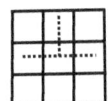

A missing Four is a sort of "floating" Pattern. These people are often not grounded in any way at all, and remain buffeted all their lives with strong emotions and beliefs that well up constantly within them. Often they can be the "Rebel without a Cause" type, but when they learn to balance out the physical practicality of living life with the often rather extreme ideals they dream of, then they get along fine.

Those with this aspect can be the life of the party when they are out and about, but at home they can be quite sullen and difficult to understand. Still, they tend to be kind hearted, even if somewhat reserved in demeanour. Alcohol can be a stumbling block in particular for this type.

Book of Number: Interpretations

"Z" Patterns

There are Four "Z" (pronounced ZEE) Patterns, as follows:

3-6-9/9-5-1/1-4-7 The Great "Z" Pattern:

9-6-3/3-5-7/7-4-1 The Reversed "Z" Pattern

1-2-3/3-5-7/7-8-9 The Turned "Z" Pattern

3-2-1/1-5-9/9-8-7 The Reversed, Turned "Z" Pattern

When this Pattern is present, it generally signifies some sort of Spiritual Opening (Mudra) is occuring in the psyche of the individual.

These Patterns are rare, and highly significant when they occur. Again, it depends on the consciousness of the individual, but when you see these in a chart, it is saying there is tremendous opportunity for awakening, growth or achievment possible.

3-6-9 / 1-5-9 / 1-4-7 Great "Z" Pattern:

Forming Energies: Two and Eight

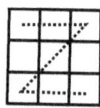

This is the Great "Z". It is one of the most powerful influences in the Noumenal Chart, yet few live up to its potential. Within its inner levels it invokes the flow of the Spiritual "stuff" through the mind and emotions, and then into this physical plane.

The Forming Energies of the Two and Eight come from the emotional level with this Pattern, and it is in the area of the emotions that much of the purification and testing of the individual will be done. This is not for punishment, but so that the individual will have the strength to carry the vibration this Pattern brings. Specifically the Two vibration will test the individuals determination, and the Eight vibration will work to develop their perseverance and selflessness.

There are few who could truly master this energy, for it requires not just the ability to rise above earthly concerns, but to also play an active role in this world. A difficult task, but not impossible. The emotions will be tested again and again, and so inner balance and discipline are of utmost importance if the individual is to rise to the full promise of this Pattern.

Both outer and inner power can be achieved with this aspect in your chart, but power can be explosive when in the hands of one not yet ready for it. Great care must be taken, for the very potential here can create real problems, especially in the area of the Ego. When the power aspect goes wrong we find the native here can cripple and isolate themselves in what can be a very deep, abiding introversion.

Something quite curious, if we overlay the name Christopher Columbus with the founding date of the United States, we find this "Z" Pattern

Little else can be said, except that the Soul so affected must find time each day for contemplation, for only by dwelling on their inner resource can they hope to gain the perspective and clarity they need to survive this "power of no-power". This is not a paradox, for the energy, though all powerful, cannot be successfully directed by the human will, and so we can only be channels for its blessings.

The interesting thing about blessings is that usually we can only give these, not receive. Because of this people with this Pattern will note that should they try positive thinking or the like to get something, that thing will tend not to arrive, or arrive at great personal cost.

This Pattern, therefore, is one of giving. But through giving we receive. The people here have the opportunity to truly understand this statement, which is perhaps, more than many will realise, both a blessing and a curse. For these people, the old gypsy saying suits. "May you live in interesting times".

3-6-9 / 3-5-7 / 1-4-7 Reversed "Z" Pattern:

Forming Energies: Two and Eight

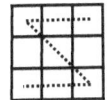

With the connecting Line of Force running from the Three to the Seven, the implications of this Pattern are of Service and Compassion. We have the Line of the Mind and the Line of the Physical present, but they are only combined harmoniously when the individual allows themselves to serve others, or a higher cause.

The Line of the Mind (3-6-9) indicates Power, while the Line of the Physical (1-4-7) indicates practicality. We have to combine these with the Line of Service, Perception and Compassion (3-5-7). This has a somewhat different aspect than we might expect, especially as this Pattern has an essentially negative feel to it. This is not fixed, or course, but the aspects of Power and Compassion which are featured here rarely sit well together.

In short, we can see dictators and would-be Napoleons with this energy, and this is not bad of itself for everything can serve a purpose, but it is not a gentle vibration at all. If an individual with this Pattern is ambitious they can cause a great deal of strife, both in the family and the workplace. There is a tendency to want to control things with arcane powers, and this is rarely harmonious. This is dangerous spiritually, and it weakens our creative energy.

The way to work most harmoniously with this Pattern is to plan with the mind, work out how the concept can benefit others beside ourselves, and then see the plan through to a physical reality. Working this way, the Pattern is exceedingly harmonious and directed towards achievement.

People with this aspect tend to like or absolutely hate the limelight. If they love it, they often tread over others to get to it. This energy works best when not seen. Obscurity and anonymity increase it's power. If the person affected is content to dwell within themselves and carry on with life, they will make remarkable observations about the true nature of things. If at peace within themselves, these people have an innate ability to see right to the heart, and often they make good communicators of the inner secrets they discover.

If they seek to use their perceptive abilities for selfish ends, they tend to develop exceedingly fine and focused minds, and often learn how to read another's mind as well.

More often this inner knowing, this often psychically obtained information is used for control rather than for enlightenment, but the understanding of Power generally involves its misuse. There is a great deal of Black Magic associated with this form, and persons so affected would be well advised to take care, for the power is not ours and comes with a price tag higher than we might otherwise expect. A warning to be at peace with your world, and a blessing if you are..

1-2-3 / 3-5-7 / 7-8-9 Turned "Z" Pattern:

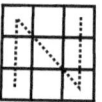

Forming Energies: Six and Four

This is a fortunate Pattern where the 3-5-9 Line of Service draws a connection between the creative energy and personal altruism. Great works can be done with this Pattern, and best done with a 'behind the scenes' involvement. These natives do not mind this, for they are naturally generous by nature, and somewhat introvert.

There is a broad outlook and an eclectic taste associated with these people. They find that travel is a always great boost to themselves, both intellectually and emotionally. They love to learn, and will be reading books till the day they die, or at very least they will be asking people questions about what their interests are. These people seem to just naturally sense that the way to obtain real information is to simply ASK people about what they do.

We will sometimes find that the curiosity derived from this Pattern leads some into scholarly pursuits, and in particular the study of history. There is much that a Soul can contribute towards the re-enlightenment of man when they understand the patterns of the past.

These folk generally disdain politics, drawing their inspiration from a contemplative approach to life, and a very solid sense of having ones feet on the ground. The only serious negative trait here being that these natives can be a little too altruistic, sometimes becoming the dreaded "helpful pest", but otherwise never learning the fact that people must help themselves if they are to develop character and strength.

There is a capacity for deep intellectual perception, but often a reticence to talk about this until later in life. Often a book will then emerge to discourse upon the subject. What is more, it is often well received if the individual has cultivated respect from his peers.

Others might perceive the general sense of silence and rectitude about these people as negative, but this is not really so. Often they are just biding their time and not wasting words. These people are as happy sitting in the sun listening to the birds as another might be with a million dollars to spend. In short, hard to find too great a fault except that they either care too little for society (which is no great problem as I see it) or too much (which is indeed a problem).

We often see a fairly self contained and self sufficient person here, but if the native veers off into self sufficiency too far, however, they can become quite callous and inconsiderate of others they perceive as less worthy. In this instance they are often impatient with the perceived weaknesses in others, and so they become quite judgmental. If so they will grow short tempered, and usually will live alone.

1-2-3 / 1-5-9 / 7-8-9 Reverse Turned "Z" Pattern

Forming Energies: Six and Four

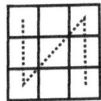

Inconstancy and uncertainty can shake your roots when this Pattern is aspected. The native will often find themselves tossing up inside with an argument about such things like the need to gain recognition, or to live a completely selfless life of service to some discipline. We often see these folk drawn to the clergy, or to some ordered and defined profession where they can see their life moving along in ordered ranks or merit.

Book of Number: Interpretations

There are many good points, but the negatives are invariably caught up with the Ego. They are not content to allow another to bask in the limelight when they feel they deserve the attention.

The connection of the One to the Nine gives a sense of urgency about things, and this type needs to learn to slow down a bit in order to allow things to grow. There is a strong accent on the Law of Completion here, and so people affected here must take care to always finish what they start. This is important for all persons, but these people are very susceptible to getting caught up with the "next great idea" without finishing the last.

This means that as time goes by all incomplete loose ends will create a sense of being lost, and this can create the sort of "rush-rush" worry mentality that is the source of many problems, for with the subsequent confusion that follows this attitude, obsessive behaviour usually sets in. Still, these folk are born under a lucky star, and things will generally go alright in the end. But the chaos in the middle can be avoided with a little more planning at the start.

There is an overall concern about the well-being of others here, which can become obsessive and hinder the life path of the native. But as the general belief grows that other peoples problems are not their own, the native with this Pattern will focus their own personal goals. In fact, they often go overboard with this attitude, and they can forget for a time that everyone else is on the same planet! Being too open or too insular is a matter to balance out with this aspect. It is part of the journey between being selfish and finding self-hood.

Generally the heart is in the right place, and the beggar in the street usually gets a coin for his/her trouble. Oddly, even though they might give a lecture at dinner about the importance of self sufficiency, these people will often give the beggar more money that the porter who carried their bags, and I can offer no explanation for this. I suspect it is because they like the dramatic more than the commonplace.

There is great energy for achievement with this Pattern, but only if the native gets serious about their specific project. If they do this they can seemingly walk through walls to achieve a successful conclusion, but there must be commitment. Too often, however, this type finds another distraction that dilutes their dedication. This is fatal to the energy and drive necessary to master this influence.

Epsilon Patterns:

There are Four Epsilon Patterns possible.

3-2-1/9-5-1/7-4-1 Epsilon

1-2-3/7-5-3/9-6-3 Epsilon

3-6-9/1-5-9/7-8-9 Epsilon

9-8-7/3-5-7/1-4-7 Epsilon

If there is any claim to a Spiritual Pattern, it is the Epsilon series. These embody a little of the Great "E" of the Greeks, which was the Sound Current that all life is based on.

Often the Pattern is Implied. This is to say, there are missing numbers, incomplete Lines of Force, etc. A Pure Epsilon is exceedingly rare. We see these active in figures that acheive prominence yet who are inwardly dedicated to a greater goal of service. An active Epsion Pattern invariably drives a person towards a goal of service of some sort.

1-2-3 / 1-5-9 / 1-4-7 Epsilon Pattern:
Forming Energy and Pivot Point: One

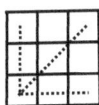

Like up reaching arms towards the heavens, this Pattern indicates a yearning, We might characterize it as the Eternal Dreamer. These people are often optimists, but the type where they drag their feet along the earth while their hearts are in the stars. When they master this two way pull, they become quite pragmatic, however, and can achieve great success in both spiritual and financial matters.

Creativity, Success and the Commonness of Man combine to form an unlikely combination where there is a drive for success, but also for creative expression and education. It combines well in those who teach higher learning of any sort, practical, or spiritual.

These people are constantly learning. The focus is on the One, which indicates they will draw all their energies into themselves in order to understand what they are seeing and experiencing. This indicates a long and sometimes arduous apprenticeship involving the scaling on many inner obstacles. These people are naturally silent about much of what is going on within them, and in keeping this silence they find a natural resource to succeed over the difficulties.

They are draw to understand their fellow man, but do not necessarily want to go out and help people specifically. Rather through education and example they would prefer to show others how to find a better life.

On the Negative aspect, these people can become exceedingly vain and self obsessed, to the point of excluding all around them.

They will continue to make mental and practical excursions into whatever interests them, but this will be a solitary journey with no friends at the end of the long, dark tunnel. Curiously, the negative type is not overly concerned with this, for they are fixed in the belief that money will buy them most things they need, and generally they are good at getting this.

It is in old age that the negative energy reverses on them, leaving them unable to cope with details and other people. They often choose (unconsciously) some illness that will incapacitate them, so while they depend on, they don't have to relate to others. This reversal of energy can happen at any time in their life, of course. But these are powerful Patterns, and usually run their course over a longish period of time.

The whole learning experience here is to learn to look outwards, not inwards, to find the way to achieve lasting happiness. There will be an inner, contemplative period that comes in regular cycles, but the idea is to take this inflow of energy and propel it into some task that reaches out to others. This is why education is such an ideal area for these people.

1-2-3 / 3-5-7 / 3-6-9 Epsilon Pattern:
Forming Energy and Pivot Point: Three

These people can feel quite tortured in their efforts to understand themselves and come to terms with their nature. The focus is on the Three, which is indicative of Creativity, but this can also mean great creativity in business or science, not just art.

The Three energy is good at planning, dreaming and building great inspirational works, but the individual must be both committed and emotionally charged with the goal they have in mind. Otherwise the Three energy will simply want to dream big things, but never actually do anything about it. Because of this Three, and the natural affinity of the Epsilon Pattern with the Law of Three, learning to act, not just dream, will be a big part of the learning experience.

Book of Number: Interpretations

The easy way to master this Pattern is to narrow down specific things to accomplish, every day, every week, every year. Without clarity of vision and clear goals the tendency is to dream impossible dreams. They can end up "fighting without reason or foe", to quote the words of the song. This negative habit can be cured with having clear goals, and the simple development of realistic focus on achieving our goals.

Impossible dreams only succeed in introverting the dreamer with a sense of looming failure, and should be avoided at all costs. However, what is impossible for one might be plausible for another, and easy for the next fellow. We need to know our inner limitations and true desires are. If we think about it, this alone is a good goal we might wish to achieve.

One of the surprising effects of this Pattern can be that of uncovering the subconscious mind and the hidden desires that play underneath the surface of our thoughts. The Line of the Mind with the Line of Creativity and the Line of Compassion combine to give the native an instrument to probe into their innermost self, with the possibility of discovering great inner power as the result.

The negative reflex is to indulge in self recrimination and failure complexes, generally to the point of neurosis and schizophrenia. An overbearing moodiness can overtake the individual, and any clear sense of perspective slips away. if so decisions and actions will become based on vague, uneasy impressions rather than solid facts.

All affected by this Pattern need to focus on the day to day finances, for they tend to be irresponsible in regard that mechanics of earning a living. When they do accept the fact that the world does not owe them lunch, they become very good at earning a dollar. They often find themselves in a position of having a good deal of free time as well.

It is one of the fallacies ingrained into the Western psyche that only hard working Souls are happy ones. The Creative Soul works continually within their imagination, and as long as they are not a burden to others, this type generally fares very well with part time and intermediate work, including such things as contract and free lance occupations.

This is one of the Patterns that are good at wheeling and dealing, and can make quite a good living from buying and selling, often travelling about in the nature of the old time merchant as they do so. The gypsy earning money by telling fortunes is a classical example of this.

If motivated to help others, these people can do a great deal of good, for by understanding their own inner motivations, they also understand what makes others tick. The greatest help we can give someone is an understanding of themselves. These folk usually have little desire for success as the world knows it, often being quite content with the simple things of life.

However, this Pattern usually craves a place where serenity and solitude are to be found, and need this if they are to function happily.

This Pattern will be seen with monks and clergy, yet also with successful business men and successful artists. The affect is broad, but remember that the Pattern works on the inner person, whatever their chosen profession. It's energy is best utilized when unlocking the secrets hidden in the mind.

3-6-9 / 1-5-9 / 7-8-9 Epsilon Pattern:
Forming Energy and Pivot Point: Nine

Silence is a powerful influence at work here, and the person affected by this Epsilon Pattern will need to develop the power of Silence. This is highlighted because the Nine interacts with the One, Three and Seven, an odd combination that strengthens individuality and the need for self. The Law of Silence (Kamit) is about knowing what is the right thing to say, rather than not speaking, as you might imagine.

A combination on the Three, One and Seven energy is excellent for the recording and demonstration of higher thought, and when governed by the Nine this can lead to very powerful influences that can help shape individuals, families, and nations. But this will almost always be done with a sense of silence, and not necessarily with a sense of comfort for the person focusing this energy. It can be quite a difficult Pattern to master.

One example for this could be the man who broke the power of the Salem witch trials. He knew he was probably going to be burned at the state, but for the sake of his family (for if he spoke and was found guilty they would lose their possessions) he said nothing throughout his trial. It was his silence that finally woke up those around him to the light of truth, and the trials ended soon after.

Silence, the inner beatitude. This is the only thing that will keep the wild horses of the One, Three and Seven in check. These are the most individual characters of the Noumenal Order, that generally prefer their own company, in a manner of speaking. But in silence they will abide each other in harmony and well being.

If all the numbers in the Pattern are in perfect balance, this is particularly significant for in this instance there will be Eight harmonious Trines present, which is hugely lucky with romance, money, and travel. In all of the Epsilon Patterns, perfect balance in all numbers will create Eight Trines in differing aspects, but none quite so fortunate as this.

Yet is this really fortunate? In the chart I have seen, perfect balance seems to create a certain lassitude. I find they can indicate a wasted life, because things would tend to come just too easily and the person in this instance generally ends up feeling both vaguely unsatisfied, yet oddly content. Too many good aspects can be as negative for inner growth as too many bad aspects, for as the Tibetans say "If bad karma be iron shackles, then good karma forms golden ones."

Individuals affected by this Pattern generally like to perform charitable acts and enjoy supporting the Arts in its many forms, but particularly in dance and poetry. They are the true Patron, giving support but not expecting reward other than the performance of the art in question.

In all, the energy developed by this Pattern is subtle and certainly not obvious to the common man, but for those with the eyes to see it, these people stand out like a diamond in a field of stones, even if they be a diamond in the rough. As such they serve well in a company, often rising to the top echelons through a combination of merit and being identified as an influential person's protégé. However, in all areas they will progress over time, and silently perform tasks allotted. It is important not to stand by idly, waiting to be recognized. This Pattern is forthright enough to present results before the people that count and will reasonably expect, but not demand, promotion.

There is a subtlety here that succeeds well if employed, and others would do well to copy this Patterns silent ability to move ahead in life. The credo here is "One step at a time."

7-8-9 / 3-5-7 / 1-4-7 Epsilon Pattern:
Forming Energy and Pivot Point: Seven

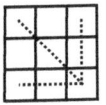

This Epsilon, being focused on the Seven, is often very self searching, and there is a distinct danger of introversion occurring. The Pattern can be very wearing, for there is a great burning off of Karmic Patterns during the lifetime of the person affected by its influence.

As such, depression can be a real problem, and so such things as fasts and careful consideration of diet become essential to clear out and maintain bodily and mental agility. It is particularly important to feed the nervous system, for it can take a real battering here, along with the natives sense of self esteem. Yet if you survive all this you will probably write a best seller telling the world of your torturous journey, and helping a lot of others as the result.

Positions of service are virtually essential for this type. They do not feel comfortable up front as a rule. These people enjoy sole charge positions, yet generally prefer roles that remain invisible, which is a specific characteristic of the Seven energy at work. You will find these people

Book of Number: Interpretations

working as technicians, repairmen, mothers, secretaries, many differing roles, but the job will never be the main consideration in their lives. Rather it is a support function that allows them to delve more deeply into themselves. You may feel that you are permanently on a quest if you have this aspect at work in your life.

As children this type can be quite impossible, for they will want their way, but never tell you what it is until they are in tears. Why the tears? Because you have not magically discovered what the problem is, and complied. I know this sounds odd, but many adults not subject to this Pattern still play this game, but this is because guilt in some form has dulled their ability to ask, and it is not a specific karmic consequence.

It should be noted that the effects of any Patterns can be felt by anyone, for they represent an attitudinal state. What is more, anyone can develop any attitude they so choose. However, a specific Pattern will indicate a specific set of circumstances that an individual will have to work out. This does not mean that they will, or course.

In most cases, social conditioning and parental expectations will overrule the natural order of things, and pervert the course of an individuals evolution. This outer energy will infect the persons auric field, and react with the existing Patterns to form sub-patterns and cross fields that can be quite injurious to bodily and mental health. It is why it is often orphans with this aspect are usually the ones who really grasp it's power.

By becoming more aware of our natural state, we help ourselves become more natural and can thus assist others along the road of their own destiny. In many cases the person with this Pattern will find they have been cast by life into the role of the student, but emerge from this apprenticeship as the teacher who can understand and assist others.

It is well to remember at this point that we are not teachers so much as reminder-ers. We are not instructors, but mirrors to help people see themselves more clearly. If we understand this, we have come to a great part in understanding our purpose, and in resolving this Pattern.

Book of Number: Interpretations

Squares: There are Six possibilities, as follows:

1-2-4-5 Minor Square

2-3-5-6 Minor Square

4-5-7-8 Minor Square

5-6-8-9 Minor Square

1-3-7-9 Great Square

2-4-6-8 Great Square

Squares are difficult Aspects, without exception. Yet so often we see them in the charts of high performing people, and in just about any field of endeavour.

This is because resistance makes us stronger. If gravity were increased by 20% tomorrow, inside a week we would all become 20% stronger. The one single thread that all Square Patterns share is that a person needs to learn to laugh at themselves and their situation before they will learn to master it's energy.

1-3-7-9 Great Square: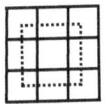

This is the only "Open" Square, and as such is open to a number of interpretations, depending on the configurations that occur with it. If the Two, Six, Eight and Four are VACANT in the chart containing this Pattern, these then become major forming influences here. In this instance, vacant positions would indicate a forming or shaping influence based around all odd numbers. This gives a masculine charge to the energy and can make the person extremely forthright and direct.

Also, we may well find a Vacant Line (such as a 2-5-8 Vacant Line) represented with this configuration, at which point the Vacant Line would take on a pivotal significance, and much of the influence of the Square should be interpreted with this in mind. As there are only two possibilities, these being the 2-5-8 Line and the 4-5-6 Line we shall look at these briefly:

A Vacant 2-5-8 Line in the Open Square Pattern indicates an emotional intensity that is in conflict with the solidarity of the Square. In this instance the person might feel driven and compelled in their chosen area of work. The choice of profession here is wide, as the Great Square has a broad influence. When the individual learns to govern their intensity here they become less obsessive in their behaviour. The intensity can be very useful, however, for these people often find that a period of emotional and mental intensity opens up to a tremendous and clear simplicity. As such, they makes excellent and kind teachers in any number of areas, and good poets as well.

If this innate intensity is not mastered, then drug and/or alcohol addiction is possible, as well as a sting of broken relationships. Even so, the good fortune that tags along after this Pattern often sees the person saved from ruin. They seem to be able to survive shocks that would crush most people, however, it does not prevent them seeking the edge once more when the cold hard sobering effect of reality wears off. These folk need to be careful of allowing fantasy to cloud their reality.

A Vacant 4-5-6 Line is a far more gentle influence. It lends an air of achievement to this person's life, and generally quite a degree of clear thinking. If anything, they can be too clear headed and as a result aggravate those who are more emotional. The type affected by this Aspect are the ones who, right at a crucial love scene in a romance movie, will say aloud, "Gee guys, these actors really do a good job with this script, don't they?" Clarity is reality, and being clear equals freedom.

It is a fortunate aspect. This Pattern will serve the person affected well as long as they continue to believe in the work ethic: a fair days work is worth a fair days pay. They are somewhat entranced by gambling, however. Usually not to the addiction degree, but enough to affect their attitude and dealings with others in a negative manner. In this way they often seek to begin large, ambitious projects, seeking finance and input from others, but not really returning an investors effort or cash input in the manner that is deserved.

How this occurs is usually through the individual becoming so self centred that they simply do not recognize anyone else's contribution, instead believing that because they were at the organizing end of a project, that they deserve ALL the glory because without themselves nothing would have happened.

This is, in short, essentially the idea of getting something for nothing. The effect of the Great Square in this instance would likely cause a certain closing off of the intimate and personal relationship with friends and lovers, creating a relatively lonely figure who constantly craves affection. We must repay confidence with confidence, trust with trust, honesty with honesty, and know enough to tell the difference when it is not there. (Either in ourselves or in another)

In the extremely unusual instance of BOTH of the 2-5-8 and 4-5-6 Lines being Vacant, (which means the 1, 3, 7 and 9 must be stated) this specific Pattern indicates a great need to serve, specifically in the religious sense. Though this aspect is possible in the Name Matrix, such a Pattern is not possible in the Birth Chart during years 2000, though occasionally possible throughout the 1900's. This is a powerful creative energy ideal for such times as Ancient Greece. (For example: 17/3/900 or 7/3/1900, etc.)

As a further note in addendum to this, much of our formed thought and social conditioning in Western culture comes directly from the forming time based roughly on the birth of Christ. This period from the Romanization of Europe through to the present have been powerful years, wrought with a Noumenal Tension.

The Great Square itself indicates the potential for stability, humour and a general ability to get on in life. It has a share of good fortune related to it, and this is due in part to a good and healthy interaction with friends who are likely to further your case. It is a well balanced Pattern, which can lead to a sense of apathy if the individual relies solely on luck and circumstance in their lives. We find a reliance and trust in family and friends can really enhance the energy here.

But there is a danger where the individual does not face the harsher realities of life because they always have familial support to carry them through hard times. In this way, their good fortune can actually prevent them from maturing. Too much good fortune, in other words, is not actually good for us. This is why I often say that the perfect chart is usually a gold plated problem.

One of the great energies of this aspect is the gift of perseverance, which in the long run is worth more than its weight in gold. It is the key to breaking through the barriers, even the self made ones, into new states of consciousness.

NOTE: If a Five is in Perfect Balance with the Great Square, what we actually have is the 1-5-9/3-5-7 "X" Pattern, and the chart should be read accordingly, but with an inference of greater mobility of thought and action being possible. (As a result of the perfect Balance and the Pivot on the Five)

A crucial lesson to learn with this Aspect is a sort of humble superiority. Know your capability, know your limitations, and listen to the direction the wind is blowing.

2-4-6-8 Major Square:

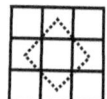

This is a difficult aspect, closely related to the "Messiah" Pattern or the 2-5-8/4-5-6 Cross. There is difficulty in relationships, and a sense of confusion with identity. As a result the individual with this aspect can project an aura of weakness and fragility. Worse, they can often attract rather negative, critical Souls into their world. These people tend to judge this Soul unjustly. The native will often prefer to just let things be, but this usually works only to their detriment. One of the lessons of this aspect is learning to stand up for oneself. At heart there is a goodness that does not want to cause problems, but building self-worth is never a problem.

Obviously, this Aspect is all Even numbers. This means that the feminine influence is strong. This Pattern strengthens the female, but tends to weaken the male. This "weakening" is demonstrated as poor social interaction, low self esteem, and a self-perception that is more passive than aggressive. This aspect, for the male, is a herald of difficulty until the Querent learns to stand their ground in a forthright manner. Words like "Maybe" and "Perhaps" would do well to be cast out of their vocabulary, and in their place use words like "Definitely" and "Yes". By simply being perceived as more definite and clear, the outer condition of criticism will change and prospects for advancement both personally and in business will improve tremendously.

The Law of Non-Interference is really at the heart of this Aspect. First step, learn to not interfere with your own process, and trust that life will take care of you. Doubt, self-critical behaviour and false modesty are practices that break the Law of Non-Interference, and have the effect of drawing interfering people into your orbit.

We often find the native of this aspect suffering from a deluded sense of personal sacrifice. The concept of self sacrifice needs to be altered to one of self sufficiency. Reversing need by not needing others, and they will be drawn to this individual like moths to the flame. Of course, we all need company to some degree, but the individual must never become the beggar of another's opinion. If you wish to find harmony in your life, be independent. It is often necessary here to strengthen one's sense of worth, and in this instance a period of isolation is likely to occur, in order to bring this self worth about.

A trip to a far away land, a drive to some quiet place in the country when you can sit and contemplate. These are the things that this native craves and needs more than any social approval, but the deep seated fear of loneliness will often prevent them from breaking out of the mould and escaping to a new and more wonderful world of living.

This is an intense Pattern, one that few really break out of, but when the individual does the world turns to favour them. There is great beauty when these people get into action, and oddly enough they often make world class athletes and sports people. They are prepared to sacrifice in order to succeed.

1-2-4-5 Minor Square:

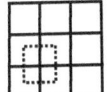

Note that all the Minor Squares contain the Five. This accents the influence of communication, and so a part of the learning experience is involved with the expression of the inner self. Often we also see a degree of excess on sexual matters, either in expression, or with excessive introversion. The energy of the Minor Squares can easily turn inwardly to the centre, which can give a great ability to contemplate deeply on a subject, yet also allows for introversion to set in.

The 1-2-4-5 Square has the particular effect of opening up the heart, for these numbers focus on Self (One), Communication (Five), Perception of Beauty (Two), and acceptance of Reality (Four). In balance this allows a good platform for much growth, but does not imply an easy life. One might view this Pattern as a step to higher energies, and certainly we see a degree of people "breaking away". We also find a degree of eccentricity with those who cannot quite deal with the energy. The Pattern indicates a certain need to express oneself, but common sense must be applied. This energy can make very vocal children, and somewhat rebellious adults, but things will generally work out in the end.

During the process of trying to communicate personal desires to the outside world, the native will often come into conflict with it. This is because the natural instinctive reaction and the trained social response usually find an argument within the individual or within society, and this provides some difficulty for these Souls. The middle ground is actually found by not fighting this, but by developing an appreciation of another's problems and difficulties. This relieves the personal pressure to succeed, and develops a sense of give and take in our day to day dealings.

Moulded by many influences, this Pattern is good for growth provided that the individual is prepared to see that another's view is as valid for them as their own is for themselves. One of the great weak points of this Pattern is that the native tends to be somewhat contemptuous of those who are not able to successfully counter the emotional and/or mental assaults of life with reasonable arguments, for there is perhaps too great a leaning towards the intellectual elite here.

Book of Number: Interpretations

2-3-5-6 Minor Square:

This Pattern involves a degree of Higher Thought, but often this is mixed with a consideration of how to make a good profit from it, to which end an emotional profit may be considered sufficient. There can be a certain amount of identity confusion related to this Square which can make puberty even more traumatic than it already is, but when a sense of humour about things is discovered, most significant problems disappear. Of course, this sense of humour generally only comes about with maturity and hindsight.

Communication once again comes to the fore with this Pattern, especially in the area of relationships. There is the odd and often strained effect of a Four energy (the Square) imposing on a Three energy (the Three itself) here which creates a dramatic tension, and these people generally have a theatrical flair about them as a reflection on this. These theatrics are actually their way of releasing a sort of "short circuit" in the Sympathetic Nervous system, and is physiologically based. The "butterflies" in the stomach for this type tend to be batwings.

There is often an overzealous personality as a result of this. It can put others off trusting them, so these individuals need to look at their sincerity, and their ethics. A lack of either will cause many marital problems. In simpler terms, they must learn to master their nerves. There is good fortune in work and pastimes, however, with generally good relations with friends and casual acquaintances. But it is a fact that the more intimate the relationship, the more open the people need to be who are in it, and this Pattern has difficulty with openness.

Trust is the keywords to consider. As a result of earlier inner and outer harassment, and due to the internal and sheltered nature of this vibration in puberty, trust becomes an attitude that can be hard to, well, trust.

With the right partner, usually in this case one known from an early age, these people find the stability their Pattern promises, and with this their lives work out just fine. It is a curious Pattern, for in this case it is Trust that brings security, which in turn brings a relief from the nagging sense of fear that plagues most of the native of this vibration.

Note that all the Minor Squares contain the Five. This accents the influence of communication, and so a part of the learning experience is involved with the expression of the inner self. The energy of the Minor Squares can easily turn inwardly to the centre, which can give a great ability to contemplate deeply on a subject, yet also allows for introversion to set in.

5-6-8-9 Minor Square:

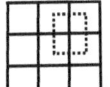

This is a powerful combination that gives a sense of dominance over the day to day affairs when focused, but an utter confusion when it is not. The Pattern lends itself to intense and considered thinking when matured, though in the forming stages this Square is more focused on simply surviving, and such things as marriage and children. Balancing the budget can be quite a task for some here! There is a need to provide oneself with the hallmarks of security (House, wife, mortgage, etc.) and over-stepping financial commitments is not uncommon.

These people are very good "behind the scenes" types, and can work well with a wide variety of persons and professions, though this Pattern is often mostly attracted to a somewhat theatrical outlook. They are not often outwardly flamboyant, but when we dig beneath the surface we usually find real rebels under the formal exterior. Many times we will discover that this type are thinking hard about subjects rarely acceptable to mainstream society.

As a result, this Pattern can serve as a resource for a writer or artist. But here it becomes curious, for this Square is rarely evident in the artist themselves, rather it is often in the chart of their partner or close friends. It is a catalyst Pattern, and many times it is endowed with good fortune financially, usually via an inheritance of some sort.

People around those with this Aspect tend to do well in life. Those who have this Aspect in their chart will die wealthy, even if it is simply a wealth of friends that they possess. On the negative side, they have a tendency to over familiarize themselves with media and the spoken word, and can quite easily become the village gossip. However, they make excellent journalist and public commentators.

These people sometimes need to be made aware that life is not for just picking roses. While their good fortune can carry them for a time, allowing them to do this, without a sense of helping others it starts to introvert. It is late in life that the effect of waste will be discovered, and it will come as a nagging regret that results in deep depression.

This aspect indicates that we should work on developing self-recognition and our sense of spirituality. To this end, a time of contemplation each day is considered necessary here. Indeed, all the Square Patterns accent a need for some sort of contemplation and spiritual retreat each day for a few minutes.

The main lesson is simply learning to laugh at life's foibles.

Book of Number: Interpretations

4-5-7-8 Minor Square:

This is an Aspect that is fortuitous for finance and friends, many of whom will be drawn to the somewhat gregarious nature of this native. A number of these people seem to pursue intellectual understanding on a wide range of topics, yet there is a danger here of introversion and isolation if a person become obsessed by any given topic of study.

If there is a strong influence relating to the One or Nine in this person's life this will not be so. They will be able to study intensely the minutiae of existence, and not disappear up their own imagination. However, if the Pattern is isolated in the chart, the tendency is for the person to be of an isolationist nature as well, even if they may have numerous admirers. A Pattern is "isolated" when there are no connecting Aspects. Specifically, in this case, if they have the 1-2-3 / 3-6-9 "L" Pattern it creates an almost schizophrenic way of behaving in social circles.

Rupert Murdoch, born 11 3 1931, has this Square, a Martyr's Cross, a 2-4-6-8 Major Square, and a Dominant One all working together. No one can argue the spectacular success he has achieved, and that he has achieved this through hard work and focus on his goals. A good example of this energy at work.

This Pattern indicates steadfastness, and people so affected rarely move about a lot, but they should do! Travel is simply the best thing for them. Generally their "travel instinct" is worked out with regular walks, which brings good health, but the native really should take the time to travel abroad if at all possible.

The solid nature of this Square gives them a sense of credibility, and strangers will often find themselves simply talking to a person with this Pattern, even though they might be cautious and guarded with others. Because of this, these people make excellent counsellors and advisors. Also they tend to know when to shut up, which gives extra impetus to this realm of service. The problem in personal relationships is that sometimes this Pattern does not talk enough! They are the strong Silent Type we love to see in the movies, but really they are often this way simply because they are shy and slightly unsure, which is why they say nothing.

There is a lot of room for growth in this Pattern, but I stress, this is only if they do not close off to the outer world, either physically or through fixed opinions and/or close mindedness. The mind is like a parachute. It need to be open if it is going to work properly.

Adventure is the keynote to the successful working out of this energy in your life. As Guru Adrian says: Half the fun is having fun.

Book of Number: Interpretations

Kite Patterns:

2-1-4-5/9 Kite

8-7-4-5/3 Kite

2-3-6-5/7 Kite

8-9-6-5/1 Kite

The Four Kite Patterns are derived largely from the Minor Squares. These need to be read in relation to this square they are connected to. The energy created icomes about because the vibration of the "tail" (attached number) is like a weight the steers the Pattern. It is like a rudder that directs the ship.

1-2-4-5 / 9 Kite:
Forming Energy: Nine   Pivot Point: One

If the Individual affected learns the art of Silence they will find the ability to delve deeply into themselves, and by doing so, come to understand the depths of every person. We are all, in essence, reflections of the same mould that constitutes the Human Being. This Pattern has the tag of the Nine over the 2-1-4-5 Minor Square, which indicates the effect of this Pattern, plus a need for Silence.

Because of this ability to perceive commonality, these people make good researchers and medical officers. In truth, this might be also called a Healing Pattern, for those with this aspected in their chart will often find they have an innate ability with healing disciplines.

If we view the "Kite" as flying downwards into the One, we will see how the energy of the Pattern is delving into the aspect of the One, which is mainly individuality, willpower and determination. Of course, if the attitude is negative, the negative aspects of the One will be unearthed.

As with "real life" kites, it is the tail that gives this Pattern stability and direction, and so the energy of the Nine is accented here. This means that the highest nature of the person will essentially be based upon the Law of Silence. A review of the qualities of the Nine will give a fuller view of the energy at work here, but overall it is based in reasoned steadfastness and commitment to achieving goals. The reverse can always occur, however.

A person with this aspect should look to common sense as their guiding light, and must be careful of becoming too highly geared in business and personal relationships. Still, there will be a reliance on the self here, and each person must define their own limits of acceptable risk. Regardless, the weight is always on keeping one's own counsel in all matters, and trusting a limited group of people with their plans.

2-3-5-6 / 7 Kite:

Forming Energy: Seven   Pivot Point: Three

This is somewhat of an adventurers and builders Pattern. The hesitancy and reserve of the Seven is countered with the exploring nature of the Three, yet it gives energy to creating by stepping back and qualifying a project before you enter into it. This is one example of how apparent opposites can work well together, for on a deeper level we find that the two aspects are harmonious. It has difficult moments, but with perseverance things will come right, and this is good because it keeps the native on their toes. People who have too good a life rarely have any incentive to make something of it.

There is only one specific and utterly clear example of this Pattern that I know: Jorn Utzon, the architect of the Sydney Opera House. Born 9 4 1918 he has a clear 2-3-5-6 / 7 Upwards Kite. It needs to be stressed, he didn't just design  one of the wonders of the world, he worked out how it could be created. The whole building was revolutionary in every respect and here is a perfect example of the energy that can flow when this Pattern is left to run free. Concept, form and practicality combined to form a "Perfect Storm".

There is a profit motive with the 2-3-6-5 Minor Square, which combined with the travelling aspect brought in with the Seven makes for an excellent market trader. There is a philosophical attitude to this Kite as it is sailing "upwards" to the Three, which loves to consider the higher plan or destiny accorded to one's life. On the higher levels the Three represents harmony through action, or a sense of purpose. Because of this, the native aspected with this Pattern has the potential to realize a great deal of progress in this life, both financially and emotionally.

The Seven tags everything with a sort of mysticism, but we often find the person affects an agnostic, or even cynical outlook. This is often simply because they do not know how to quite deal with this energy. In this instance, the person will be drawn to science rather than religion, to lots of friends rather than intimate relationships, and to outward recognition rather than inner peace.

The downfall for these people is often based on their flirtatious behaviour, which destroys many intimate relationships. Other than this there can be a sense of indecision that confuses both themselves and those around them until some degree of inner confidence is found.

4-5-7-8 / 3 Kite:
Forming Energy: Three   Pivot Point: Seven

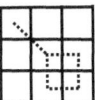

The person with this Pattern will want to escape responsibility, but in a mature Soul this will evidence itself as a desire to utilize one's time in useful projects. An apparent turnaround, but understandable when we realize that the motivating influence is to not be caught in mundane and superficial surroundings. Though travel is highlighted, it is for the education as much as the pleasure of the journey. If there is a spiritual need, there is a likelihood of the person devoting themselves to pilgrimages and the like. In fact, there usually is some sort of spiritual reward in store for these people whenever they step outside of themselves and explore the possibilities life offers.

This holds true in business and personal relationships, and is not confined to travel. Also, there is an influence of "establishment" about this Pattern. Society, and being a part of this, is often very important to these individuals. However, there is also a general disdain for the rules and regulations, and a definite rebellious streak in there as well. For those born into lower classes, this will give a great incentive to "make good". If not for the money, then for the prestige. The governing Three is not a creative so much as an organizing influence with this Pattern, which is an interpretation rarely applied to the Three.

If we think about it, to create something, we need to organize ourselves to do this. However, if we look at most artists we will see a characteristic disorganization. this is simply because they have not mastered the energy they are working with. We mistakenly think that it is the creative process that is causing them pain and confusion. This is true to a point, but in reality organization solves most of the disorientation that comes from stepping into new "thought zones". (Which are real and actual things in the higher planes)

And so we find that a keynote energy to resolve with this Pattern is organization, with natives often finding themselves comfortable in roles which require this. The negative aspect comes when the dreaded "Pillar of Society" disease strikes. This destroys the natural sense of humour and isolates the person in a need for recognition. It creates a large ego problem, one that is hard to alter because it is entrenched by the natives own sense of righteousness. Self-righteousness is a difficult poison to recognize in ourselves, let alone cure, and is often fatal to inner growth and any sense of personal satisfaction.

The overall effect of the Pattern is "Downwards" into the Seven, and so indicates a degree of introspection, but the Three prevents it from becomes too intensive. The Three, if the Forming Energy overrules the Minor Square, can become somewhat flippant and thus creating an impression of brittleness of character. Yet underneath a real person is hiding. Acts of unspoken kindness will be done by all natives with this Pattern, for despite their outward gregariousness, inside they have a passion for silent service to others.

Many times, if they are financially blessed, they become the patron of a worthy charity or social institution. If not so blessed, they will often take time out to help others, finding a great balance here for their need for social standing.

5-6-8-9 / 1 Kite:

Forming Energy: One Pivot Point: Nine

This is a powerful "Thought" Pattern, with the danger of the individual so affected becoming so enthralled by the "perfection of planning" that they entirely forget about reality. There is a warning to not allow dreams to take over, and a message that the task is to make our dreams a reality

One example I saw of this energy was of the fellow who came in with wonderful architecturally drawn plans for an expansive house. He asked my opinion on building it, and I simply said "How?" He did not understand, until I pointed out that his architect had drawn a beautiful design, but one that required building products that did not as yet exist, such as a single wooden beam that would stretch 130 feet without support, yet take a 35 ton roof.

I could almost bet that the architect had a this Kite Pattern in his birth chart! However, if the One aspect is well grounded this does not occur. It is really letting your ego gets involved with your dreams, and the result will always be mistakes like this. Ego is part of the executive function of the mind, and is not a planning function. It has a definite use in developing the ID, creating big ideas, and developing the impetus towards success. Yet vanity is a huge stumbling block for these people.

Logically, when our decisions are based on appearance maintenance or what the neighbours think, it is almost certain that we will try to buy that house we can only just afford, or that new car when the older one was still quite serviceable. It is decisions like these that stretch the budget, and the nerves. This inevitably creates fertile ground for irrational behaviour, with possible emotional and/or financial breakdown.

Practicality is the keynote for success here. With this grand designs will be employed, but they will be ones that actually work. These people are designers, and on the negative side they are schemers, but even so the general goal is to build something. If we build in life, the very Law of Life states that we will not be repaid in a negative manner, and so even the schemer somehow often manages to make their plans come good. As long as they are practical!

These people are attracted to organizations, but usually leave when qualifications and/or contacts have been achieved, as they prefer to work on their own. They like to be in a sole charge capability. They can deal well with success, and rise to the occasion when given a project beyond their present means.

Exuding an aura of talent, they can encourage jealousies in other without realizing it, for they have an innate capability not to notice anything but their goal. Socially they are rarely comfortable with anyone but those who share the same pursuits. They are not open and inviting to change, and generally prefer to modify or alter an existing habit, design or way of life rather than try a new one.

With the Pivot on the Nine, these people need to be quiet about what they are doing until the whole thing is ready to be seen by the public. The One as Forming Energy gives direction, and these people have no trouble about being single minded. They often have a pig headed belief that everything they do is right. The modifying Five, Six and Eight soften this, however, and give the Pattern greater breadth of vision.

The One/Nine combination indicates the beginnings and endings of many things throughout this person's life. Take care with dealings in life, for hidden enemies are often accented here.

Parallel Patterns: There are Eight in all:

1-2-3/4-5-6 Parallel

4-5-6/7-8-9 Parallel

1-2-3/7-8-9 Parallel

1-4-7/2-5-8 Parallel

2-5-8/3-6-9 Parallel

1-4-7/3-6-9 Parallel

1-4-7/2-5-8/3-6-9 and 1-2-3/4-5-6/7-8-9 (Triple) Parallels

Parallel Patterns are amongst the most contrary within the Noumeal influence. They are difficult to work with, and harder to understand or quantify, because they are extremely open and changeable. Often the effect most acutely suffered by those under their influence is indecision. Just finding a natural direction seems impossible.

We tend to find natives externalise extreme behaviour. This is similar to a child trying to find it's limits under the parental roof. Many diagnosed bi-polar clients in the psychiatrists office have this influence in the background. The effect tends to be either ON or OFF. Forward, or not moving. Happy or miserable.

And yet, we also find priests and mentors will also carry this energy. To explain, the frequency has to be in balance, or harmonic, for it to work. Out of balance, it drives people to extremes, but in balance it pulls you towards the heart and into a sincere depth of contentment.

The Triple Parallels are not as rare as you might imagine, and even when they are only implied, they have a tremendous influence in the life of the individual. We tend to see these only in Overlay Matrix charts, however.

1-2-3 / 4-5-6 Parallel:

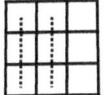

This indicates an ability to understand people and life. The general implication for this Pattern is a degree of detachment, to the point of being a sense of coldness towards the "common" man. This then might be said to be the aristocrats Pattern.

There is an indication of being unable to deal with the mundane issues, and a certain degree of vagueness, but this is largely because the person affected by this Pattern would be disinterested in day to day affairs. It is excellent for the researcher, but bad for the housewife, so to speak. We will note that the Pattern looks like an Eleven! This Eleven value lends itself to a tendency to burn the midnight candle. If the person is not of robust health, short-sightedness and a pale demeanour will follow.

When a person is not in charge of the energy here, the tendency is to revert to a Two vibration (Two Lines of Force), with a sense of double mindedness, and double standards. A weak willed person with this Pattern will create many difficulties, for its energy will be such that plans and projects will fail unless strongly organized and pursued. But once focus is brought to bear, there is little these people cannot achieve.

Even so, they tend to stand alone throughout their lives, and really need to develop the ability to share in some way that which they have gained. If this is done, life will be full and complete, and many joys will come. However, this generally comes late in life, with the first part of adulthood often being marked by the struggle to survive and harness the energy behind this Pattern.

This is an odd combination of the dreamer and the achiever, and as we can understand, it requires a very strong person to truly master this Pattern. We find that there are many here who find the middle road, and manage to do quite OK for themselves in life, but tend to have this lurking fear that they could have done better. Acceptance of ourselves is therefore the lesson highlighted here.

Acceptance means you set yourself free from judgement, and it also means you are free to use all the tools in your toolkit to build a better life. It is extraordinary how people hamstring themselves by non-acceptance of their own nature.

This Pattern is very much a case of moving forward by simply not opposing yourself. Self-doubt, self-criticism can all be set aside, and you can embrace each day as a new beginning. Do this, and the energy is remarkably fortuitous.

Book of Number: Interpretations

1-2-3/7-8-9 Parallel: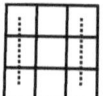

Here we find an ability to mould and create great plans, but also we often find the power to put them into practice as well. The power here is not so much authority, rather an ability to motivate others towards a common goal, and thus by the strength of the group behind them, these people forge forwards. However, they also know how to survive on their own, but this means a lack of recognition, and generally this is very frustrating for these people.

This is not a vanity, but a deep need. This Pattern loves to work with others, but on Its own terms. This might seem selfish, and indeed it can be. Yet if we consider that there are many, many souls out there who look for a strong leader, people who are more than happy to be told what to do as long as it serves what they perceive as a common and useful goal, then we can see that there is a role for this energy to play.

Thus this Pattern is good for preachers and politicians, and all who rely on the energy of the group to complete their large and grandiose schemes. If the Five is vacant it indicates that the person so affected will need to develop powers of oratory, which they will use to great effect when influencing others. Obviously, there is great potential for menace here as well, but this is always the case with anyone who is gifted. Talent rarely makes life easier, in fact it is usually quite the opposite.

A more negative effect comes when a real craving for power over takes their life, and this generally means they want power over others. Such a thing allows little freedom for others, and the person can develop a type of bully boy attitude. However, this energy can completely reverse, and this will be because the individual is mature enough spiritually to understand the need to not interfere in another's space.

There is a somewhat dogmatic side effect from this Pattern overall, and this is that the people affected like to set rules for themselves and their families. If they have power, they loves to set rules for all under their influence, the problem being that these rules will be based on their own concepts of right and wrong, and so there is a dictatorial element here. If benevolent this is good, but obviously there have been very few benevolent dictators.

Of course, the basic lesson is to allow others their physical and psychic space. The Law of Non-Interference must be adhered to if a person is to have a productive and happy life. And always remember the old adage: The road to hell is paved with good intentions.

4-5-6 / 7-8-9 Parallel:

Sharp and edgy, this energy can be frantic and disturbed, and it takes real strength to conquer the nerves and thus maintain a human relationships with greater harmony. A lot of times, those strong with this frequency choose to live alone, preferring pets to people. Charm and personality don't get you far with this type, and they tend toward being somewhat sombre and inflexible

If a person affected by this Pattern has no goal or purpose, their lives will constantly go from bad to worse. But when they start setting reachable targets, life suddenly takes on new meaning and they begin to discover how all things have a capacity for rapid change. This also indicates an ability to turn on a sixpence, both to the positive and negative, yet not to lose momentum in life.

The Japanese characterizes this ability, with their ability to turn from a peace loving nation to a nation of warriors in a matter of years. And yet there will seem to the Japanese no paradox in this. Thus people affected by this Pattern can be both kind and ruthless, all in the same day, and feel no sense of regret for actions that have hurt others.

Actions may be wrapped in noble ideals, but there is a trait here I call the honourable thief, which is that a person can be a criminal, yet also be proud of this, and be quite dedicated to the task before them. We see this with a lot of evangelical pastors who are quite happy to be good shepherds, while at the same time they will be fleecing the flock.

Reason is a powerful rational, and is often used by these people all the time. However, things can turn, and the next minute they can be entirely unreasonable, with strange and odd demands that are quite impossible to fulfil. As a side effect, there are a number with this energy about them who end up schizophrenic, but more in the way that they have a high spiritual value, tied in with a low moral sense. An example of this is the religious person who goes to church on Sunday, but has deep sexual repression's that drive him/her to deviate behaviour.

One of the points worth noting with these folk: They can reach for the stars, but like others to pay for the fuel to get there. This might sound negative, but if they can associate themselves with like minded people, many are happy to have leader who will do just this, just so they can bask in the glory of their leader's achievement.

The person with this Pattern may suffer from being a "Pay-Martyr" (guilt and shame drive them to pay too much for everything) or they may become a "Play-Master". A major lesson here is with non-judgement.

Book of Number: Interpretations

1-4-7/2-5-8 Parallel:

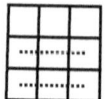

This is a very grounded Pattern, very unlike the upright Parallels, which largely deal with power and influence. The horizontal Parallels look to balance and understanding the human condition, yet they still often have a negative aspect involving manipulation and deceit. Parallel Patterns are always connected to polarity and balance, and so swing from positive to negative in their effect.

This Pattern is connected with earth and emotions, and as such tends to influence the person affected to look at these areas of their lives, but often forgetting the mental area and such things as common sense. Because of this we might see rabid conservationists here, people who fail to regard the other half of the story. The overall concern with this Pattern is that the person affected gets drawn into the logical arguments of others, and so becomes involved with, and controlled by, mass thought, which operates on the emotional band. This is a sort of herd mentality.

It is interesting to note that every thought, emotion and physical reality all operates on specific wavelengths. In the Physical world we see this, in part, as stereotypes: the body builder, the executive, and all manner of specialization's, but we also see this in body types. Each person is one of twelve mineral types, vibrating to the numeral associated with that mineral. In all: Each individual possesses specific frequencies that, as a result of natural cohesion, attract specific and predictable consequences.

Each person is also of a specific emotional wavelength, and here we have the mass mind Jung spoke of (not the instinctual mind, which is on a higher level) as well as other types of assorted emotion frequencies such as anger, love, greed, fear, nobility, etc. Any word we have that describes an emotional content is a key into this frequency, that operates in an area of thought on the emotional plane. (called the Astral Plane)

This Astral area is the most potent of the lower planes that affect man, for through this area the power to energize the mind and the body flows. So a soul with a confused or twisted emotional consciousness (and there are many walking around) is virtually incapable of clear and reasoned thought. Guilt and fear are the perversions in almost every instance, either from this life, or carried over from a previous incarnation.

After such a long digression, I come to the point that the people who share this Pattern must learn to rise above the emotional level of thought, and come into the clarity of BEING-ness that is part of their destiny.

All of this is to highlight the importance of the emotional plane, represented numerically as the 2-5-8 plane. In this particular Pattern there is a choice to make: to allow the emotions to rule the body, or vice versa. Both have a positive or negative possibility. The positive aspect is to allow common sense, combined with love, to rule our actions.

Even so, this must be governed by an equal emotion that allows us not to love, if we so choose. An ability to detach ourselves is a major and necessary freeing influence in life. Thus we can see how the negative and positive are not good and bad, as we are led to believe, but different ends of the same tool. This is one of the great learning experiences offered by this Pattern, the ability to truly have our emotions and understand them, but also be able to use them as required.

Also the same can be said for the physical body. Because of this, harmony with environment and correct diet are very important with these people. There is an indication of a breadth of thought and action being given here, with the possibility for developing tremendous "Lateral Thinking" abilities that allow the individual to solve almost any problem with an astoundingly clear perception.

We can view this Parallel as a series of steps to the mind. It is very important that these people clear themselves of such habits of guilt and insecurity. The best way to do this is through directing our energies into useful pursuits, and in this case, areas which directly benefit humans and animals. Conservation and environment causes are suited to this type.

The negative effect is quite significant. It is to live in squalor. The body consciousness and a subsequent laziness will utterly rule if allowed to do so, and so a degree of discipline is very necessary for the peace and harmony indicated by this Pattern to manifest.

2-5-8 / 3-6-9 Parallel:

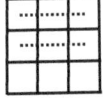

Here we find a Pattern of Completion. One that can signify enormous difficulty in life and relationships, because it is bringing the individual to the end of many outer influences. In order to master your destiny you need to develop a quiet understanding of life. By coming to an inner agreement with the the universal energies, both of the mind and spiritual, the person affected by this Pattern learns a way to be more at ease with the constantly changing circumstances of living.

A big part of the process is developing an attitude of allowing others to live as they will, as long as they do not infringe on personal liberties. This requires a high degree of non- judgment. Patience is the keynote, for once this is achieved, non-judgment comes more easily. The core lesson here is: Take nothing personally. If the person under this influence can master this, there is a tremendous freedom waiting for them. But this is not easily found, let alone held.

Often we find great difficulties arising with this Pattern, for a big part of its influence is to present to the individual a wide gamut of human expression. The problem here being that so much of human expression is of a negative nature. It must be remembered that this is a negative world, and that we live in training camps striving to discover our own beingness. When individual finds an inner balance, natural grace and poise will follow. This will resolve the often tumultuous energy within this Pattern.

If successful, the person will find they are able to complete their destiny for this life, and discover the Jivan Mukti, or Spiritual Freedom so many have sought. In this case, there is often a large degree of financial freedom that comes here as well, even though the native generally appears to be somewhat disconnected from the world.

The negative aspect here is one of passivity, and the subsequent loss of identity this entails. Often when these people are forced to confront someone with a strong negative personality they crumple. But the problem will simply re-surface somewhere else. The test of freedom will simply replay again and again till the person stands up for themselves.

We can see this energy as coming initially from the emotional level, but as Soul matures in this incarnation, the energy will come more clearly and directly through the mind. Focus and clarity are essential tools to temper here. These qualities are invaluable for these people.

The overall lesson is one of purpose. If the individual carries a clear sense of purpose that benefits the whole they will find much of the drama appearing simply as the stage show it is, and they will find themselves above the misery that is the lot of so many.

1-4-7 / 3-6-9 Parallel:

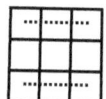

Between heaven and earth all things are made equal, eventually. But there is a lot of work balancing them out in the meantime. This Pattern requires a great deal of understanding and humility to work itself out, and many will never even guess at its true meaning, but suffice to say we are working with differing levels of mastery here.

There is a great tendency for this native to "Blow Out" and lose everything a number of times during their lifetime, but always there is the resource of both inner spirit and the will to live that helps them recover and start again. This then is the key to mastery, that when everything is lost, we can know that we are whole within ourselves.

If the 2-5-8 Line of Emotion is in the Vacant position, this adds tremendously to the energy that the native must contain, and this is akin to trying to ride a wild horse. What it indicates is that the person so affected will be brought back to basics again and again, until they learn what the heart of the situation within themselves actually is. Power is the lesson here, but power contained and trained in silent service to a higher ideal.

Power is the protector of the true heart of man, not an attacker of the weak, nor is it necessarily the ability to influence... But the native of this Pattern must learn an understanding of Power for themselves. It is rarely an easy road. In time a sense of beatitude comes about, usually only when everything else has been tried and the person just gives up and says "Your will, not mine". Only then can the healing energy of life flow freely through the emotional plane to give succour and sustenance to the whole person.

Here we also discover the dichotomy of life, that we are divine, and yet common. When this paradox is resolved, (and it is resolved by seeing the light of God in every Soul we meet) then we will be freed from confusion and be able to make our way forward to meet our destiny. This then is the key to this Pattern, that here we will meet our destiny, but only when we have prepared our inner selves to face this.

If not, we will be thrown back to the vagaries of fate, and generally suffer from the blindness of too many opinions. Bodily health should be carefully watched by these people, for if they become weak or anaemic it will affect their thinking . This in turn will create mental unbalance, and stress will rule our actions. Our thoughts and feelings then become increasingly abrasive towards the flow of life.

A major lesson here is to do with combining the inner person into a cohesive, functioning unit. The end effect, if the person is successful, is to become completely normal. This might not seem much of a reward, but when the individual comes to this point, they will feel axons of conditioning fall away, and they will truly come to know, love and understand themselves and those about them.

The Triple Parallels

(1-2-3 / 4-5-6 / 7-8-9 - 1-4-7 / 2-5-8 / 3-6-9)

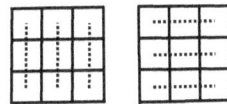

These are rare in the Name Matrix and extremely rare in a birth matrix, but they do occur, especially in Overlay Matrix charts.

In theory, someone with a Triple Parallel should contain all the possibilities for any sort of life they choose. In reality, the person is often paralysed by too many options. As a point of observation, the more complete the Pattern appears, the more perfectly balanced it is, the more difficulty people seem to have resolving the energy.

Book of Number: Interpretations

A clearly defined Triple Parallel is possible in the Birth Matrix in the years such as 2 11 2033. Line of Balance on the 1-2-3 line, two Vacant Lines on the 4-5-6 and 7-8-9 lines and in this instance it would indicate a tremendous degree of flexibility in resolving problems. However, we generally find this Pattern represented in the Name or Overlay Matrix.

The problem with the Triple Parallel is that it has no specific impetus or inertia in any direction. As all the numbers are represented with an equitable weight, the energy often feels stagnant. Yet the Triple Parallel has an ability to combine and recombine things in new ways, and as such it acts as a catalyst for change. Flexibility and adaptability are the great strengths to develop here. This greatly enhances survival abilities.

The Triple Parallel occurs with the combination of Lines of Force, Lines of Balance and Vacant Lines. When this is present in a chart then we would say the influence has a POTENTIAL, much like a rock sitting at the top of the mountain. When it gets rolling it can have tremendous force, but unless it does it is just another piece of scenery. This is the whole secret to the Triple Parallel: Get things moving.

What is required to get the rock of consciousness mobile in this instance depends very much on the circumstances and weights in the chart. These we find described in the various Lines and Trines present, and the real effect of the Triple Parallel is to make the POTENTIAL of all of these that much greater.

Usually when an individual has worked through the Patterns they have been presented at birth, and is living their life according to the way they wish, only then does the effect of this Pattern really come to the fore. If a person can master their internal process and external circumstances, then they have a tremendous resource on their hands with this Pattern. If not, a Triple Parallel can be a bit of an albatross.

I would say that for most a Triple Parallel is an unattractive situation. Combined with the natural tendency towards the negative that this world holds, it implies a lack of motivation. Getting motivated is therefore the key to feeling good about yourself if this Pattern occurs in your chart.

Where the Pattern has incredible power is when the OVERLAY MATRIX creates a Triple Parallel in relation to company takeovers, new ventures being formed. Where there are large projects being planned, and many people involved, working under the influence of a Triple Parallel means that their is an almost unlimited power to achieve available. In this instance the Director and Executive are key to success.

A curiousity: If we overlay the birthdate of Christopher Columbus (Oct 1451) on Independance Day (4 7 1776) we get a Triple Parallel. His day of birth is not known, but if he were born on the second or twelvth, it would make a perfect Triple Parallel. (1-4-7 LF / 2-5-8 LB / 3-6-9 VL)

PATTERNS: Summary

Patterns in the Matrix are archetypal energies, that reflect in the numerical combinations that occur in charts. Most commonly, these occur in the Overlay Matrix that comes about when you combine various charts.

They give a broad stroke insight into the energy at work behind any given combination. It is an amazingly fast way to gain a comprehensive insight into the meaning of a chart, or combination of charts. This is information that has not been in print for centuries.

The Interpretations given in this text are condensed from the original course published in the early 1990's and as with all aspects of Pythagorean Numerology, the reader must strive to assemble and resolve each chart in a way that makes sense.

Cutting and pasting verbatim text is not the best practice, but it will suffice until a reader gains an insight into how the various Aspects work together.

You can even give an individual the various Aspects to read through, and make sense of for themselves. So often I have simply gone through the various Aspects for an individual, and seen their jaw drop in amazement with the accuracy of the description.

This, I expect, will be something you too will experience with clients and friends. For now, we close this book with a look at interpretations for Doublets.

Doublets (Oppositions)

This apparently simple Aspect of Oppositions and Doublets within the Matrix is an area that can become quite complex. These represent internal alignments of energy, and often highlight areas of conflict within the psyche of the individual.

This is most significant when there are a series of three or more oppositions in any given chart, and the most curious part is when these are shared with family members. If an individual has a one/six opposition highlighted, and this is shared with a wife or parent, it clearly decribes part of the karmic tie between them.

ONE/SIX Opposition

The One/Six Opposition is often one that creates personal difficulty in the home and in business. The essential lesson here is to respect the inherent value of life, and then life will respect you. As the individual learns to modify their behaviour to be more inclusive of others, and to trust that life works for the benefit of all, the negative energy of this aspect becomes very positive. They literally turn over a new leaf. This transformation of energy usually occurs with a symbol, such as a marriage or significant change of work or address.

ONE/EIGHT Opposition

A combination that often indicates personal karma being worked out in personal relationships. If the individual is unaware of this effect and how to deal with it, there is a tendency for a breakdown in communication and thus multiple marriages. There can be great difficulty with finance until the individual learns the Laws of Wealth, especially the concept of creating a greater value to the self. (Much gathers more, less gathers loss)

A study of finance and investment will pay dividends. Essentially, the overall lesson here is that other people reflect the lessons we need to learn, and so we must not criticize or chastise perceived faults in another. Take the log out of your own eye before you criticise the splinter in another, so to speak.

TWO/SEVEN Opposition

This Aspect indicates a potential to resolve the male and female forces within the individual. The overall lesson is to do with balancing and understanding these opposing energies within ourselves. A person affected by this Aspect is often withdrawn of nature, and usually prefers quiet reflection over strong argument. In it's early stages, this is a very unbalanced energy, and those with this aspect can be very changeable. A great deal of inner searching seems par for the course, or otherwise the opposite attitude of careless abandon can be displayed. The message here is: You must learn to deal with common problems before you will be able to deal successfully with life. Acceptance of self is a very important step towards the resolution of the energy here.

As this frequency wakes up, the individual often feels the need for argument or competition in order to define themselves. Definition is the key note here, for this energy looks to split hairs in the search for its personal truth. The only problem is that this attitude tends to also split families and friendships, and so a major lesson here is to learn to be more forgiving and understanding of others. Acceptance of others as they are follows on from acceptance of self, and this sets you free.

THREE/FOUR Opposition

A curious Aspect that has a creative fatality to it. This is where the individual can simply think too much about the why's and wherefore's of things, and in doing so forget to live their life. There is a tendency to want to create great dreams, but to worry about the details so much that the dreams never eventuate. It is an argument between the creative self and the practical self that is highlighted, and the individual must learn to make their creativity pay when this aspect is strong in the chart. Freedom comes from a practical application of the dream. This is the lesson to be learned here.

A very common issue faced with the Three-Four opposition is how to make creativity pay. It is really a question of internal dreams meeting external reality, and working to make the two harmonious is the basic task before those with this Aspect. Yet in truth, this is everyone's task. What the numbers are saying is that it will be a specific question the querent will have to answer in this life.

Book of Number: Interpretations

THREE/SEVEN Opposition

The name of this Aspect is the "Liberty Bell". The question is: Does it toll for thee? When the Three - Seven is aspected in any area of any chart, it is a wakeup call that will be paid attention to. You cannot slumber through this cycle. It like a Letter of Demand from Spirit, saying that you need to claim your spiritual and emotional freedom or else. Or else what? You simply fall asleep at the wheel and have a directionless life.

Spiritual Freedom is the goal and purpose of this energy, and so a person will find themselves pushed through many barriers if this becomes accented in their life. You must demand your spiritual liberty, and usually there are blockages placed in your path to test your resolve. You really cannot compromise on the need to be free when this Aspect shows up. If you do, life just never seems to work out.

FOUR/NINE Opposition

You will need to prepare for war. This Aspect demands a warlike spirit, and we often see warriors carrying this combination. Of course, now-a-days the swords have been swapped for pens and our shields have turned into with legal arguments, but the principle of waging war, especially for justice, is the same.

The lesson here is in learning when to fight and when to leave things be. This energy can put a pressure on the individual that clouds their judgement. And so a major lesson is actually to do with discrimination and knowing how much is needed in any given situation. A great deal of good or a great deal of harm can be done with this energy in the chart, and as a result the person tends to avoid it's power. The personality can turn inwards towards passive agressive behaviour, and there is a tendency to self destruct if no positive outlet is found for this energy.

SIX/SEVEN Opposition

Remember the old saying "At Sixes and Sevens"? The individual tends to be at odds with themselves until they learn to focus on a single course of action. Distraction and indecision pull at the attention, and there is little progress that can be made until focus and clear goals are put in place. When this is done, the barriers fall away and much forward movement can come about.

Book of Number: Interpretations

The overall lesson is one of "added value" though, which is going one step more than is absolutely needed. This is like buying an apple, but keeping the seeds and planting them. This breaks up the frustrating energy that tends to keep the person affected by the Six - Seven at a level under their true ability.

The barriers of self limitation are the only prison, and the best way to break through this is through service to life in some manner. The simple answer to the energy of this Aspect is to look to altruistic professions (doctor, nurse, fireman, teacher, etc.), and to carry an attitude of "Added Value" in all you do. Always look to go one step more than others consider necessary.

THREE/SIX Opposition

This is an energy of the mind, and of willpower. People tend to feel tthey can create life as they want it through purely mental focus. When we make things happen through force of will, the personal consequences are things like broken marriages, distant family relations and blood pressure issues. Why? Because it is an isolating energy, and it generates vibrations that seem like arrogance and agression to those close. By simply allowing life to shape things, not personal will, all reverses and the individual learns true intimacy and friendship.

In the end, learning the Law of Kamit (silence) is essential. Knowing what to say, when to say, and remaining diplomatic even when the temper is frayed are the lessons of this aspect. Patience is the cure for most of life's ills, but never more-so than with the Three - Six opposition.

THREE/EIGHT Opposition

Finance and worldy concerns weigh heavy. This is a very Saturnian energy, one of sombre grey tones, and it tends to rule the personality, creating an aura of deep traditionalism and dullness. And yet this energy flips to an almost manic sense at the flick of a button. Really, the mania is in the background, and the seriousness is a way to contain it.

Allowing the inner nature to run riot is no solution, but accepting there is a child-like part of ourselves that wants to run free, and finding areas where it can, does work. So often a simple hobby which absorbs our total attention is all that is needed to balance this combination.

Book of Number: Interpretations

OPPOSITIONS: Summary

Other Doublets/Oppositions exist, in fact any combination of two numbers can form an opposition, but they are relevant to the Patterns and Aspects around them. I list the main ones here, and they are (apart from the Three-Six) the numbers that reach "across" existing lines in the Matrix.

These are the areas of greatest tension, and the oppositions are a message from Spirit similar to the sound of an orchestra tuning up. There is no clear song, but in tuning up the tensions within a chart, we can prepare a harmonic base for the song to be created.

The smallest adjustment in the tension of a string can make an extraordinary difference in the overall tone of the instrument. These Oppositions, when they occur, are a little message saying "Fine tune the instrument".

In life, these adjustments are mostly by way of changing an attitude, looking at something a different way, accepting another as they are, or just remembering we are not the centre of the Universe. Simple things change the inner tension, and can radically alter the song we are to sing.

I remember when I first learned a musical instrument how hard it was for me to tune it. It took forever, and was rarely really correct. Yet a professional musician would turn up, and in seconds have it in perfect harmony. The guitar sounded fantastic when it was tuned.

This is how it is. The first step is in learning to tune our instrument. As a Numerologist, I can look at someone and quickly tune them up because I know the correct tensions, but learning to do it for ourselves is the real journey. This is the purpose of this book, to help you "tune in".

Once you have this attunement, the song you have to sing will flow naturally from your heart. It is something you were born to sing, but the lack of harmony within the heart and mind has prevented you from recognising your own latent perfection.

In many ways, we have taken on a virus in our upbringing. The "rules" of society and attitudes of our parents have infected our natural state, distorting the simple, clear song we have to sing by bending us a little out of shape. By finding our natural self once more, we also find a release these tensions, and come to find the correct state for ourselves. Thus we find the natural harmony within.

Oppositions are simply a message to ourselves to find that harmony.

The Harmonic Nature of Number

Perhaps the single greatest technological break-through of the 20th century is the computer. Advances in science and medicine have been remarkable, but the computer has crept into every avenue of our existence. They are running cars, used in robotic manufacturing, and almost every house has a computer connected to the net. We even use them to call people, because the new smart phone is really a computer. Even refrigerators and sewing machines have one. And the remarkable thing is they all work on just two signals: Zero and One.

Just TWO signals are running our entire civilization: One and Zero.

But let's extend this outward, and consider the view that existence itself has a mathematical basis. Planets spin in a perfect symphony of movement, the rise and fall of the tides is a clock, etc. The extraordinary connection between nature and seasons, the migration of birds, all form part of an interconnected series of cycles that create the pattern of existence as we know it. Is it all just coincidence? Or does it follow a mathematical pattern? The Pythagoreans firmly believed in the latter.

I wondered how I would close this book and drifted off to sleep looking for the words that would encapsulate all I have been trying to convey. That night I had a dream where I saw the universe as a living machine, but instead of operating on Binary, it operated at Base 12. In other words, not just Zero and One, but every parameter and permutation running through One to Twelve were the variables. It was like watching a huge multi-dimensional clock with trillions of interlocking dials, all working together in harmony. Such a thing clearly involved a technology that was far beyond our human capacity to construct.

As I awoke, the full depth of what I had seen faded. It was like trying to put 12 dimensions of wisdom into a 3 dimensional bucket. But the essence remained, and that is that we are ALL part of an incredible process. We are part of a universe that moves with the clarity and articulation worthy of the finest Swiss-made watch.

Of course, sceptics look at books like this one, and when they hear statements like I have just made, they snort and scoff. The entire concept of Numerology is utter hogwash to these people. They say: How can a little thing such as the day you were born or the name you carry give any real insight into the potentials you carry within you?

Yet they will happily respect computers and pay heed to the programming that models future projections of weather, the economy, and the prediction of election results. Everything they believe in is based on a Zero and a One. This strikes me as somewhat ironic.

They will argue there is no correlation, The climate scientist putting in thousands of random figures is looking for the computer to process the details, and draw a conclusion based on evidence. It does not predict the future. And yet, what people do at the weather bureau every single day is to try and predict the future, and they do this by using numbers.

Think about this in a little more detail: The computer I am typing this book on is relating the signals from the keyboard into a series of Zeros and Ones. This then sends the mathematical process to a program that reinterprets these signals as pixels. These are sent as mathematical particles to a printer that converts them to letters and words, and recorded as a book you can read. This original signal is now transferred via reflected light to the optic nerve, which converts the light patterns into Fourier curves and THIS signals to the trained cortex what these patterns on paper actually mean. Simple reading alone is remarkable example of ourselves as living math in a living computer.

The Universe is a Living Computer

We ARE living in a computer! Regardless of what you choose to believe, life works to a pattern. You may not see mathematics at work in the growing of the plant, but it is there. Seeds with specific DNA are being modulated by water, soil and sun, and the net result is the plant you see growing. But it is not growing in some random burst of life, it is growing to a very specific plan. EVERYTHING in life grows and passes away in a very specific series of cycles, governed by internal mathematics.

If there is a pattern to things, then it is predictable. Just as a computer operates and performs on a series of Ones and Zeros in a predictable manner, the universe performs and operates with a numerical series in a manner that is predictable, albeit at a far more complex level. In Pythagorean Numerology we have a system at work that is based on the harmonic principles Pythagoras proved: This is that there is a mathematical perfection based on the ratios of 1, 18 and 12.

Did you know that One divided by 18, multiplied by 12 equals .666 ? The biblical number of man (not the beast) is in fact a mathematical perfection. 12 divided by 18 equals .666. 666 divided by 18 multiplied by 12 equals 444. 1 divided by 18 equals .0555 and so on. So why are the numbers 18 and 12 so significant? Because they create harmony.

What is more, Pythagoras clearly demonstrated how this harmony comes about, and proved it 2500 years ago. He proved that by ratio and math alone we can arrive at universal constants. Specifically, he demonstrated this with music and harmonics. He took blacksmith hammers, three in tune with each other, one out of tune, and reformed the shape of these, but kept the original mass. No matter the form, metal of equitable mass (based on a ratio dividable by 1/18th) generated audible harmonic resonance. Anything not within this ratio sounded dissonant.

Every luthier uses the principles Pythagoras laid down when creating a fret-board. Take any flat piece of wood, divide the length by 18, and then subtract this figure from the overall length. Mark the wood at that point. This is the position of the first fret on a musical instrument.

Now we simply repeat this process by measuring the length of the first fret to the remaining length of the wood. Divide this length of wood by 18, and subtract this figure, and similarly mark it. This is the position of the second fret. Do this 12 times and you will have the EXACT interval structure for a musical instrument. This is the ratio for ALL fret-boards for guitars and other instruments. ONLY this ratio, which we evolve from the division of a length by 18, will work.

Ratio is the Secret to Harmony

More over, even when expand or compress the 12 frets on a fret-board, to get maybe 13 or 11 notes, they all sound perfectly fine, individually. But there will be no harmony between any of the notes created by any instrument that has fretting not based on the division of 18 over 12. Only the ratio created by the division by 18 allows the creation of harmony. Only the the interval structure of 12 to this ratio allows the creation of harmony. And lo and behold! This just happens to be the exact, same ratio present in the expansion of a ripple of water on a pond, or the radiation of light from a star, or the waves created in the cortex by the voice of a mother speaking to her child. It's a living computer.

We humans did not invent music, the universe possessed that secret long before we knew it. Everything in the universe is frequency, and *harmonic* frequency is the building block of life. All life is based on a harmonic principle wrapped around a theme based on a mathematical principle. As the Pythagoreans said: There are no coincidences, there is only the song we sing, and what we become by singing it.

The Music of the Spheres is a term created by Pythagoras. It is the harmonic interchange of life itself. Harmony is core to the very nature of the Universe. If you slow down the "random" sound of crickets, you hear a perfect harmonic chorus worthy of Beethoven. Watch the moment by moment growth of a plant, and you see a perfect mathematical equation expanding in, and as, a living universe of harmonic being.

Book of Number: Interpretations

Humans like to think they invented music. We did not invent anything, we simply DISCOVERED it. Likewise, the harmonic principles of life have always existed, just as the internal math that allows a plant to grow has always been there. And yet, while every aspect of our entire existence is so clearly governed by math, the sceptics will still deny there is a divine plan at work. This avoidance of the obvious amazes me. The concept of God or Spirit, or some other great harmonic principle, at work in the lives of each of us is seen as some sort of witch-doctor belief, and the fact that we live in a universe governed by perfect mathematical harmony is purely a thing of random chance. Well, each holds true what they will.

OCCAM's RAZOR

Occam's Razor tells us that, if there is an overriding code to the entire universe that is measurable, clear and constant, then it is most likely that something wrote it. Yes? Or did it just write itself? Every aspect of nature demonstrate clear, unmitigated mathematical principles at work, and yet the sceptic still tries to believe it is "pure coincidence" that slime could evolve into intelligent beings who can build and fly space craft.

I have no interest arguing with blindness. And if an individual cannot see the obvious, they are as good as blind. It is obvious that the universe works on mathematical principles. Let's forget the concept of God, but it is clear SOMETHING is an organising force. WHY is it so incredible to accept that this ALSO occurs in our personal experience of life as well?

In essence, all Numerology is comes down to an acceptance of the mathematical cycles at work in each individual's life. Just as there are predictable cycles in every aspect of creation, so too are there cycles at work in our personal life. Denial of this is like saying the Earth is flat, or that the universe revolves around ourselves.

The only real question is whether, in our human form, we correctly discern the divine proportions. Can we grasp the great currents that flow through all life and which are equally at work in our own? We live in a vast computer that works, not on Binary, but on a range of Zero to Twelve. Everything, every atom, is part of the program *and it is running right now,* creating form and shape in both the universe and in our life.

The entire purpose and focus of this book is simply to offer you a way to gain an insight into what this program is saying to you.

This Book of Interpretations has evolved from a long, personal study into the nature of number. I have written each interpretation guided by the nature of each number represented in each Aspect. And this is not a closed book: It is a living computer with immeasurable variables.

Book of Number: Interpretations

I have sought to be both as comprehensive and concise as I can be in this extraordinary wide and every changing subject. The simple fact is, my personal presence will not be here to help you understand the intricacies. I have recorded all this, therefore, in such a way that you can pick up the "resonance" of the subject, and in due course tune into the reality of the Pythagorean way of thinking

Please remember this: The Book of Number exists within YOU. It is open or shut, alive or dead, according to how you see things. Trust me, when it is open, and alive, you will amaze yourself with the clarity of understanding it brings. I have one simple request to make of you, dear reader. Please read all within these pages more as a travel guide rather than as a "bible" of absolute truth. The point of writing all this down is to give you a direction to travel, to offer an indication of potential and possibility, rather than present a stagnant, ossified tome of past wisdom.

We know life works on a mathematical model. We know that we can deduce future probability from past events. What we don't know is who, or what, constructed this vast machine we call life. One thing is certain, however. As you master the skills needed to read a numerical chart, and begin to see the extraordinary accuracy of Pythagorean Numerology, you will come to recognise that there is some sort of intelligence behind it all.

Whatever you call this, be it Allah, Spirit, or just life itself, it is something that is IN you. The name isn't important, only the recognition of IT at work in your life matters. So often we come to understand this by seeing how Number plays out in the lives of those around you. A simple truth: when you are doing this correctly, no one learns more about themselves when doing Number Charts than you, the reader.

Now, with my keyboard and my body wearing out, I close this chapter on the last 30 years of study and practical application. I find I have but one simple greeting and farewell to offer to you.

May your journey of discovery be long, and your trials be short.

Michael Wallace (Raven)

Cudgen, Australia - December 2014

Be Your Own Oracle!

Did you like the Book of Number?
Did you want to know the next step?

Yes, there's more! Go to
www.divinitydice.com.au

Discover the extraordinary books on Dice Divination by this author

DIVINITY DICE

"Any one who is interested in Dice Divination MUST read this book"
— Luke Rhinehart, The Diceman

Researched for over 30 years, the divinations given to you in this series are simply remarkable, both with their accuracy, and their layers of depth and meaning. Using knowledge that has laid dormant for 2500 years, Michael Wallace has brought to light the ways of the ancient Pythagoreans in a simple, easy to understand series of games.

Fascinating, and extraordinarily accurate, the Divinity Dice series is something right out of the box. Want to know more? Go to:

WWW.DIVINITYDICE.COM.AU

For those who wonder about the Raven Pen Name, it came about because for a time, every place I went anywhere in the world, there would be a Raven looking at me from a post. I asked a Hopi Elder what this might mean, and he said "A storm is coming".

Some years earlier, a remarkable musician, Gerry Bull, had commented to me about an inner experience he had, where he saw a vast storm rolling in. He wondered what it meant, and someone said to him "Storms create an opening between the worlds". He realised energy was flowing down and into this world as a result of the titanic forces being released.

It occurred to me that the true Pythagorean System had not been recorded in modern times, and I realised that the awakening of this ancient wisdom would call forth an opening between the planes, and so the name Raven was used.

I trust it wasn't all just a storm in a teacup!

COPYRIGHT 2014

This book is published under the Berne Convention. All rights are reserved. Apart from any fair dealing for the purpose of private study, research, criticism or review, as permitted under the Copyright Act, 1966, no part of this publication may be reproduced, stored in a retrieval system, or transmitted, in any form or by any means, electronic, electrical, chemical, mechanical, optical, photocopying, recording or otherwise, without the prior permission of the copyright holder.

Enquiries should be made to the publishers at this Email Address.
Info.numberharmonics@gmail.com

ISBN: 978-0-9756994-6-1
Copyright 2014 Michael Wallace
Publisher: Ladder to the Moon Productions

Michael Wallace (Raven)

Michael Wallace is a remarkable individual. He is a Master Musician, Master Body Worker, Master Numerologist, Dice Master, Recording Artist, Songwriter, and Publisher. On top of all this he is also a prolific writer with over 17 titles in print.

Known as "Raven", or what the Hopi describe as the Storm Bringer, he is a catalyst for change and renewal.

www.ingramcontent.com/pod-product-compliance
Lightning Source LLC
Chambersburg PA
CBHW052058300426
44117CB00013B/2187